Dok ✤ Mai ✤ Thai
The Flower Culture of Thailand

*For Brigitte & Joerg,
With Good Wishes
Jiri & Fay
Bangkok 2012*

Dok · Mai · Thai
The Flower Culture of Thailand

SAKUL INTAKUL

Photographs by JIRASAK THONGYUAK

Flower Culture

This edition published in Thailand in November 2009 by
Flower Culture Press
52 Rajavithee Road Soi 2, Samsennai, Phayathai,
Bangkok 10400 THAILAND

In collaboration with
Sakul Intakul, Pawo Company Limited
52/1 Rajavithee Road Soi 2, Samsennai, Phayathai,
Bangkok 10400 THAILAND

The first edition was published in Thailand in August 2009 by
Flower Culture Press
In collaboration with
Sakul Intakul, Pawo Company Limited

Copyright © Flower Culture Press 2009
Text copyright © Sakul Intakul 2009
Book design and layout copyright
© Flower Culture Press 2009
Photographs copyright © Flower Culture Press 2009
or as indicated otherwise

Publisher / Project Director / Creative Director: Sakul Intakul
Editor: Rungsima Kasikranund
English Editor: Peter Myers
Design: Be›Our›Friend Studio

Author: Sakul Intakul
Photographer: Jirasak Thongyuak

All rights reserved. No part of this publication may be reproduced or transmitted in any form or by any means, electronic or mechanical, including photocopying, recording, or any other information storage and retrieval system, without prior permission in writing from the publisher.

ISBN 978-616-90326-0-1

Printed in Thailand

✤ Contents ✤

	7	*Foreword*
ดอกไม้ไทย	8	*The Story Unfolds*
มาลัย	16	**Malai**: Floral Garlands
เครื่องแขวน	34	**Khruang Khwaen**: Floral Pendants
พานดอกไม้	50	**Phan Dokmai**: Floral Arrangements on Pedestal Trays
กระทงและงานใบตอง	68	**Krathong & Ngan Baitong**: Floral Floats, Leaf Containers & Banana-Leaf Works
บายศรี	84	**Baisri**: Offerings to Divinities
งานดอกไม้เล็ก	102	**Ngan Dokmai Lek**: Small Floral Works
เครื่องแต่งตัว	118	**Khruang Tangtua**: Floral Accessories
ล้านนาและอีสาน	136	**Lanna and Isaan**: In the Regional Realm
สมุดภาพดอกไม้ไทย	152	**Dok Mai Thai Galleries**: Variations on Thai Floral Designs
	168	**Floral Glossary**
	172	**Board of Advisors**
	173	**Sponsors and Partners**
	174	**Acknowledgements**
	176	**Team Acknowledgements**

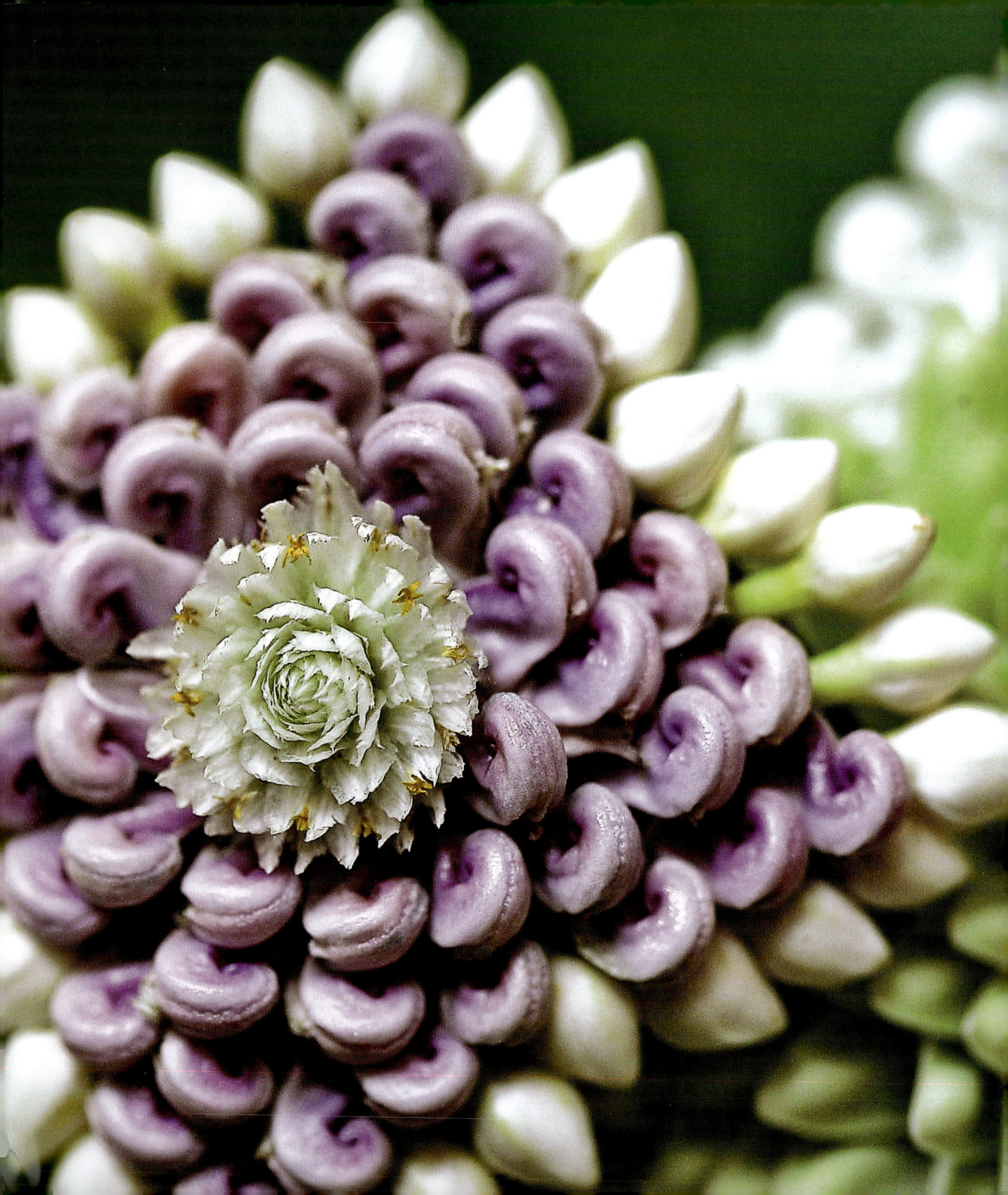

✦ Foreword ✦

In celebration of Her Majesty Queen Sirikit's 77th birthday and shaped by a huge sense of pride in the Kingdom, *Dok Mai Thai: The Flower Culture of Thailand* invites you to join us on an Asian floral journey.

Through *Dok Mai Thai*, we explore and chronicle the floral art of Thailand across each of its sub-categories, featuring fine samples of works spanning both the traditional and the contemporary. Some pieces illustrated in this book are faithful reconstructions from images of past floral works found in the country's National Archives; other interpretations are inspired by century-old mural paintings and bas-reliefs.

Several hundred Thai florists joined their hearts and hands to create the floral materials appearing on these pages, and the stories that accompany each chapter aim to provide insights into the Thai way of life in accordance with a particular type of floral art.

My heartfelt thanks go to our solicitous advisors, my dedicated pre- and post-production team, ever-supportive sponsors and partners, and all others who had their hand in making *Dok Mai Thai* a reality. Above all, and of utmost importance to the Thai people, is the core that holds the hearts of everyone on the project together – Her Majesty the Queen of Thailand, without whom this book would never have been possible.

I hope for *Dok Mai Thai: The Flower Culture of Thailand* to serve as the Thai ‹flower ambassador› to the world, bringing with it the heart, soul and goodwill of a nation, while encouraging new interest in and appreciation of the Kingdom's rich cultural heritage.

Join *Dok Mai Thai* and the rest of the Kingdom in paying tribute to Her Majesty for her tireless dedication to the conservation of Thai arts and culture. Let *Dok Mai Thai* always blossom in the Kingdom of Thailand.

Sakul Intakul

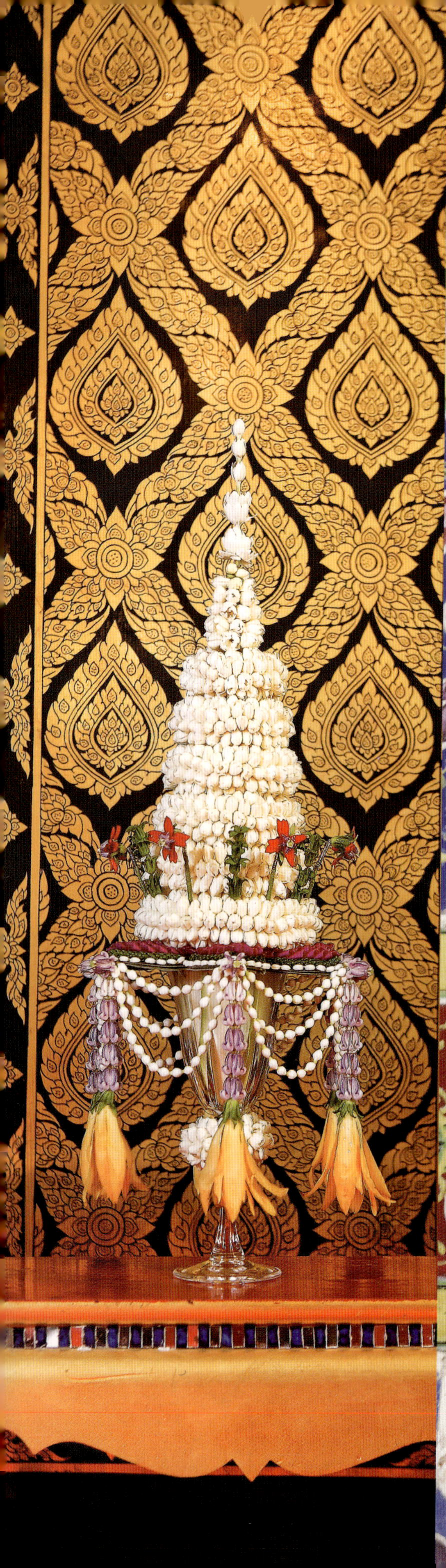
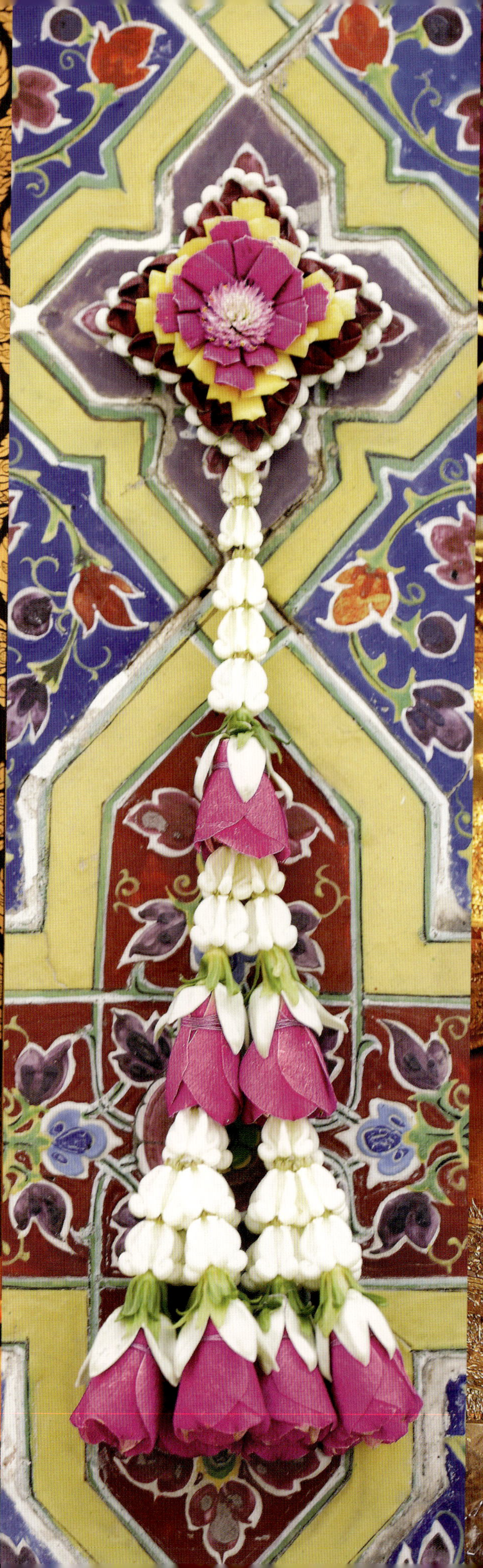
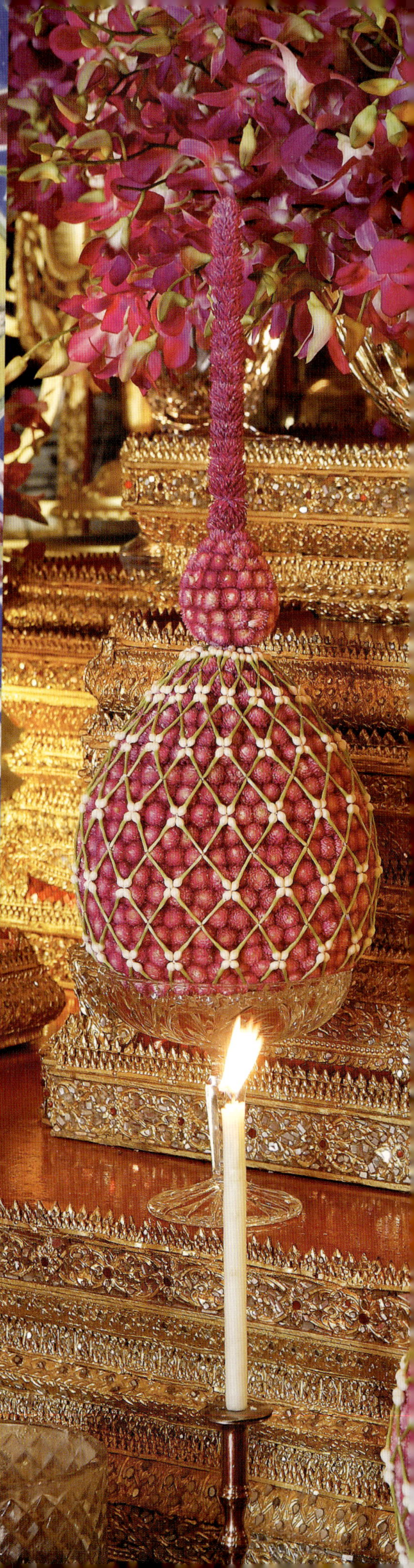

ดอกไม้ไทย

❖ The Story Unfolds ❖

Flowers, **the most delicate, beautiful, natural creations are also a source of deep fascination and spiritual refreshment. Indeed, the degree of artistry applied in floral displays is a good measurement of a nation's cultural depth and sophistication; it takes skilled craftsmanship to add artistic value to such natural beauty.**

Dating back to ancient times, there is a rich flower arranging tradition in Thailand; floral art is an integral part of birth celebrations, royal feasts, and cremations and other religious ceremonies. Thai flower culture has been passed on from one generation to the next since time immemorial.

The oldest remaining historical record of flower arrangement in the kingdom can be found in a book written in the Sukhothai period, around 700 years ago, by a noble lady at the court of a great king of the Sukhothai period. *Memoirs of Lady Sri Chulalaksana*, better known as *The Story of Nang Noppamas*, notes the king was very impressed by a striking floating lantern made by Lady Sri Chulalaksana, which was subsequently presented to him. Comprised of multicoloured fresh flower petals sewn together in the form of a full-blown lotus, the lantern was made for «*Loy Krathong*», the full moon ceremony held on the night of the 12th lunar month's full moon.

Another passage in the book tells us of Lady Sri Chulalaksana's floral replica of a golden double-decked tray. The arrangement was covered with a delicate netting of flowers, and she presented it to the king during the royal ceremonial bath that took place in the fourth lunar month. The tray was used as a receptacle for betel nut, yet so refined was its craftsmanship the king decreed that the tray should be used for entertaining guests on important occasions, especially wedding ceremonies. He named the tray «*phan khan mak*», a wedding dowry tray.

The absence of written records means that the flower arrangements of the ensuing Ayutthaya period may never be known to us, though floral art must have been practiced and perpetuated throughout this thriving period in the nation's cultural and commercial development. Evidence comes in the form of mural paintings found at Wat Ratchaburana, a monastery built in the early Ayutthaya period. «*Malai*», or floral garlands, were portrayed in these paintings.

Source materials increase during the early Rattanakosin period. According to HRH Prince Damrong Rajanubhab's historical records, Chaokhun Tani, a concubine of King Rama I, was known as the greatest floral-art practitioner of her time. Her skill and technique can still be traced among her descendants – the Bunnag family – in present-day Thailand.

The golden age of Thai-style floral art came during the reign of King Rama V (King Chulalongkorn the Great). As the king showed a great interest and delight in floral art, the ladies of the court were driven to become more attentive to this delicate art, competing with one another to achieve ever more exquisite craftsmanship. Old techniques and designs were revised and adapted, while new ones were created for greater variety, complexity and beauty.

Although the popularity of Thai floral art went into decline during the reigns of King Rama VI, VII and VIII, the result of economic crises and the World Wars, it was revived by Her Majesty Queen Sirikit, beloved Queen Consort of HM King Bhumibol Adulyadej (King Rama IX). Since featuring in Bangkok's 200-year-anniversary celebrations in 1982, Thai floral art has benefited from the Queen's continued support into the present day.

Dok Mai Thai: The Flower Culture of Thailand was consequently created in honour of HM Queen Sirikit, who, through her royal duties, has long played a significant role in the preservation and development of Thai arts, craft and culture. *Dok Mai Thai* also celebrates the auspicious occasion of the Queen's 77th birthday in August 2009.

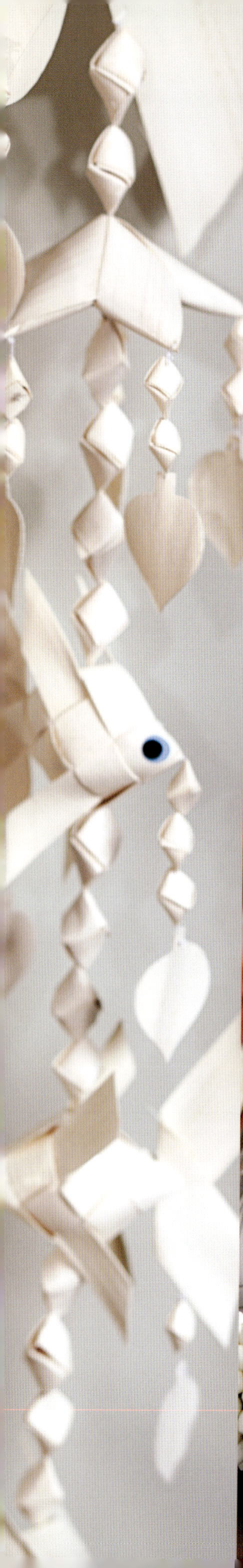
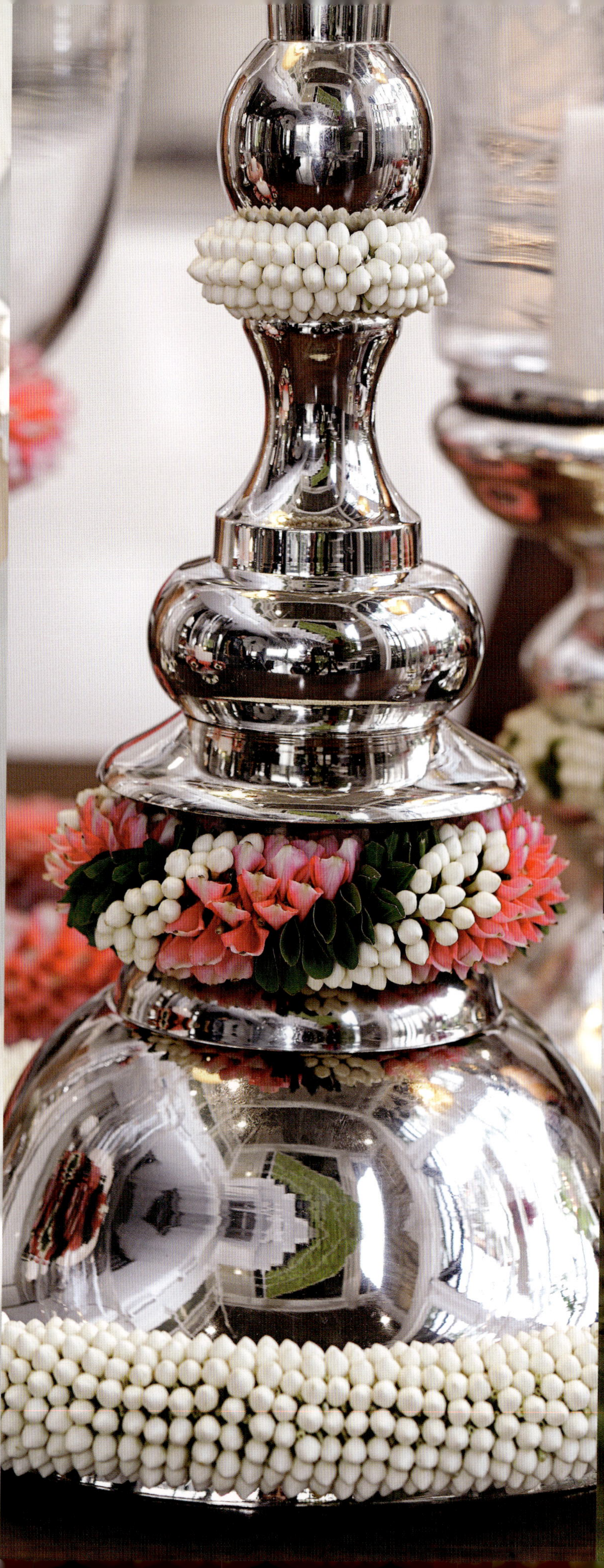
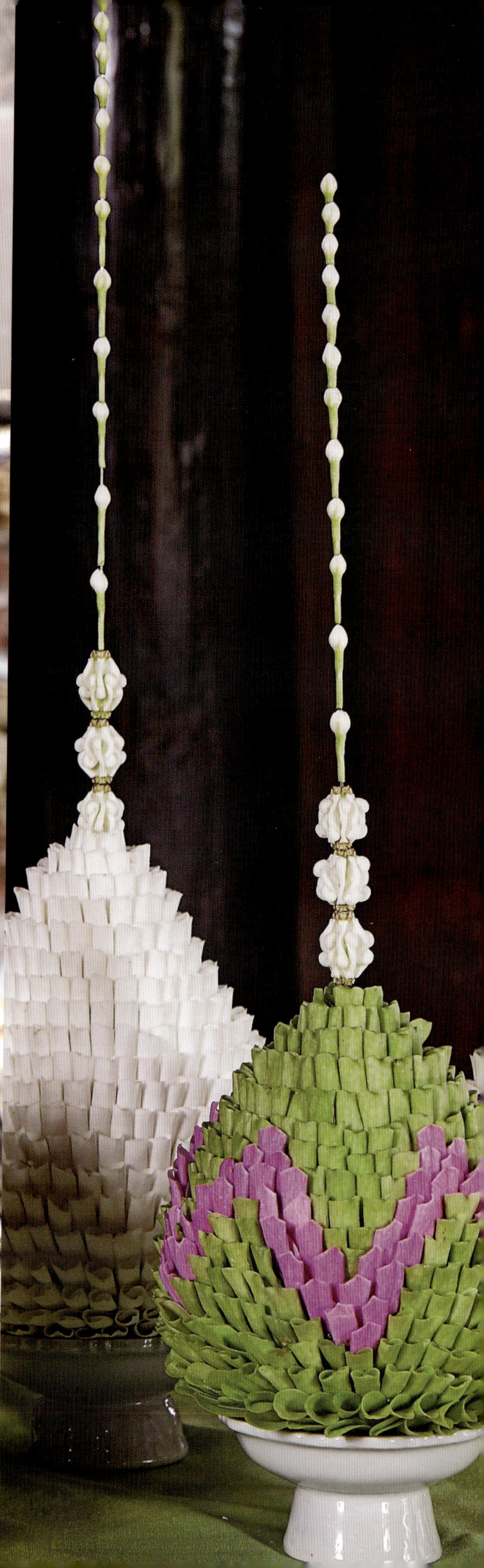

This book aims to rediscover the beauty of Thai flower culture, a culture which has become the pride of the nation, as well as part of its identity. *Dok Mai Thai* serves to record and preserve this exquisite art form, while at the same time bringing its artistic and cultural value to the world's attention. We explore and illustrate Thai floral art as an offering, a decoration and a gift in both its original contexts and contemporary interpretations. All illustrations printed here were photographed in Thailand's spectacular palaces, traditional residences and contemporary homes.

The Thai phrase « *Dokmai Thai* » translates as « Thai Flowers »; for the purposes of this book, however, we have infused the words with another layer of meaning, to include the elaborate art of Thai floral display. *Dokmai Thai* may not yet be well known to the Western world, but it truly evokes the essence and soul of Asia. ❖

Opening Spread (from left to right)

«*Malai thao*» – a set of jasmine garlands on a pedestal tray – are normally used in ordination ceremonies, or as an offering; «*thad hu*» tied with a dangling floral tassel; and this «*phan phum*», made from globe amaranth flowers, is covered with a floral net made out of small gardenias.

Previous Spread (from left to right)

A contemporary interpretation of «*phan dokmai*» decorated with jasmine and crown flowers; a century-old example of «*kruai up-atcha*» – a form of *phan dokmai* – used in an ordination ceremony (image courtesy of National Archives of Thailand); «*toom dokmai*» made from orchid petals; and a floral tassel, as seen from below.

This Spread (from left to right)

A fish mobile made from dried palm leaves, normally hung above a baby's cradle; a contemporary floral-garland display; and a modern day collection of *phan dokmai* made from colourful folded orchid petals.

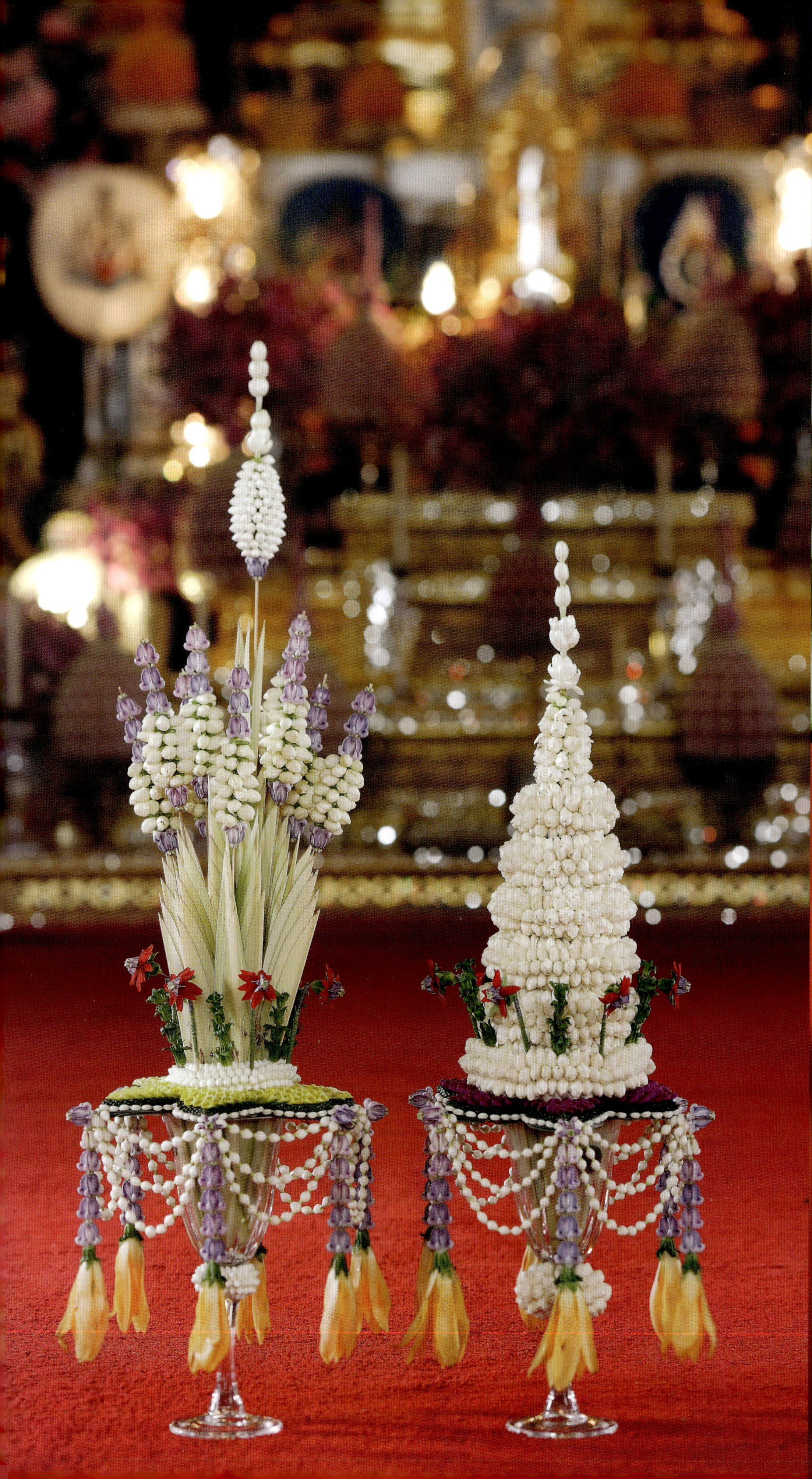
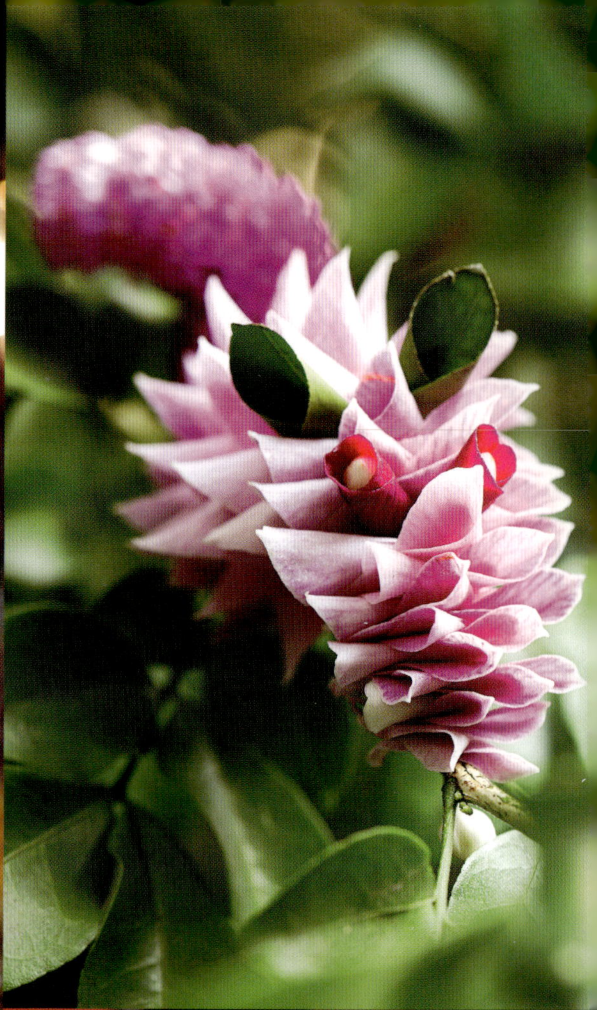
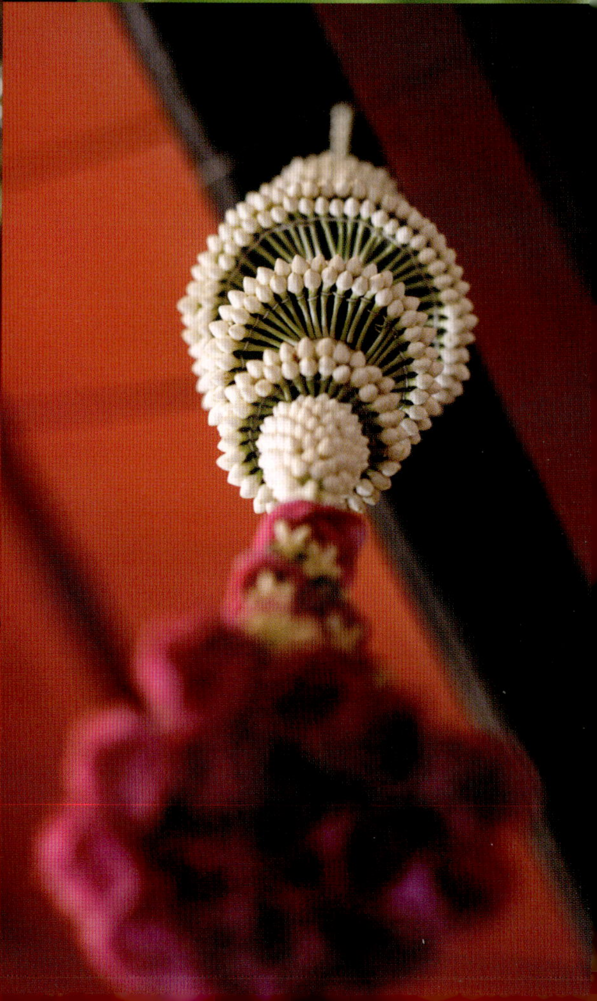

This Spread (clockwise from far left)

These traditional floral arrangements on pedestral trays are used in Buddhist ordination ceremonies; «*kratae*» – a floral squirrel made from orchid petals, small gardenias, rose petals and orange jessamine leaves; detail of «*phan dokmai*» covered with an intricate floral net of small gardenias; a floral tassel – part of a floral pendant – as seen from below; and «*khruang khwaen*» – a floral pendant tied with a floral tassel.

Malai
Floral Garlands

Before a group of Thai traditional classical musicians plays, each member will «wai khru», or pay respect to their teachers, using a «wai» gesture with a «malai», or floral garland, in their hands. They will then gently place the garlands onto their musical instruments.

The smell of «*dok champa*», orange champak (of the magnolia family), soon permeates the air. The *wai khru* prepares the minds of both the musicians and their audience. A brief moment of quiet follows… then the music starts.

Malai are the most common Thai floral feature; visitors may notice them soon after their arrival in the kingdom. From the simplest *malai* at Bangkok's central flower market – Pak Khlong Talad – to the most intricate creations at the Inner Court of the Grand Palace, these garlands serve as decorations, offerings and gifts in Thai flower culture.

Rounded garlands of small white flowers can be seen on the wall murals in the centre of the small crypt inside the tower of Wat Ratchaburana, Ayutthaya, complete with «*uba*», or tassels, of water lilies. Being one of the oldest mural paintings in the kingdom – dating from the early Ayutthaya period; the crypt was sealed off from human sight in 1424 AD – this serves as a rare record of Thai floral art.

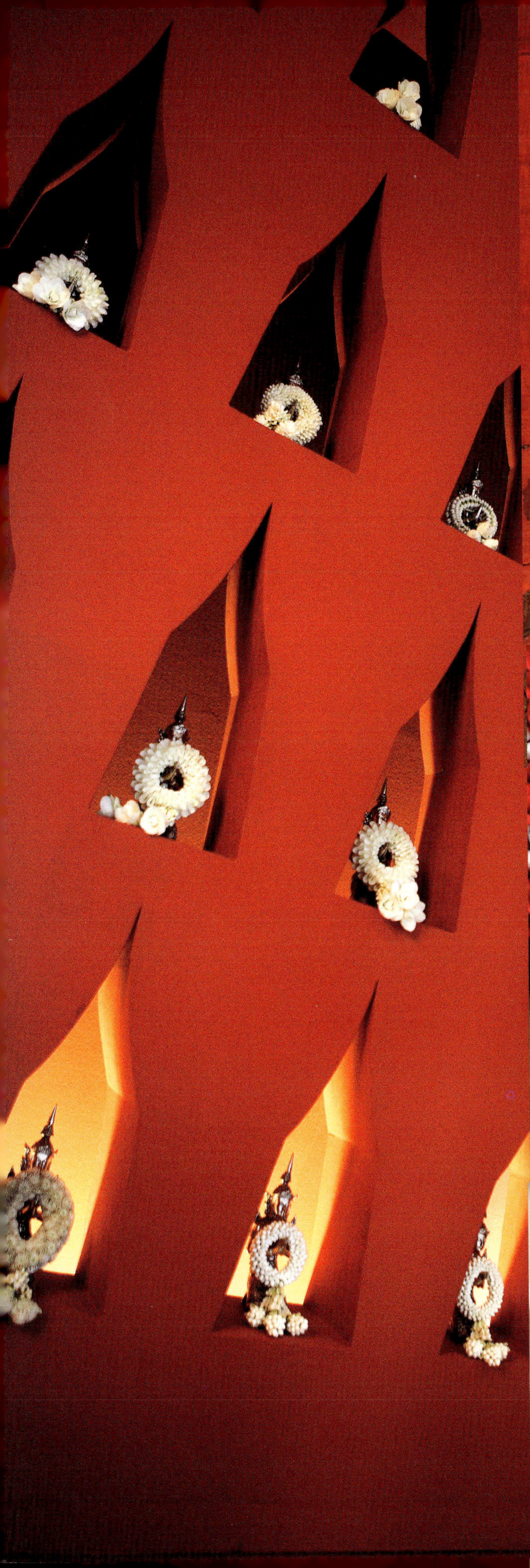
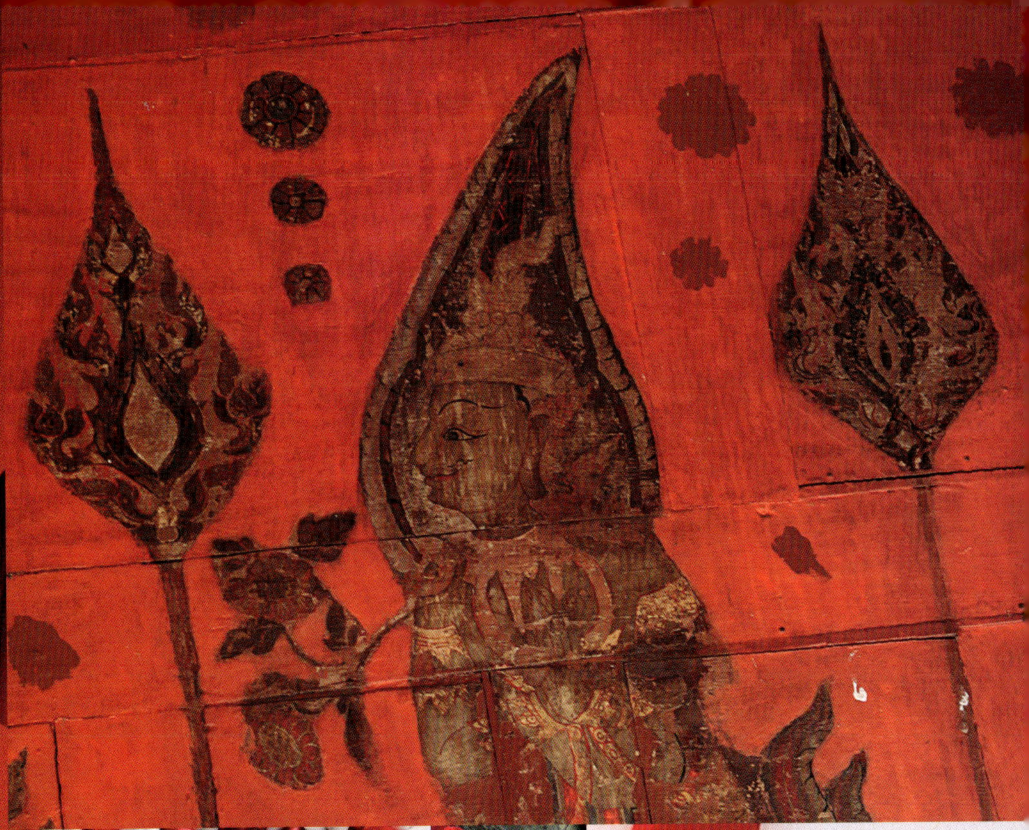
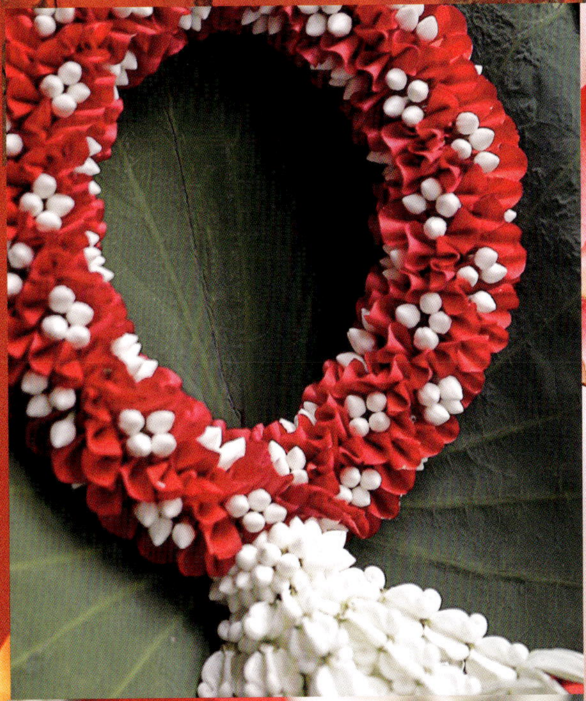
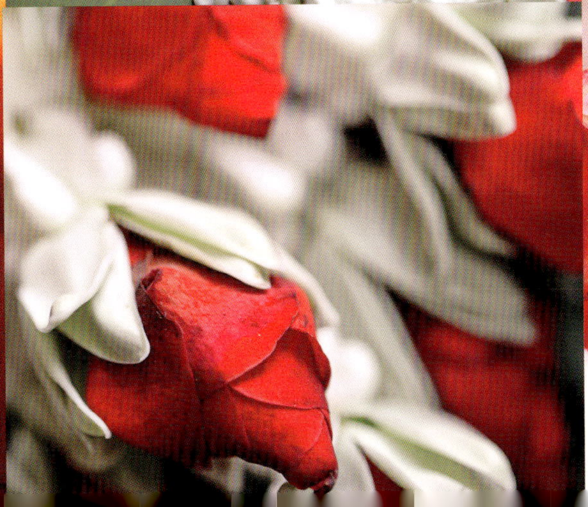
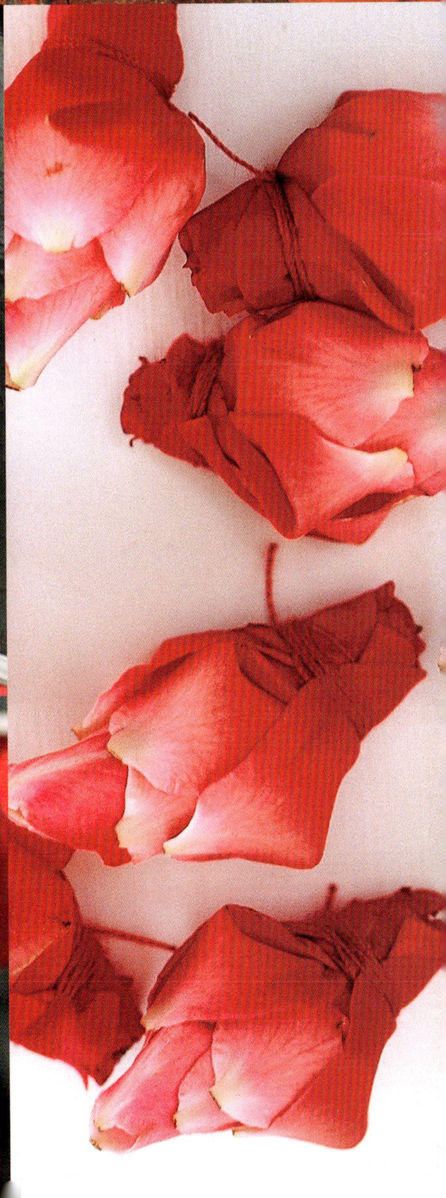

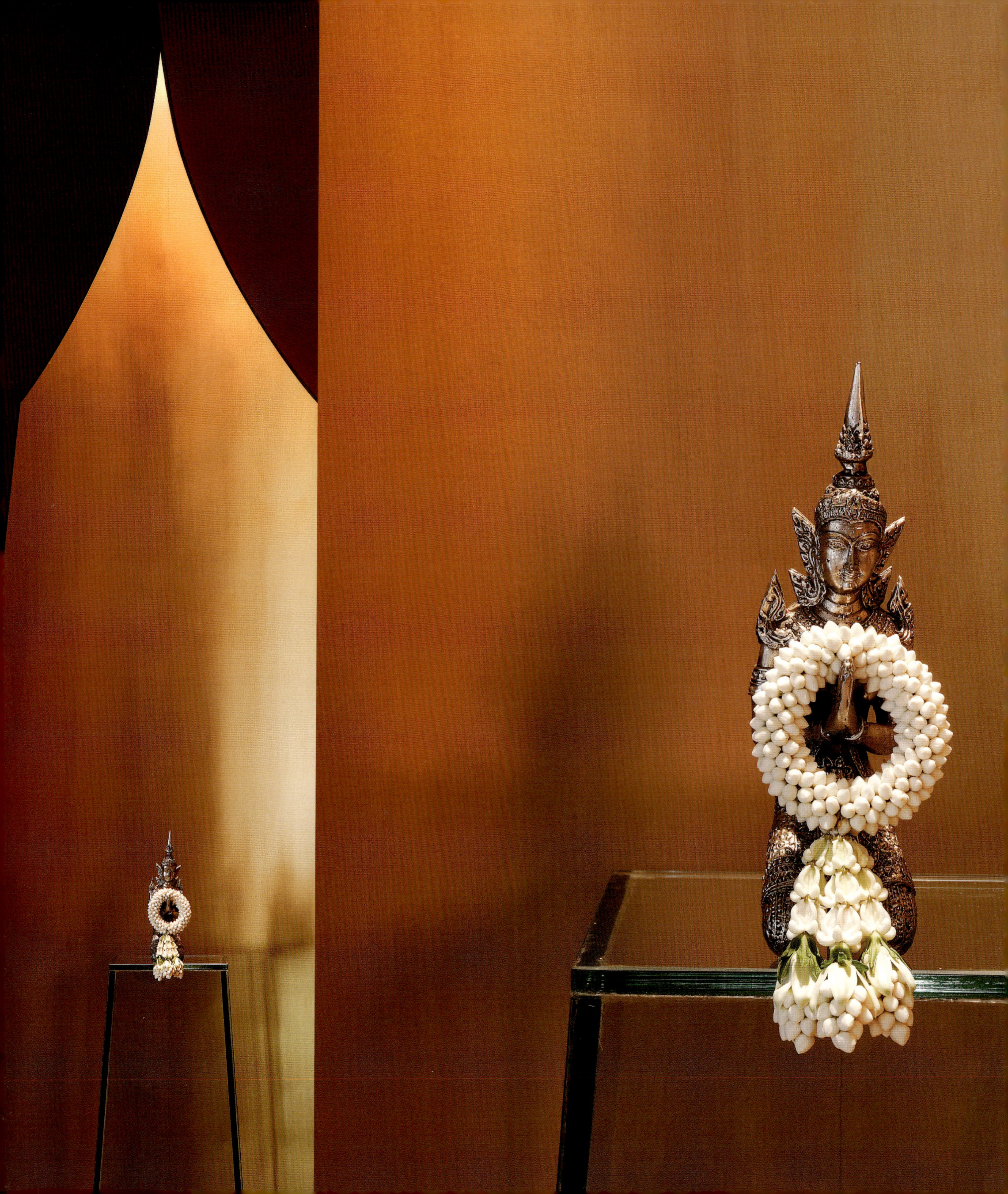

The *malai* are painted clearly on a red background, serving as part of the wall decoration among other plant and flower motifs. This is similar to the manner in which *malai* are used in the present day. Often punctuated by «*thad hu*» (patterned banana leaves sewn with fresh flower petals) and *uba* (floral tassels), *malai* can be seen decorating the sides of dining tables, walls, handrails and other architectural features.

Opening Spread (clockwise from left)

Jasmine, crown flowers and orchid petals can be used to create these small white garlands which decorate Devarana Spa in the Dusit Thani Bangkok; a mural painting at the former residence of King Rama I, Tumnak Chan, at Wat Rakhang Khositaram monastery; «*dokkha*» are made from rose petals, each one held together by a delicate thread to form a small lotus-like bud; the *dokkha* are typically sewn as the ending of floral tassels; and a hand garland made from rose petals and small gardenias.

This Spread (clockwise from far left)

A small white garland graces an angelic statue in Devarana Spa's yoga room; a similar garland constructed from small gardenias; crown flower petals are sewn into these round garlands, with orchid petals made up into *dokkha* for the tassel endings; small garlands crown the princes and princesses at King Rama V's inner court; simple garlands made from globe amaranth flowers; and orchid-petal garlands are a modern addition to traditional floral art.

20 *Malai*

Another frequent use of *malai* is as an offering, for purposes both religious and reverent. In a Thai temple, together with lit candles and incense sticks, flower stems or *malai* are placed in front of Buddha images as part of the offering. In the same way, Thais will adorn revered statues – of kings and Buddhist monks, for example – with floral garlands to express their respect. *Malai* also comprise a significant part of the daily alms received by monks.

This Spread

Four garlands made from different plant materials: the dark green leaves of orange jessamine; light green «*dok khajorn*» flowers, with a small gardenia at the centre of each; red rose petals and small gardenias are used in this garland; and a pinkish red garland of rose petals is patterned with gardenias and orange jessamine leaves.

Far Right: This «*thad hu*» – patterned banana leaves sewn with flower petals – is made from crown flowers.

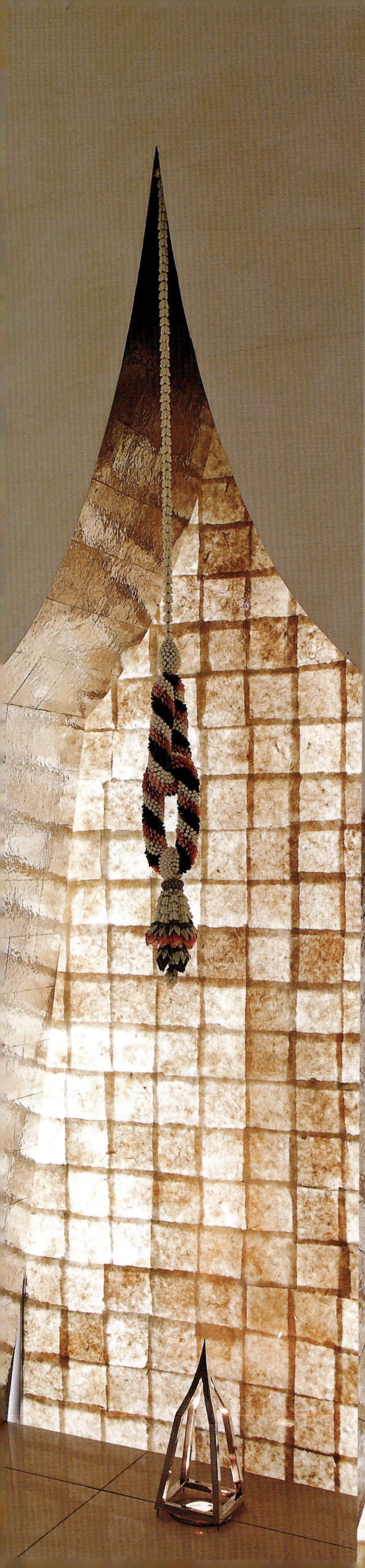
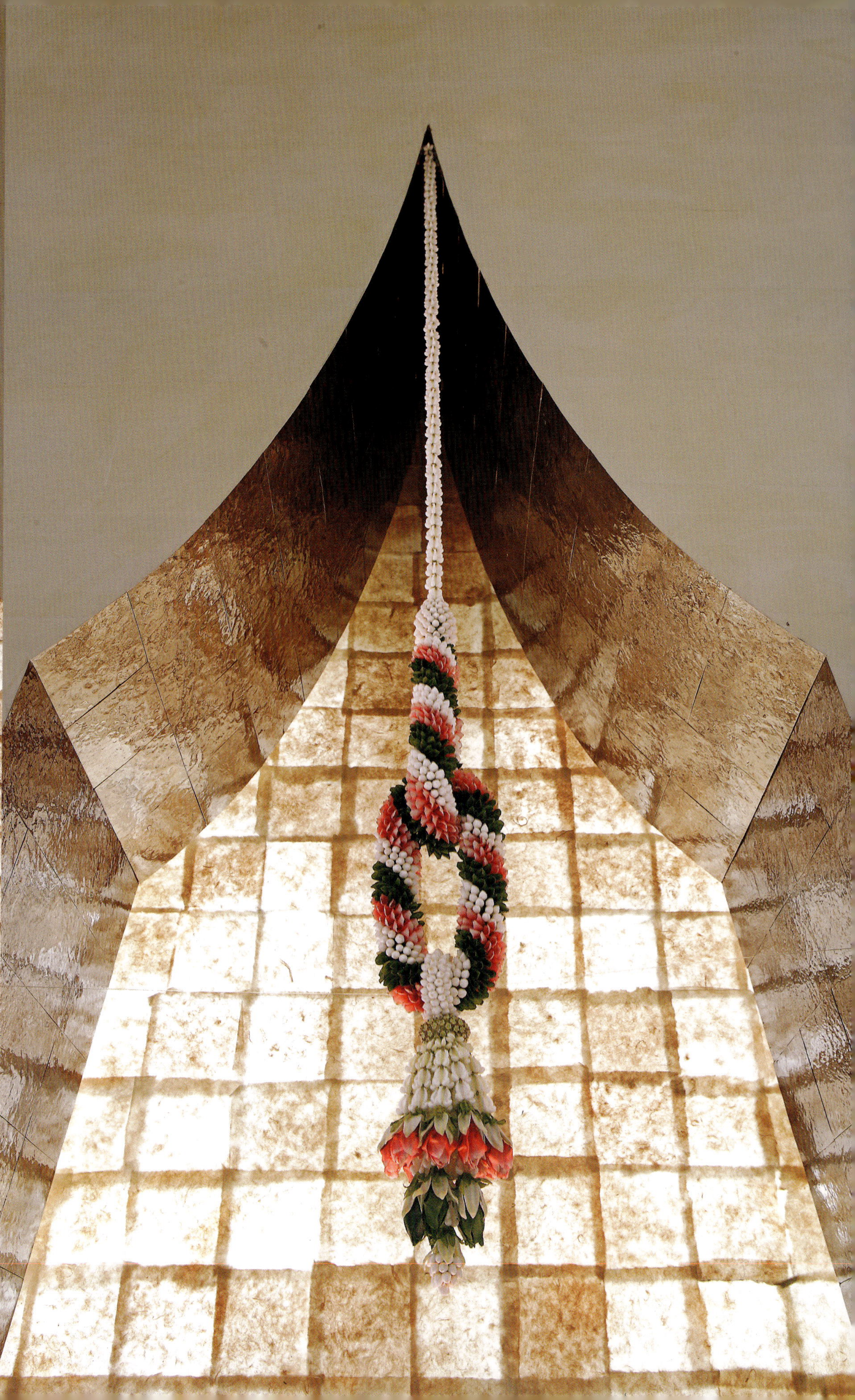

Greeted with a fresh flower garland, no one, be they foreign visitor or Thai, can but admire the beauty of these petite flowers or loose petals sewn into complicated patterns and finished with floral tassels. Carefully crafted by dextrous hands, and with attention to the smallest detail, *malai* is an excellent welcome gift. Small and simple garlands, mimicking the shape of small animals like squirrels, are sometimes also given to departing guests. Long string garlands, with a tassel at each end, are given to people on special occasions to wear around their necks – like the bride and groom on their wedding day, or a victorious athlete.

This Spread

These «*malai gleow*» are made from orange jessamine leaves, rose petals and small white gardenias.

Left: Two interlinked garlands make simple floral pendants.

This Spread

Floral pendants constructed from triple-chained garlands decorate one of Tumnak Chan's gilded windows at Wat Rakhang Khositaram – orchid petals give the white and pink colours, orange jessamine leaves the green.

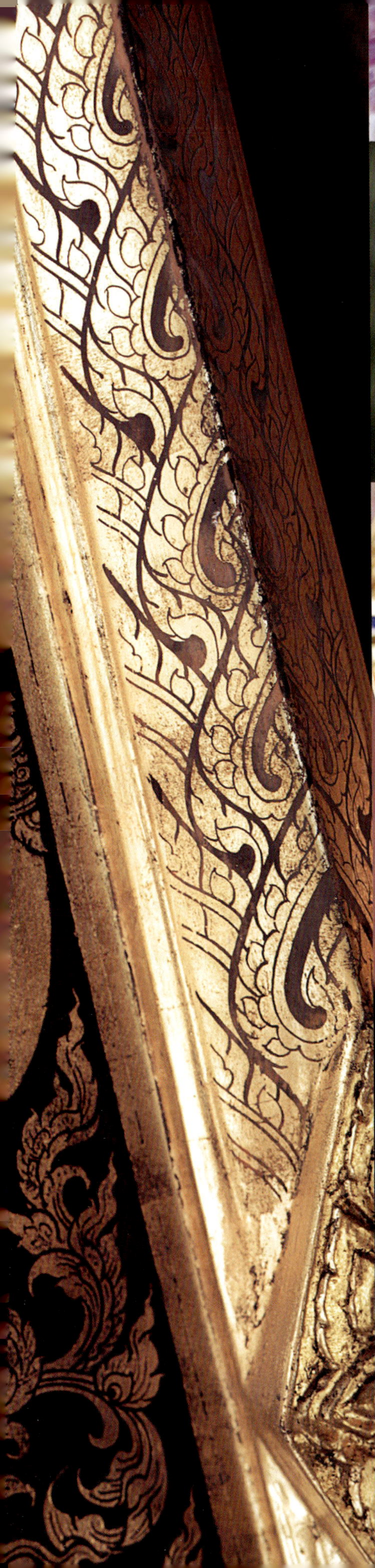
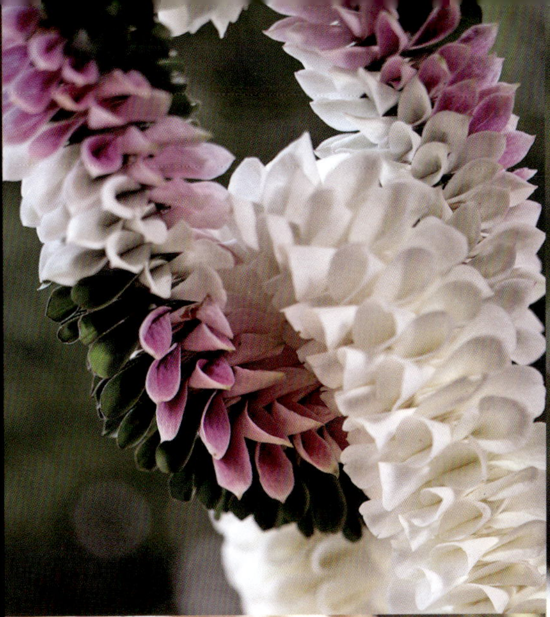
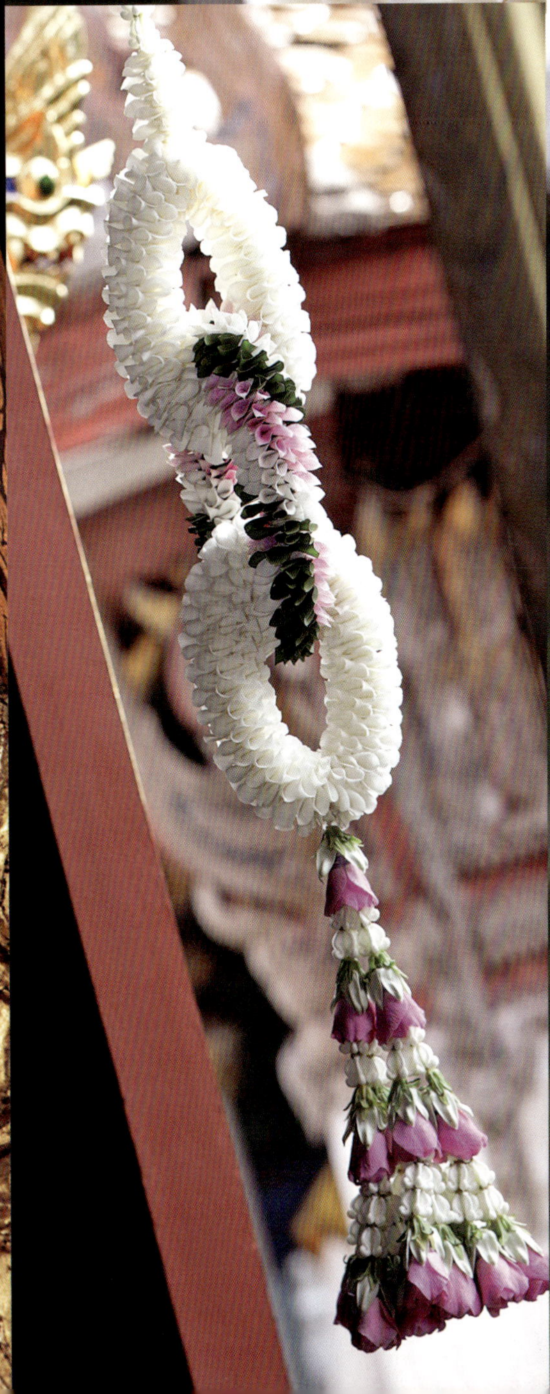
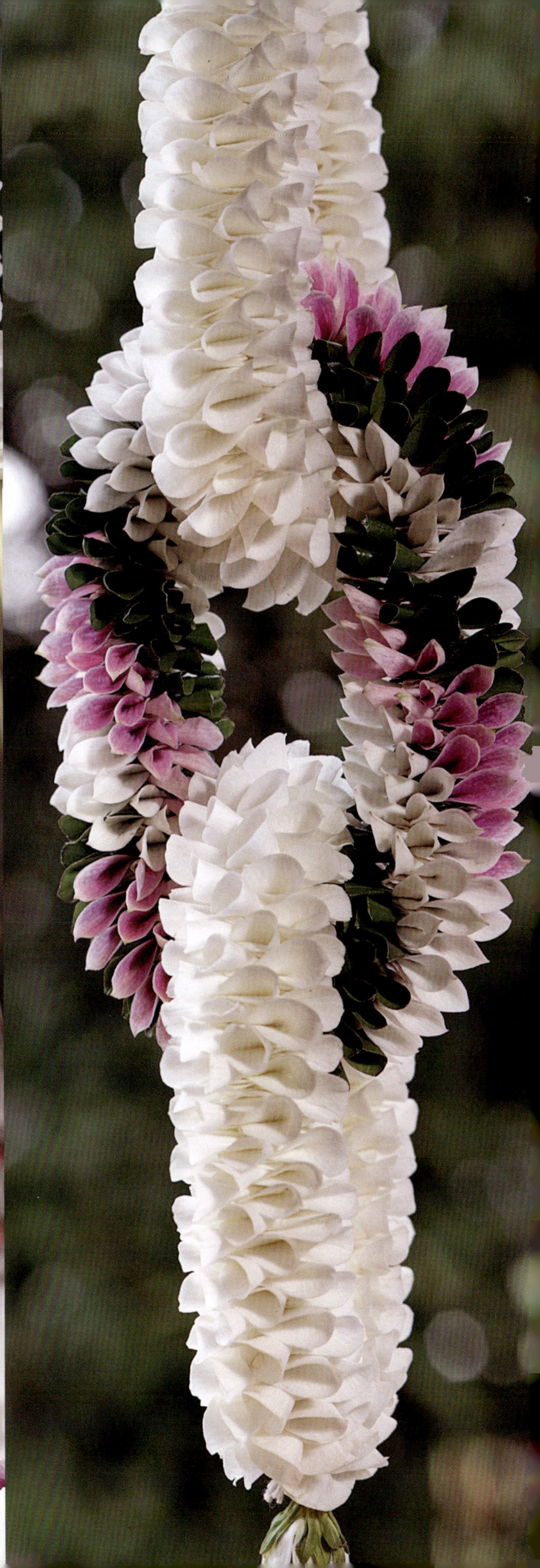

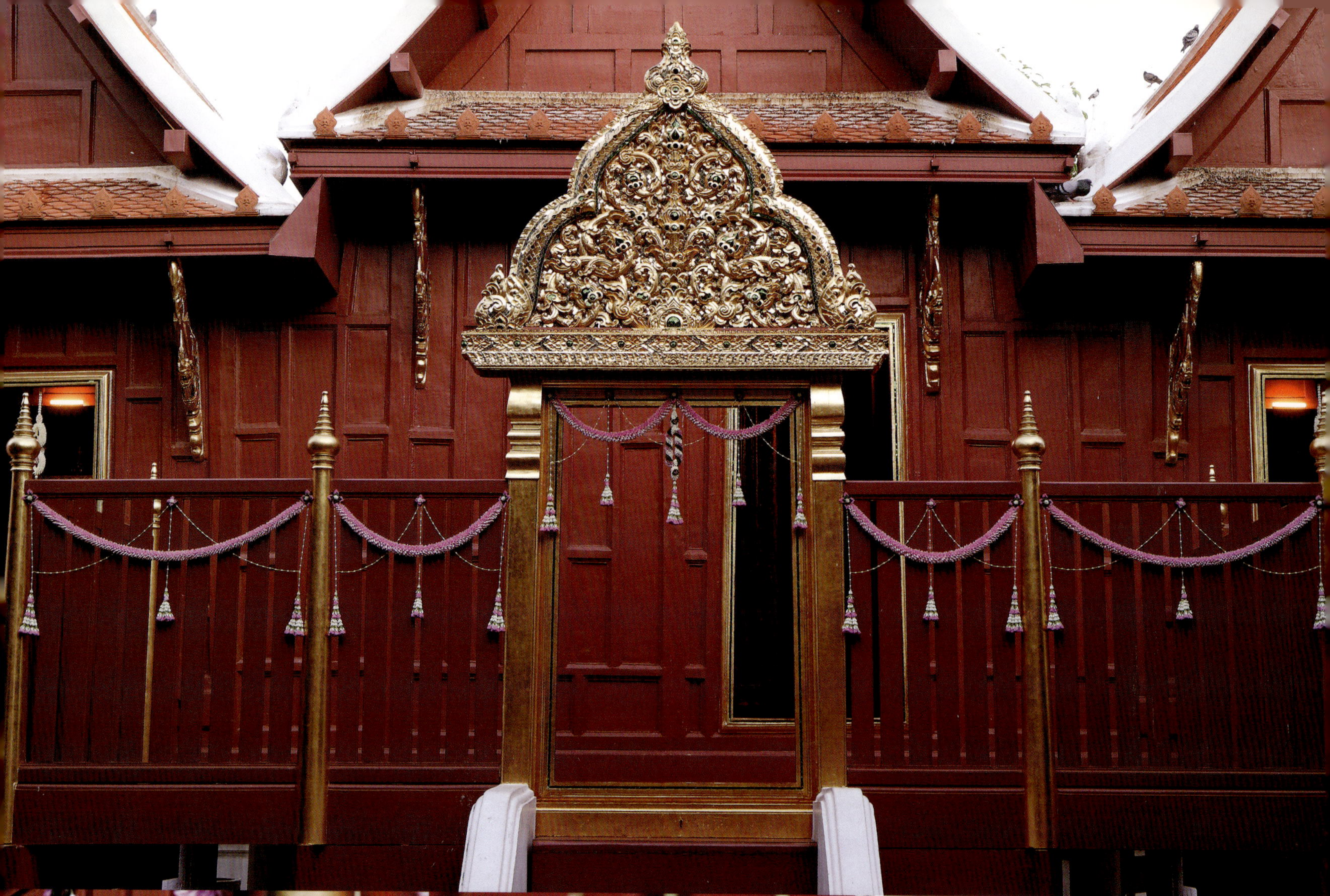

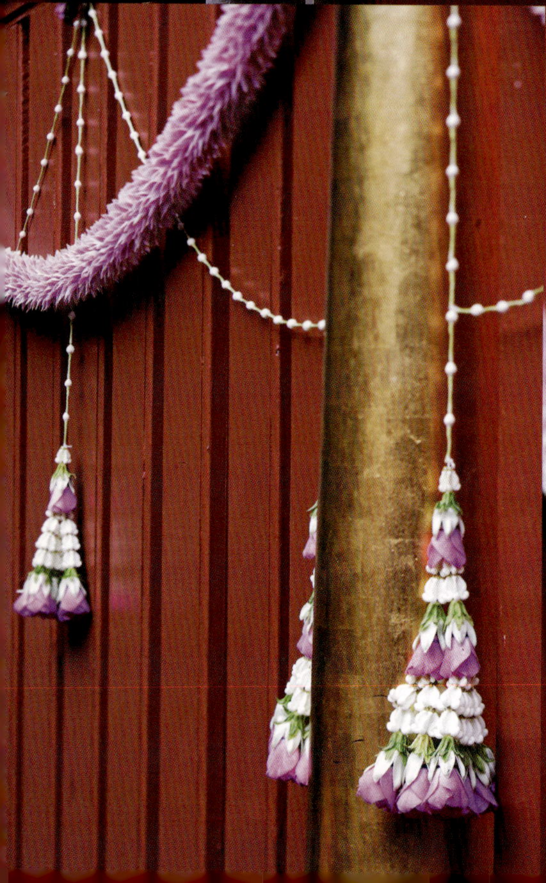

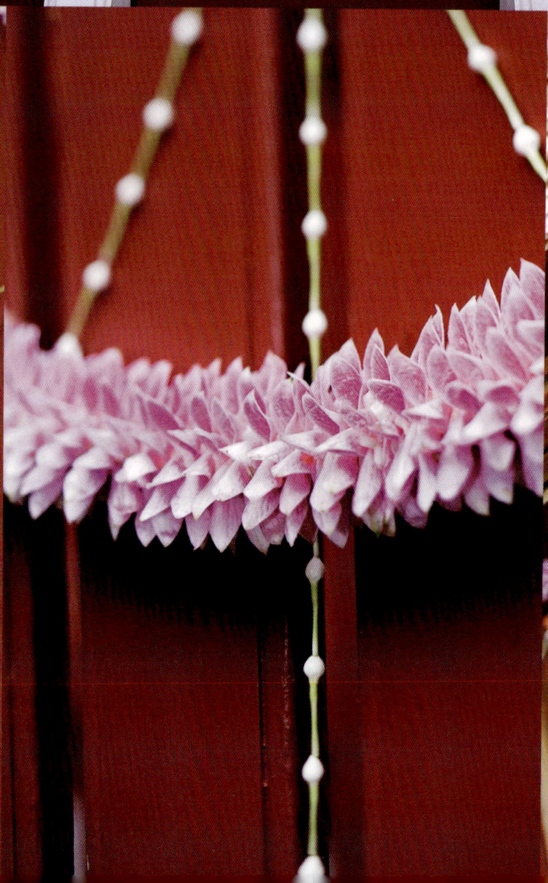

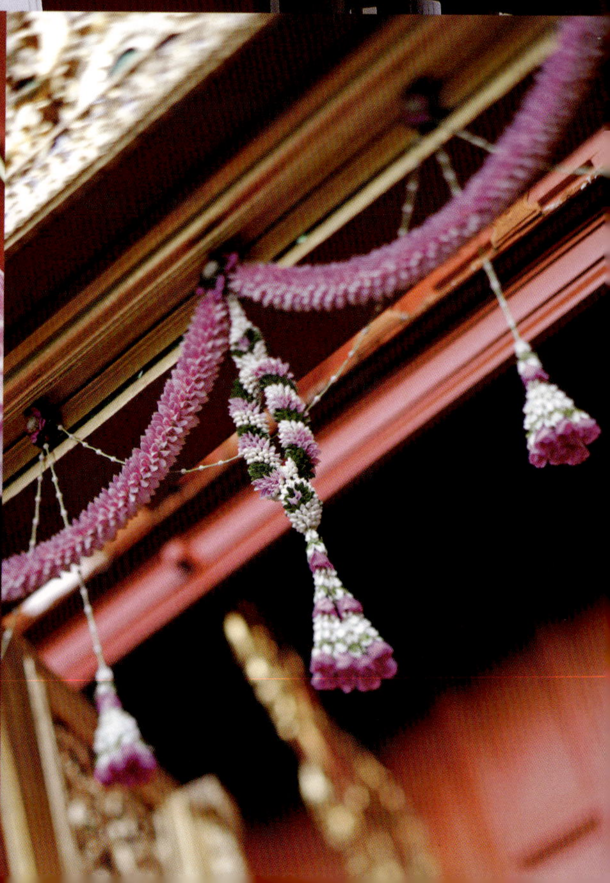

Records show that *malai* had reached their golden age during the reign of King Rama V (King Chulalongkorn the Great). The ladies of the court spent hours each day arranging flowers. Each then taught the designs to her ladies-in-waiting. Also educated in *malai*-making were the young girls who lived in the palace, who received 'finishing school' education under the royal ladies' patronage.

This Spread

As well as their use as gifts or offerings, *malai* can also be utilised for decorative purposes. Two different types of garlands adorn a royal residence's gate and fence; the pink garlands are sewn from orchid petals, the petite white strings from small gardenias.

Top Right: A special garland named «*malai khruie*» was conceived by Chaokhunphra Prayurawongse in the reign of King Rama V, to be worn as an accessory by a male court official.

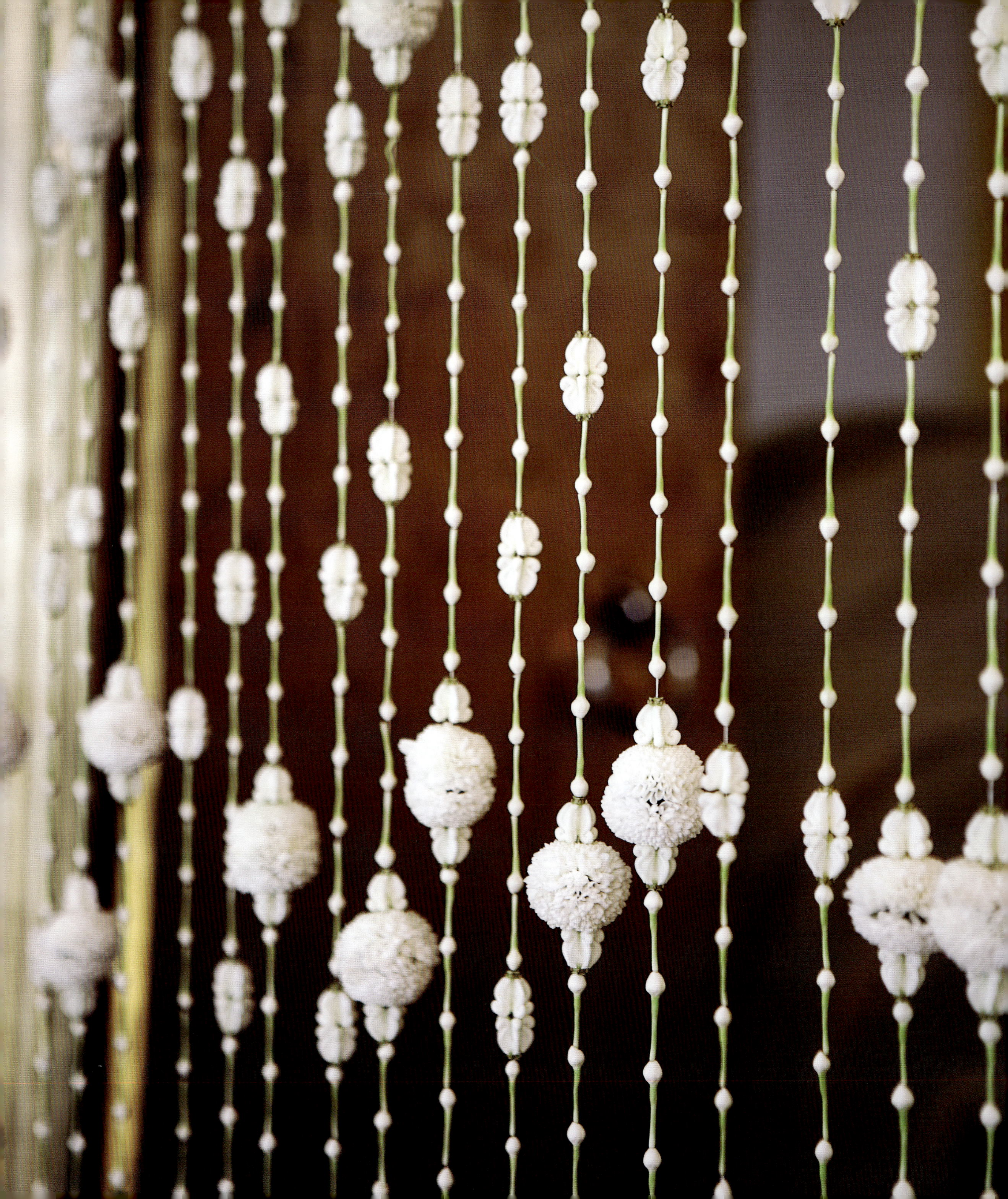

This Spread

These contemporary-style floral curtains by Sakul Intakul are made with crown flowers, small gardenias and chrysanthemums.

Her Majesty Queen Saowabha Phongsri, mother of King Rama VI, was particularly accomplished in *malai* art. She transformed traditional *malai* design – plain rounded shapes made solely with jasmine – by creating myriad beautiful and complicated patterns, along with elegant designs using loose petals and leaves. These royal inventions are believed to be widely practiced even today, adding another layer of intrigue and significance to the art and ensuring that *malai* culture is very much alive in the lives of Thai people.

This Spread

A modern interpretation of floral garland usage by Sakul Intakul, inspired by the traditional floral headdress, as shown *top left*.

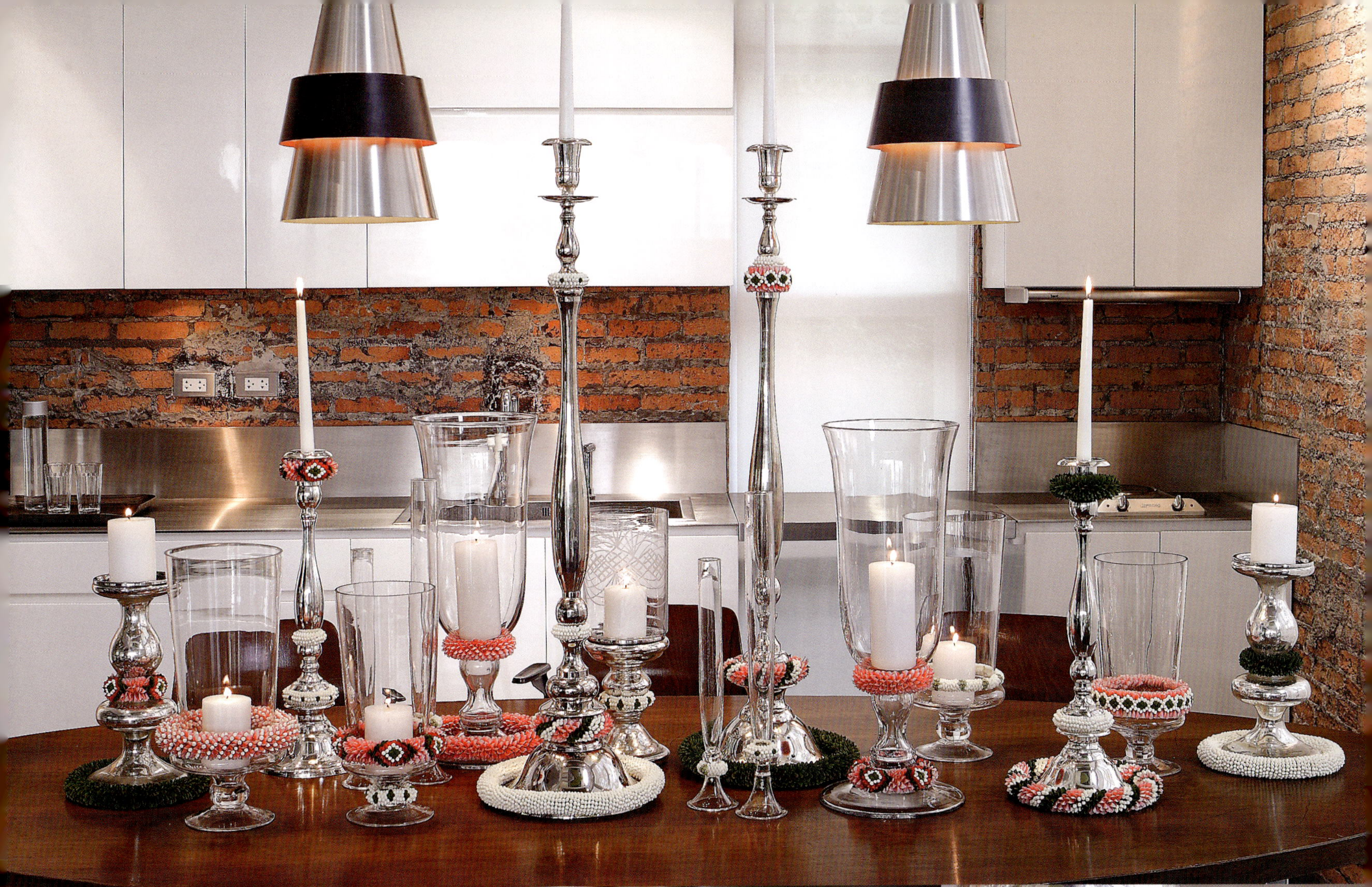
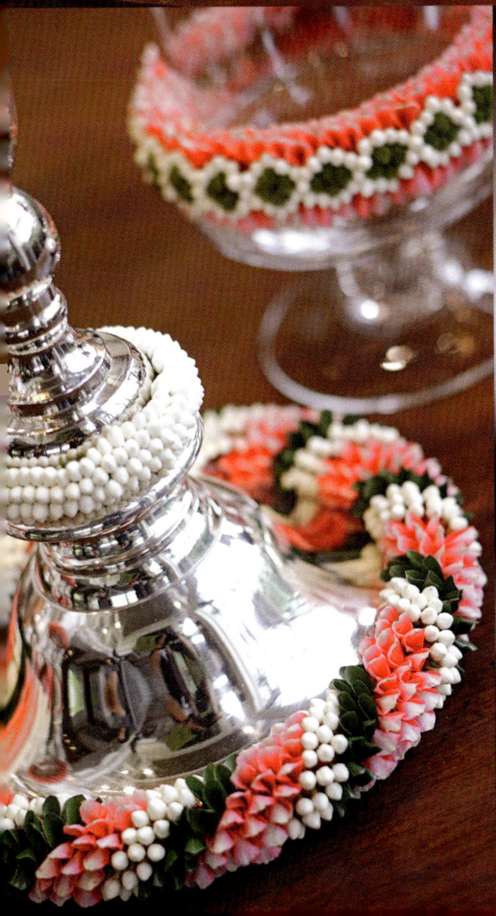
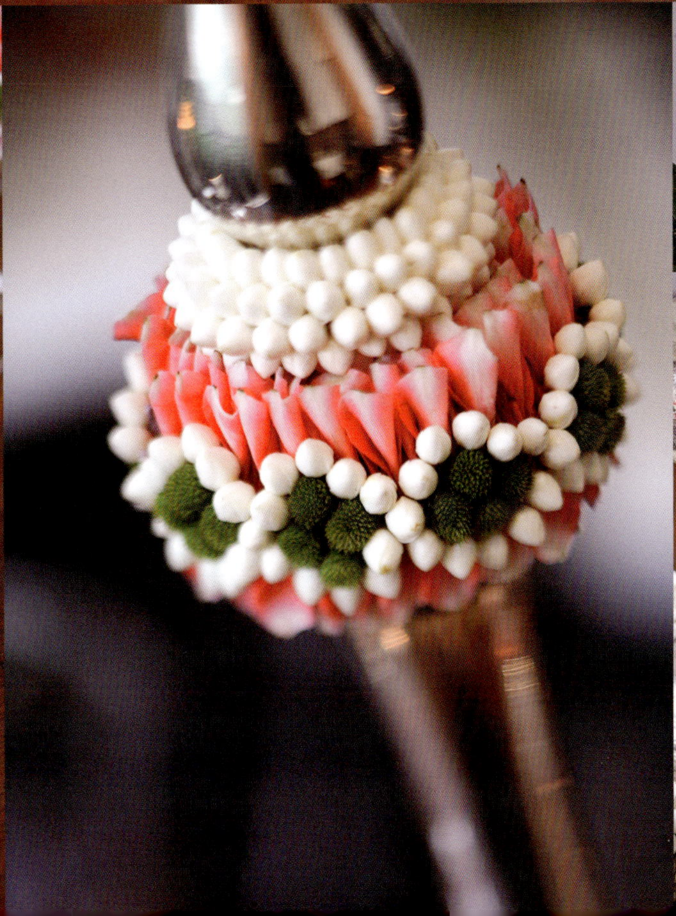
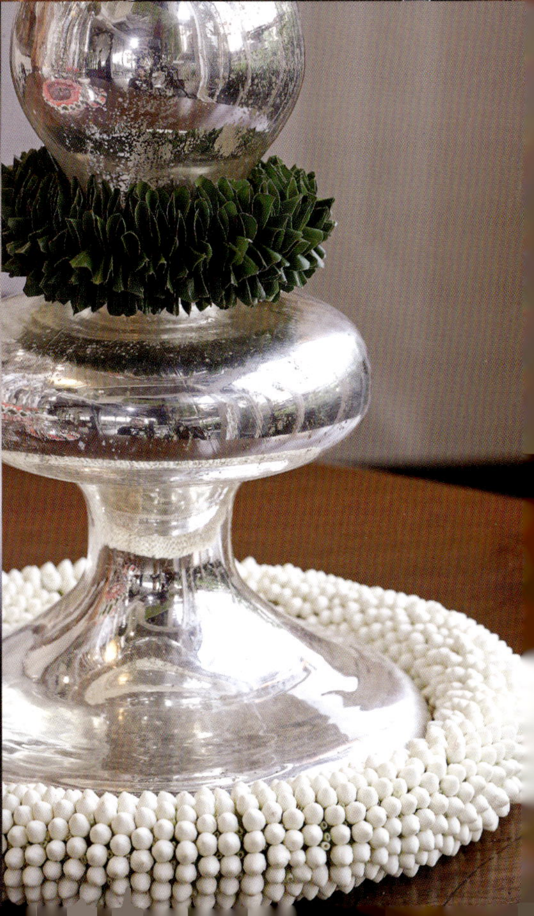

This Spread

Modern garlands made from green orchids decorate stairway handrails at the modern home of Satit Kalawantavanich.

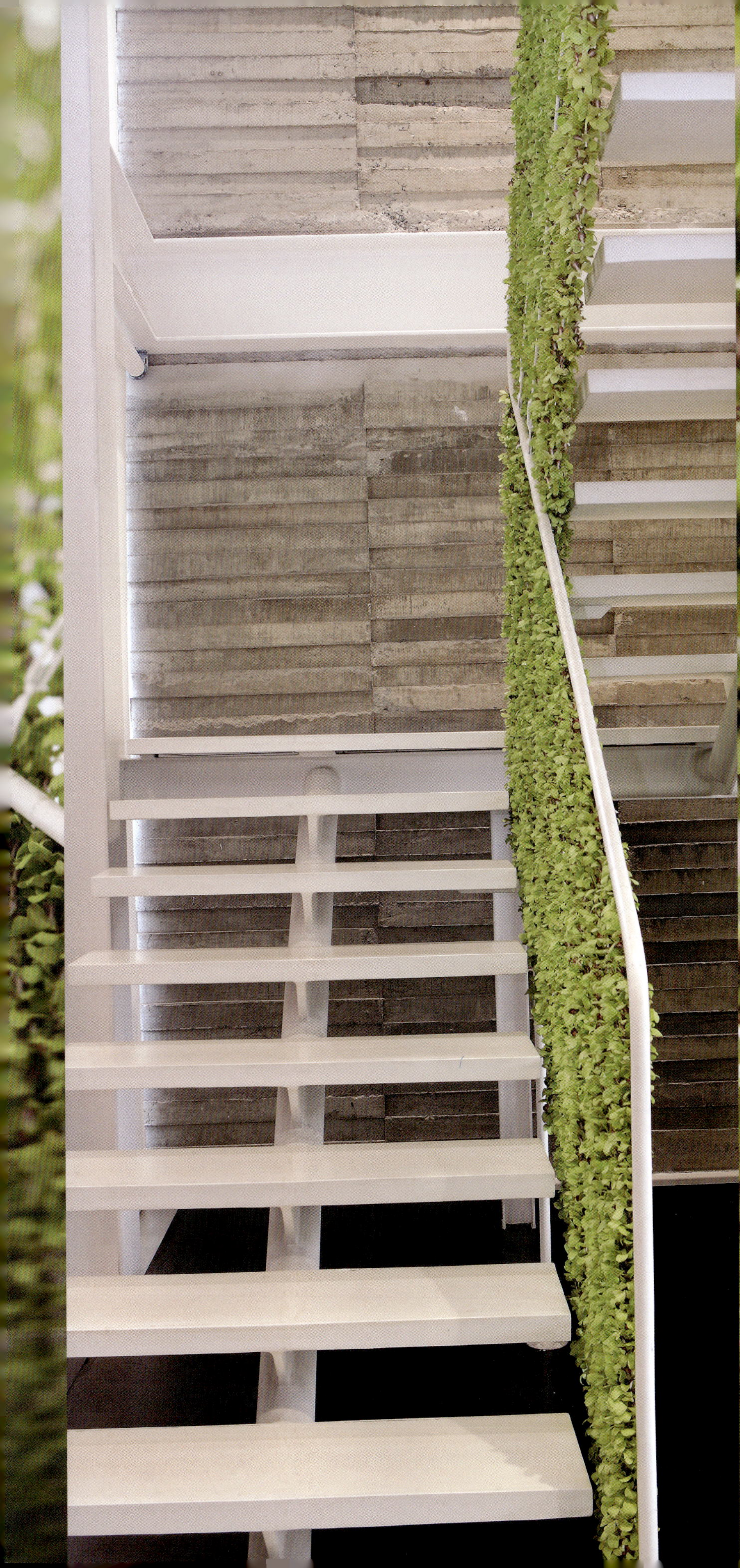

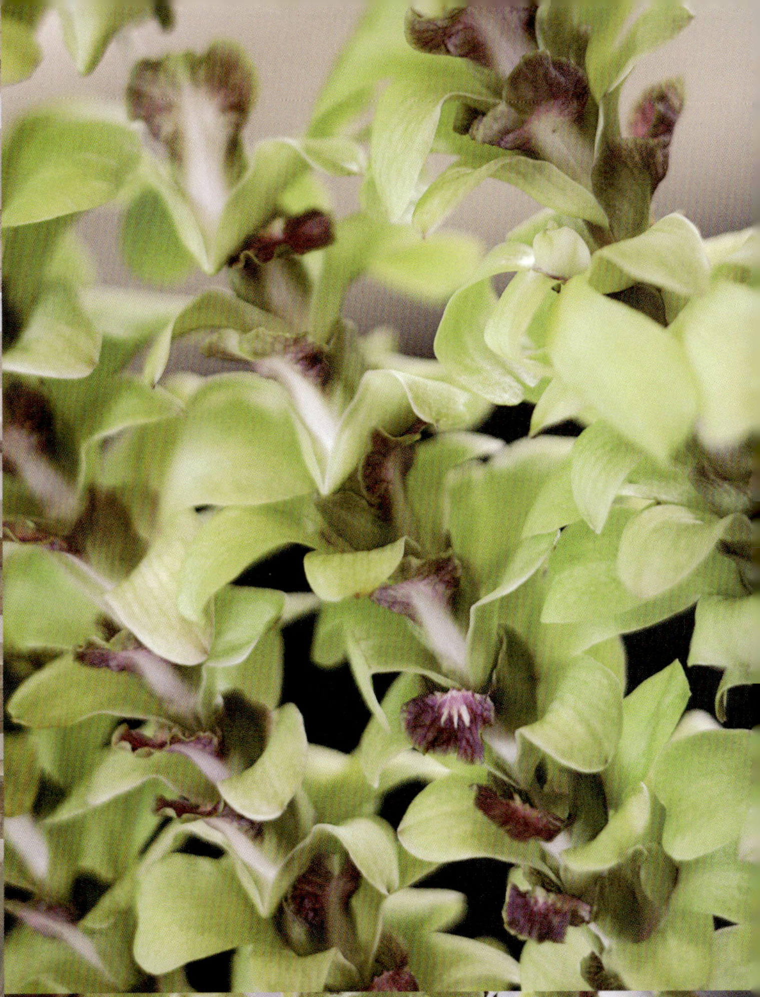

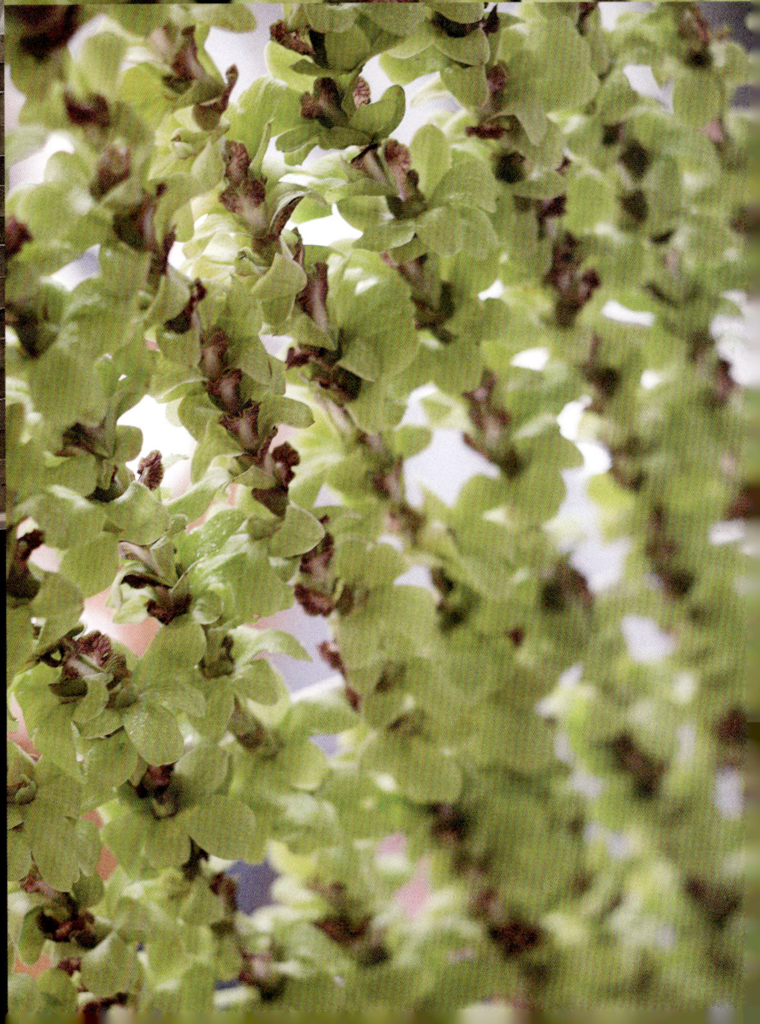

เครื่องแขวน

Khruang Khwaen
Floral Pendants

During summertime, there is an old and very common Thai saying that goes "Dad rom lom tok", which literally translates as "When the sun is gone, the wind blows".

Around February, the cold, dry winds from the South China Sea that sweep across the north-eastern highlands and central plains of Thailand cease to blow. As the winds drop, the mild climate they created rapidly warms. It is now the turn of the southwesterly winds, which signify the approach of summer. At the same time, sweet-fragranced flowers, (such as «*dok champa*», or orange champak, and «*dok mali*», or jasmine, both used in Thai floral art) are in full bloom after a period of low yield, due to the cooler climate.

Rural Thai folk love to grow «*ton champa*», orange champak trees, near their houses. The wind carries the delightful scent of *dok champa* into their homes come evening when they're back from working the paddy fields, making summer evenings in Southeast Asia's hot and humid climate incalculably more pleasurable.

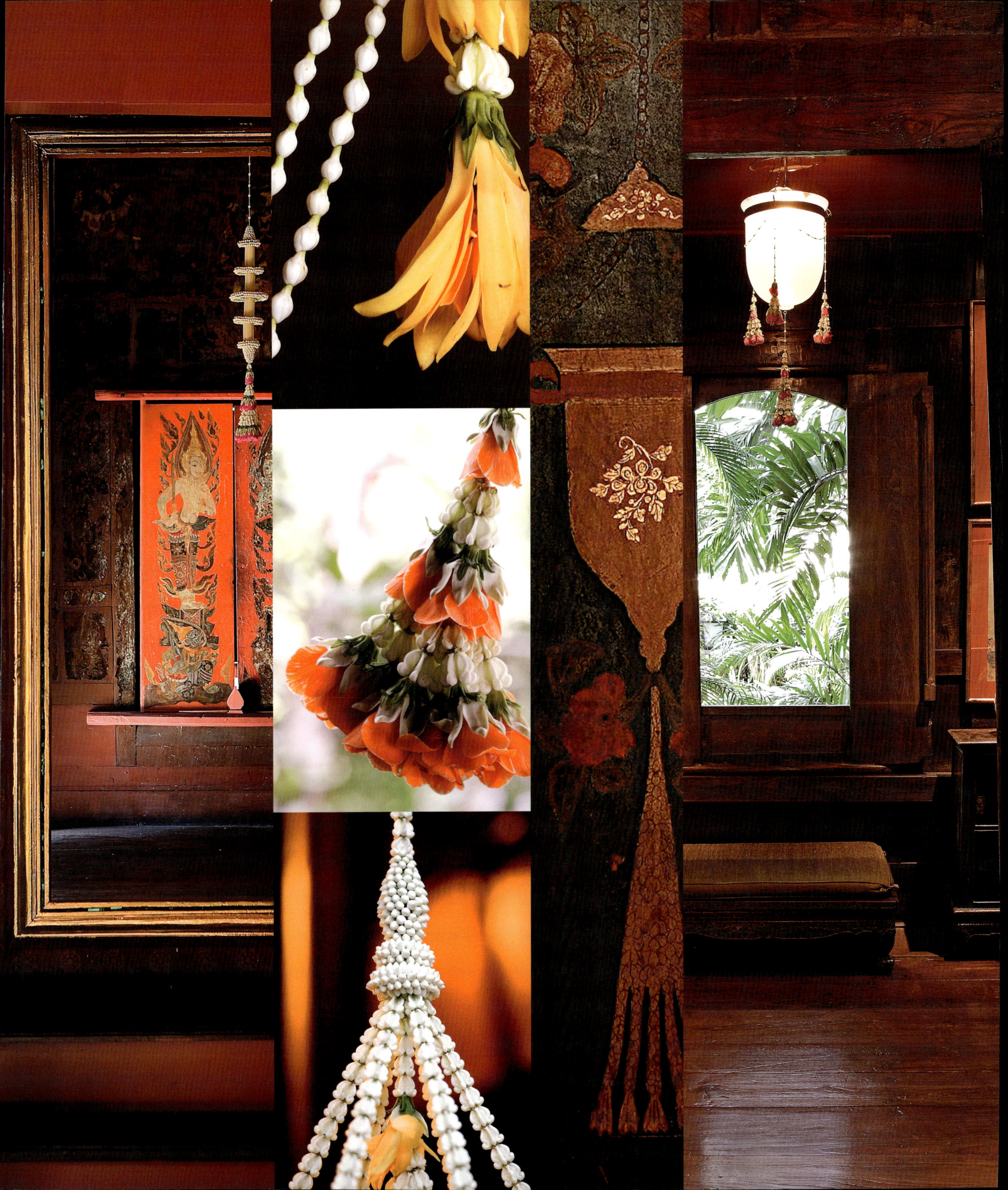

This Page

The two-dimensional floral pendant «*Chorakhe*» is made from a net of small gardenias.

Opposite Page

The small but extraordinary hexagonal floral pendant «*klin ta-khaeng*» is constructed from rare purple crown flowers. Three long needles are used to create its inner structure.

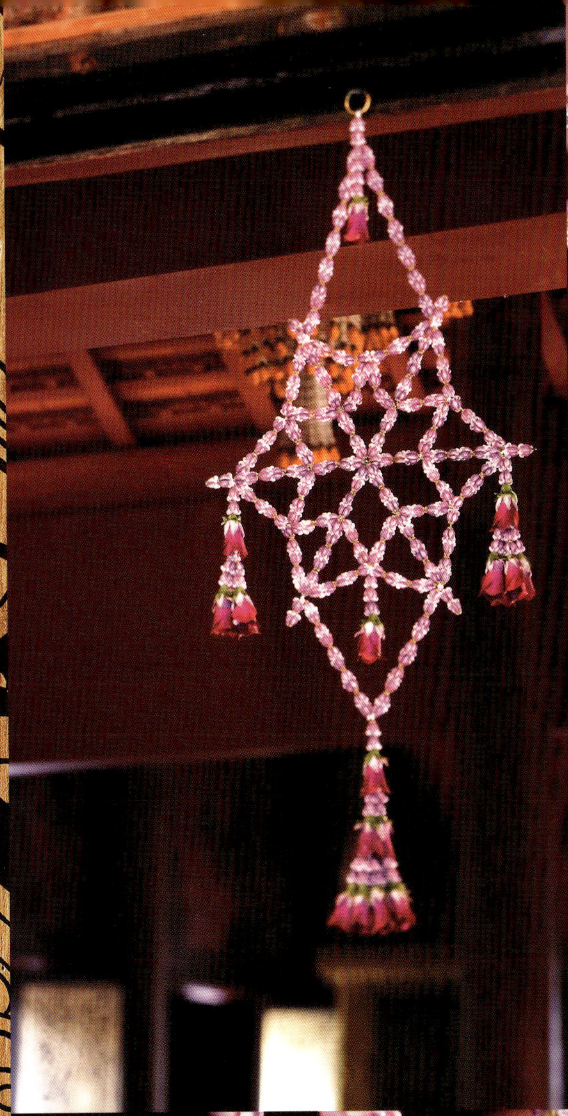
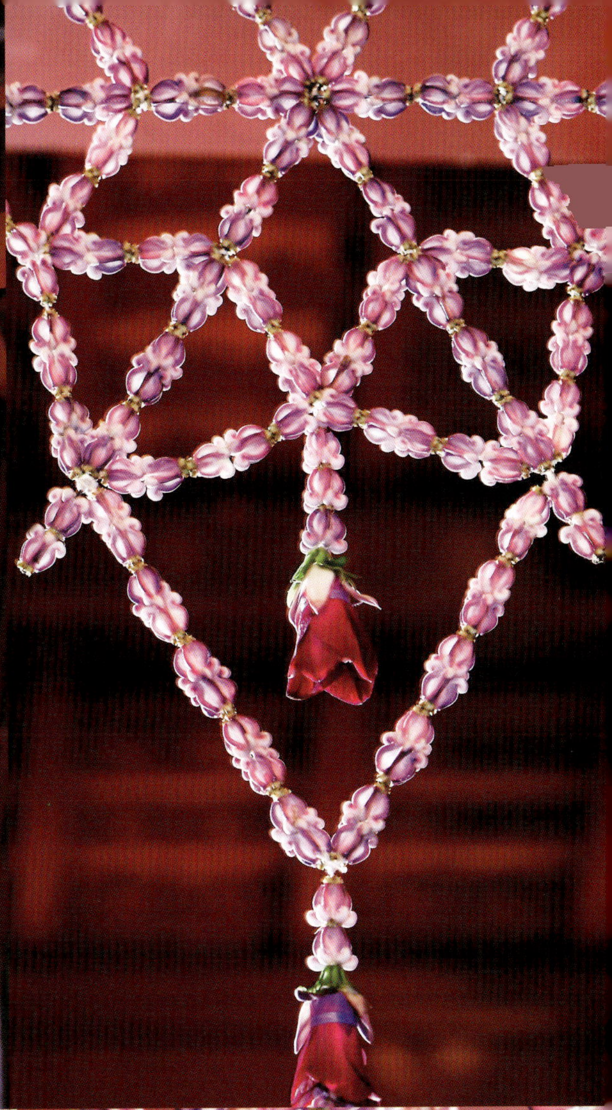
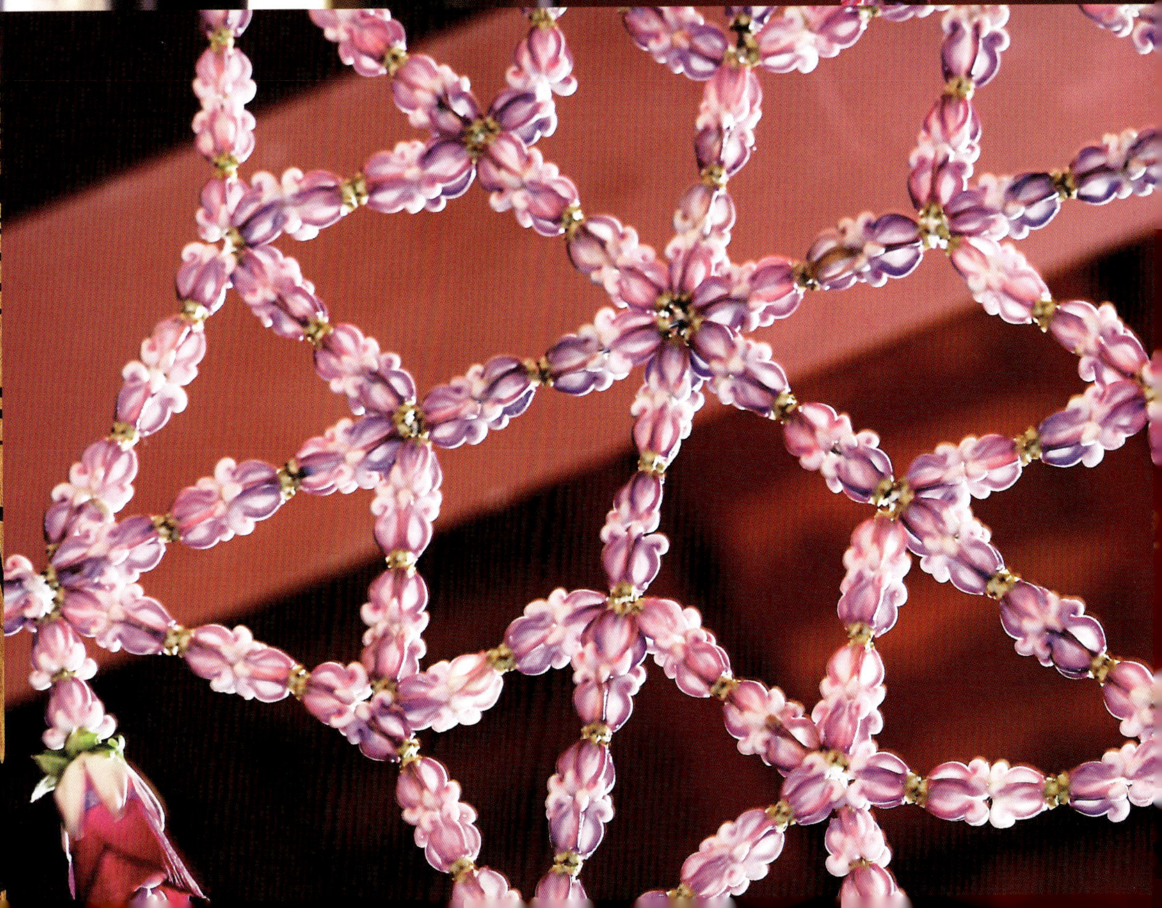

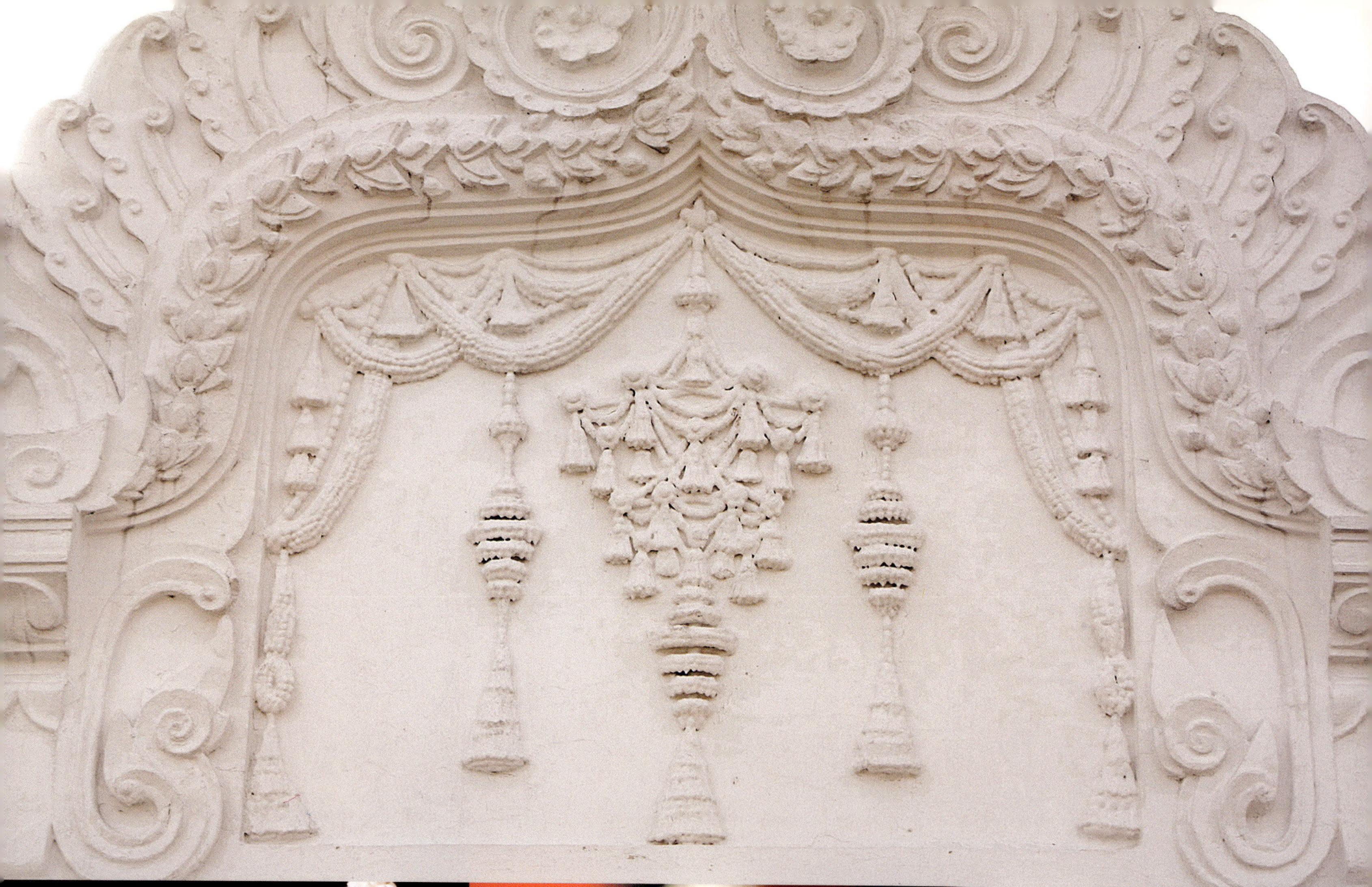
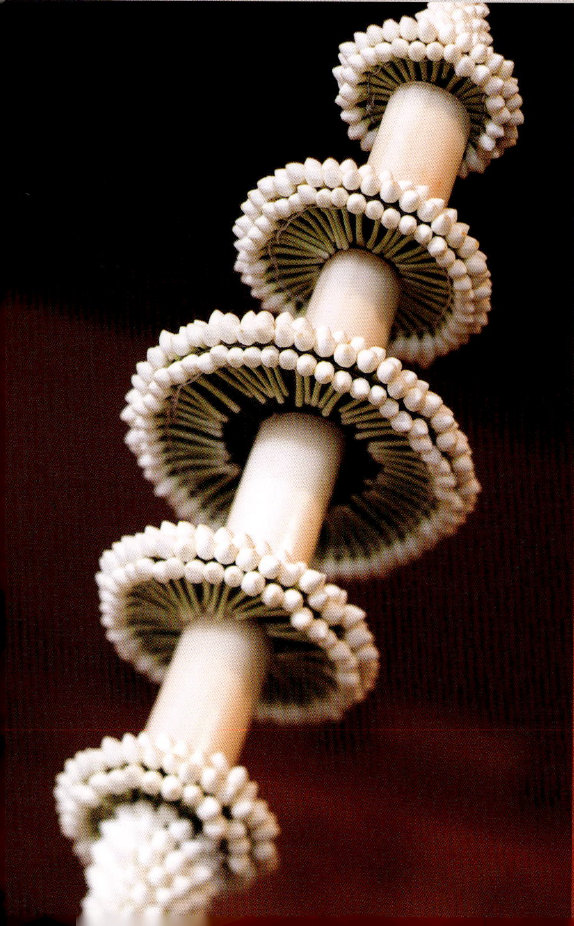
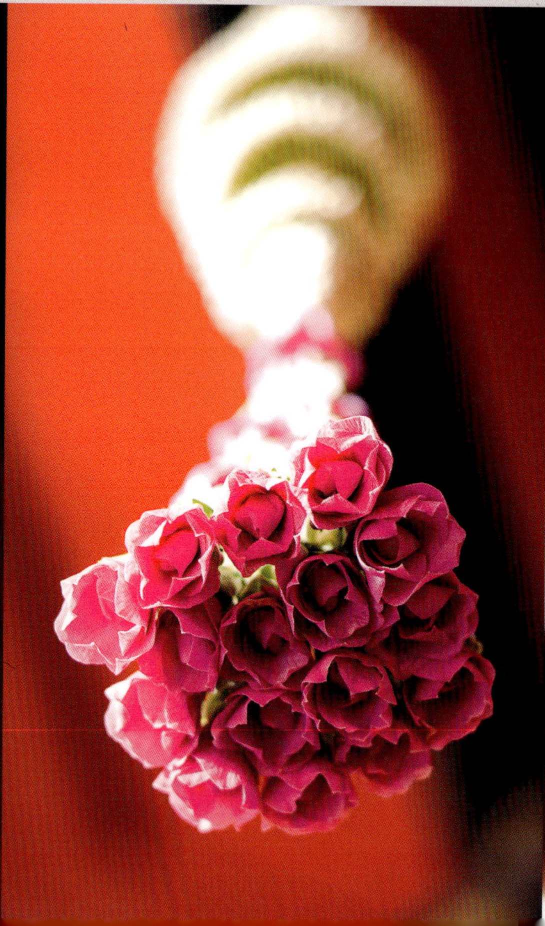
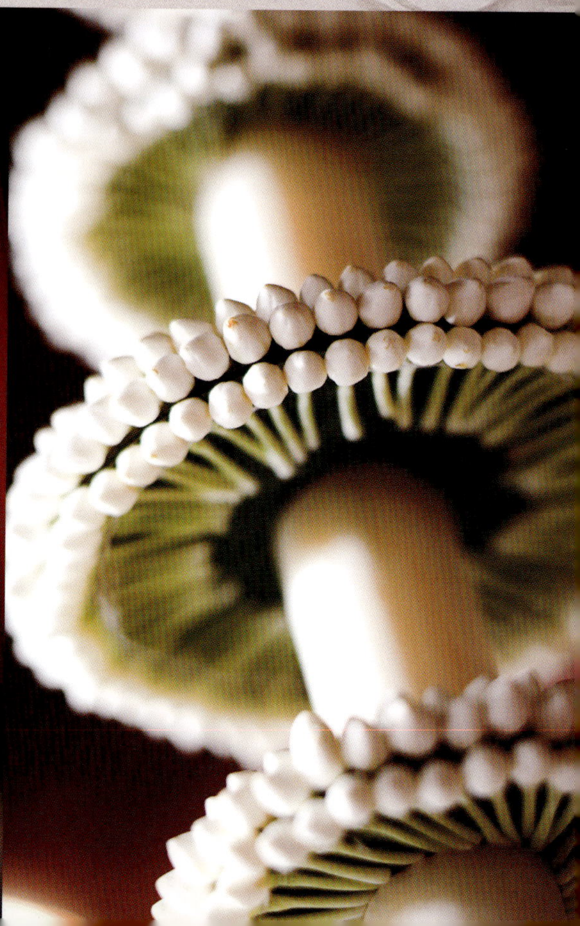

Opening Spread (clockwise from left)

Small pendant «*phu klin*» decorates a living chamber of Tumnak Chan at Wat Rakhang Khositaram, Bangkok; «*dok champa*» (orange champak) is a favourite perfumed flower for tassel endings; mural painting from the reign of King Rama III at Wat Thepthidaram, Bangkok; floral tassels decorate a suspended lamp at The Jim Thompson House and Museum in Bangkok – the floral work was inspired by the mural paintings pictured here; the top section of a floral pendant crowned with «*malai toom*» traditional decorative garlands; and «*uba song-khruang*», an elaborate tassel tied with orange-dyed orchid petals.

This Spread

Diminutive pendant *phu klin* is made from small gardenias sewn on five circular pieces of banana leaves; four pieces of banana tree's central core hold it together.

Top Left: A bas-relief on a pavilion's gable at Wat Benjamabhopit in Bangkok displays a set of traditional floral pendants, including three *phu klin*.

Khruang Khwaen

There is another more delicate Thai invention for perfuming the airflow into their living quarters – using the fragrance of fresh flowers. This is «*khruang khwaen*», one of the most distinguished forms of Thai floral art. *Khruang khwaen* means "things to hang"; floral pendants are hung in the centre of the window or door frame, allowing the sweet scent of *dok champa* or *dok mali* to drift straight into the house.

This Spread

Large and sophisticated pendant «*phuang kaeo*» is inspired by the European chandelier and is laced with hundreds of orange champak floral tassels that perfume the air with sweet fragrance.

Top Left: The picture of this elaborate three-dimensional pendant, which evolved from the traditional «*raya noi*» floral mobile, was taken in the century-old reign of King Rama V.

Centre: A pillar mural at the chapel of Wat Somanasviharn in Bangkok depicts traditional Thai floral pendants.

Khruang Khwaen

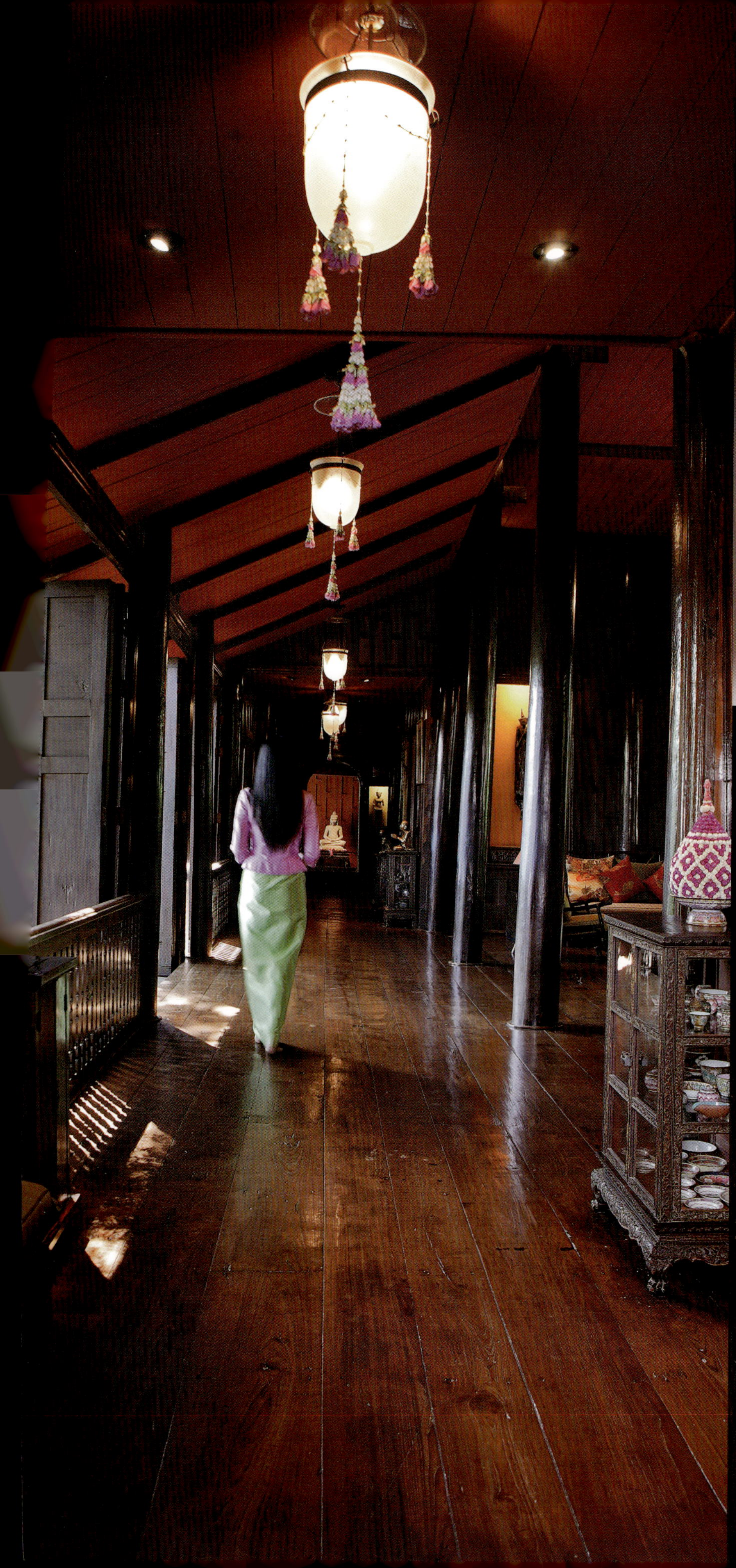
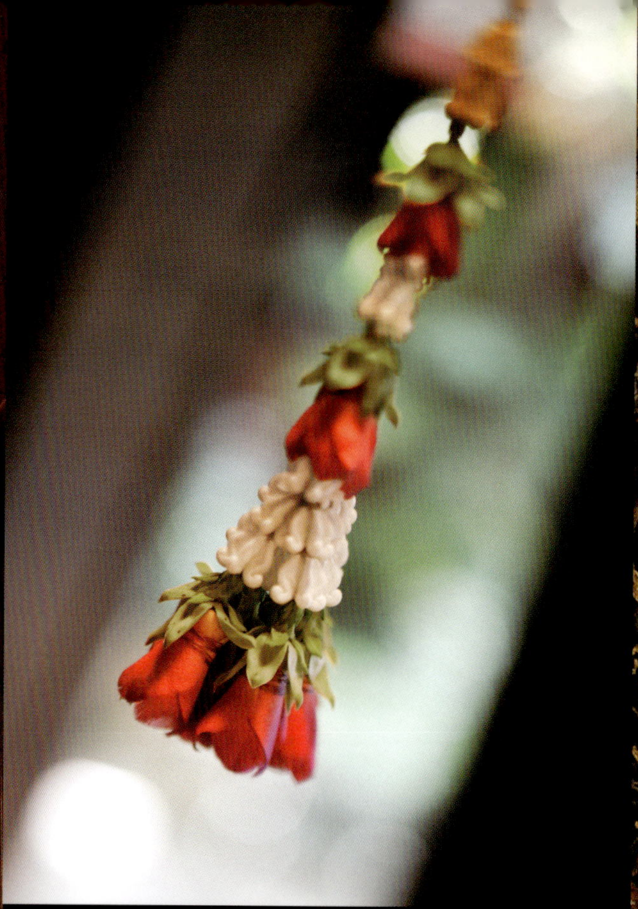
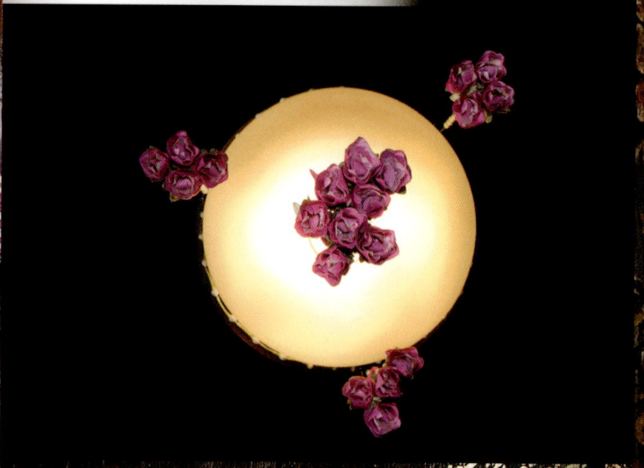
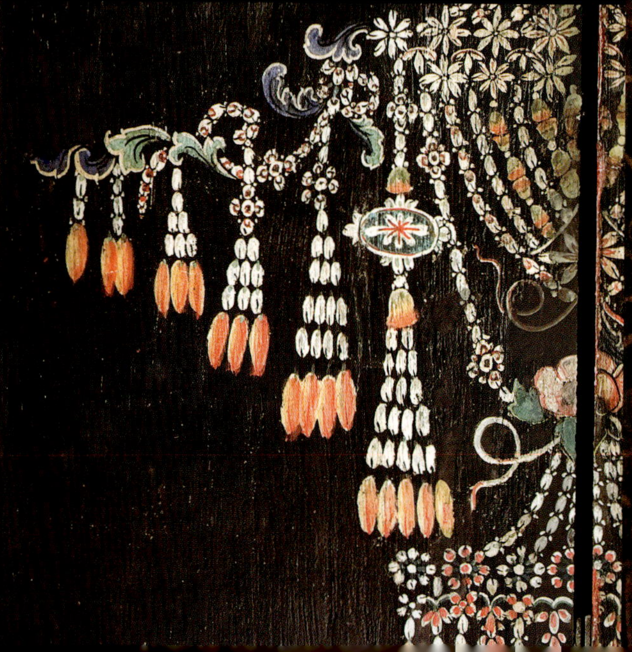
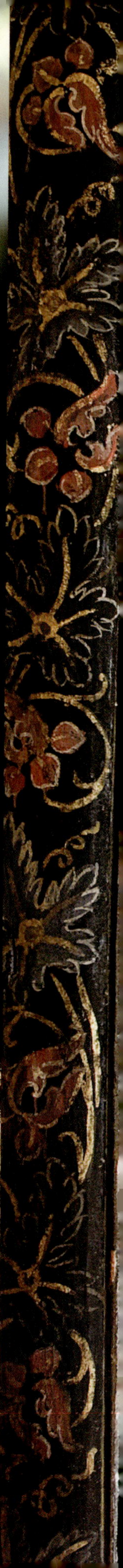

Delicately decorated with Thai floral elements such as floral nets, tassels, garlands and petals (which are sewn onto cut banana leaves to create different patterns and designs), *khruang khwaen* carry a sweet fragrance but are also a real delight to the eyes. Their aesthetic beauty means that *khruang khwaen* perfectly complement Thai architecture, and are used to decorate the windows, doors and passageways of houses, palaces and temples on ceremonial days.

Records of *khruang khwaen* can be observed in murals at Wat Thepthidaram and Wat Somanasviharn in Bangkok. Dating back over 150 years to the reign of King Rama III of the present Chakri Dynasty, the Chinese-style murals on the window and door panels of Wat Thepthidaram depict the use of «*uba khaek*» (intricate floral tassels) as floral pendants decorating glass lanterns, complemented by other Chinese floral ornaments. (Chinese architecture exerted significant influence during that period; Wat Thepthidaram being one of the best examples of the era's architectural style.)

Opposite Page

Floral tassels decorate a line of suspended lamps in the hallway of The Jim Thompson House and Museum.

Bottom Right: Painted in the reign of King Rama IV, this Wat Somanasviharn mural was inspired by a European crystal chandelier.

This Page

Traditional «*klin ta-khaeng*» pendant

This Spread (from left to right)

A small floral tassel adorns a wooden ornament depicting a mythical winged creature; designed by H.H. Princess Smararatna Sirijeshtha in the reign of King Rama V, this large, elaborate floral pendant evolves the traditional «*raya noi*» floral mobile by joining three sizes of *raya noi* together; and Sakul Intakul's interpretation of «*chorakhe*» is made with a metal frame and decorated with floral nets, floral pendants and «*thad hu*».

Following Spread

Left Page: Details of Sakul Intakul's contemporary *chorakhe*.

Right Page: A design variation of Sakul's *chorakhe*; all pictures were taken at the throne hall of Bangkok's Ban Moh Palace.

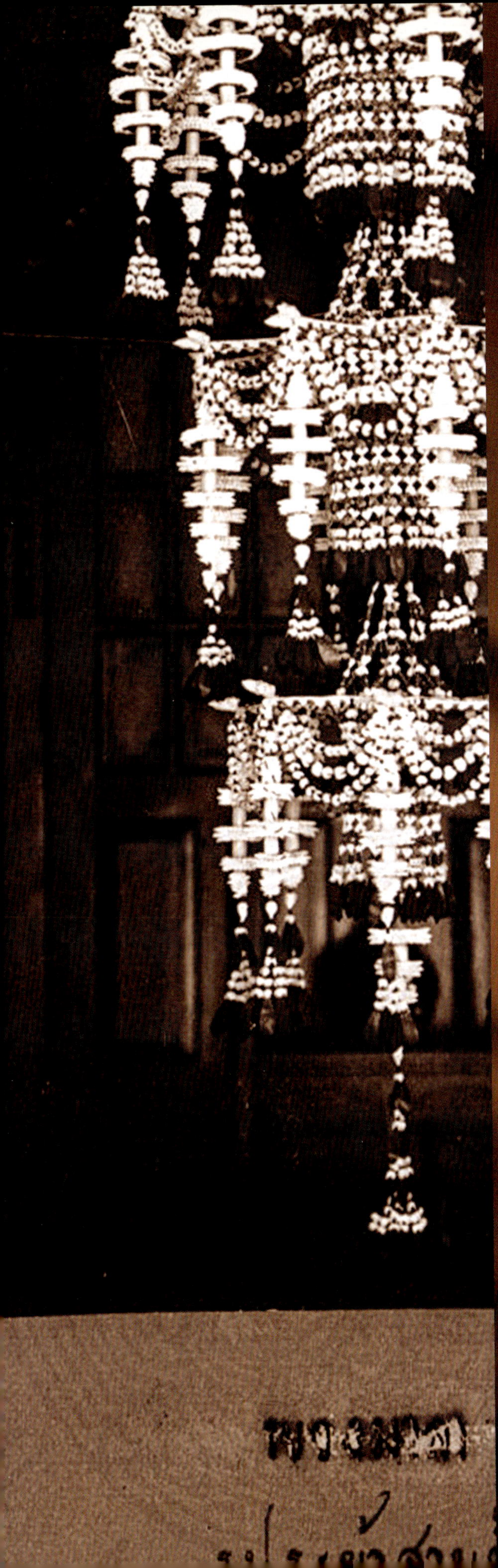

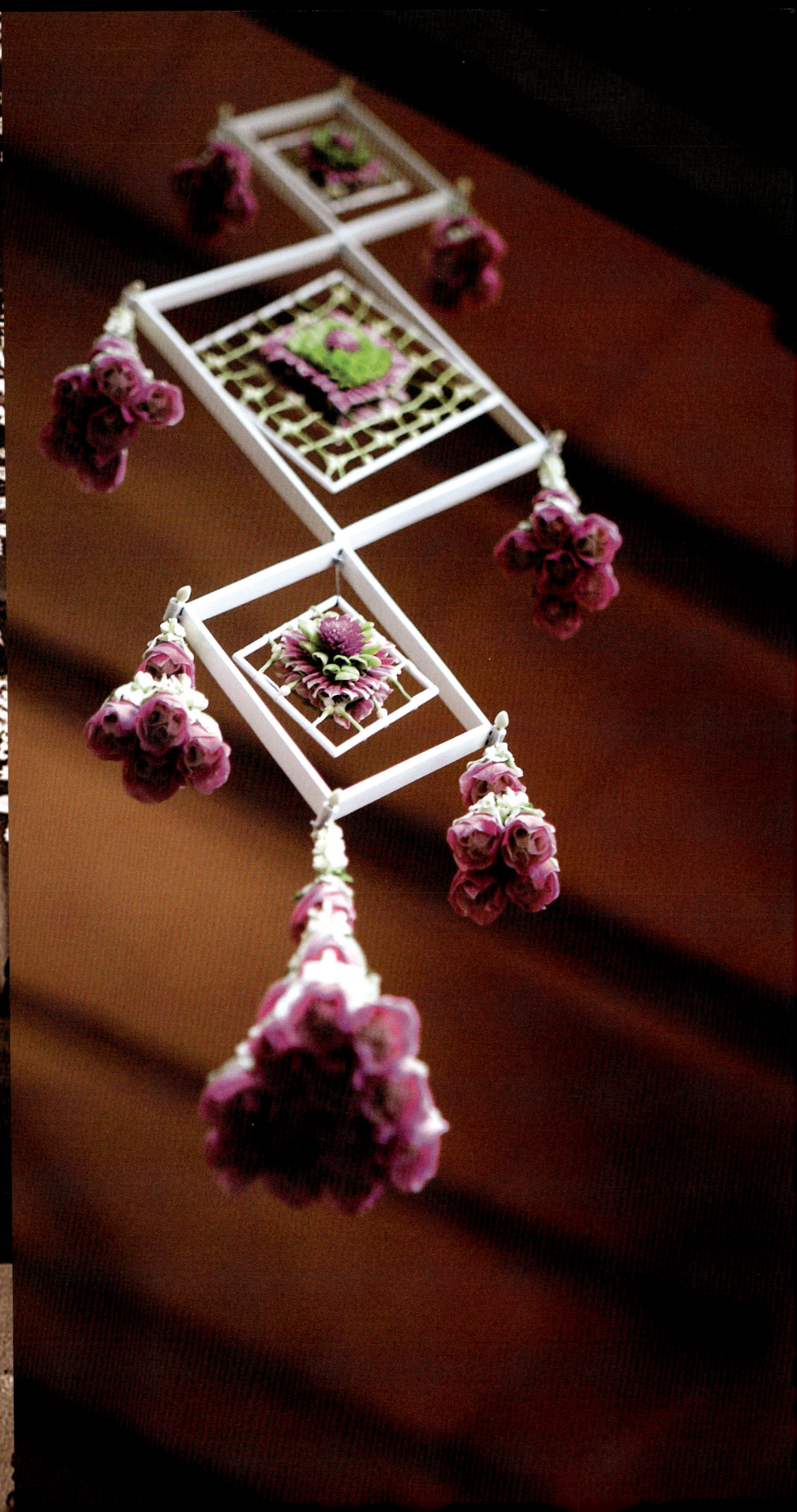

The murals found at Wat Somanasviharn are of a later period, dating to the reign of King Rama IV when Siam opened her doors to the Western world. The floral pendants depicted in the murals on the door and window panels of the chapel clearly took inspiration from the European crystal chandeliers popular in Siam at the time, utilising aspects of their form and structure.

There are basically two ways to categorise Thai floral pendants. One is by size – small or large – and the other by design – two or three dimensions. Although not all types of *khruang khwaen* are illustrated here, the samples of Thai floral pendants shown in this chapter cover all the categories.

Two-dimensional floral pendants are sub-divided into «*chorakhe*», «*klin ta-khaeng*», «*wiman phra-in*» and «*wiman thaen*». Three-dimensional pendants are either «*phuang kaeo*», «*phu klin*» or «*raya noi*».[1] The space in which the *khruang khwaen* are to be hung dictates which type of pendant is to be used. Also included in this chapter are Sakul Intakul's own interpretations of *khruang khwaen*, applying traditional pendants into contemporary floral designs, in both traditional and contemporary settings.

«*Dad rom lom tok*» … How pleasurable summer evenings in the Land of Smiles can be when the southwesterly winds blow, perfuming the air with the sweet, refreshing fragrance of Thai floral pendants that turn slowly in the air; a fleeting pleasure forever remembered.

---

[1] Turn to the glossary for translations of these terms.

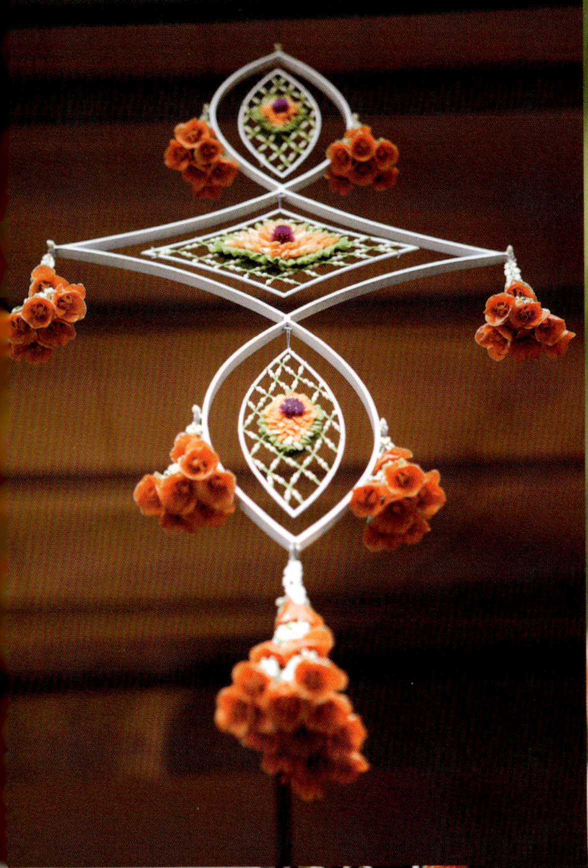
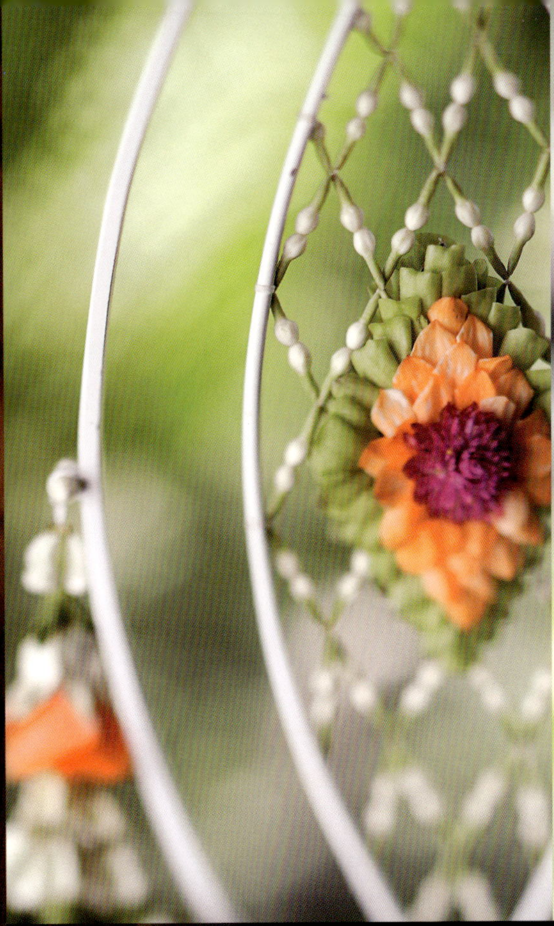
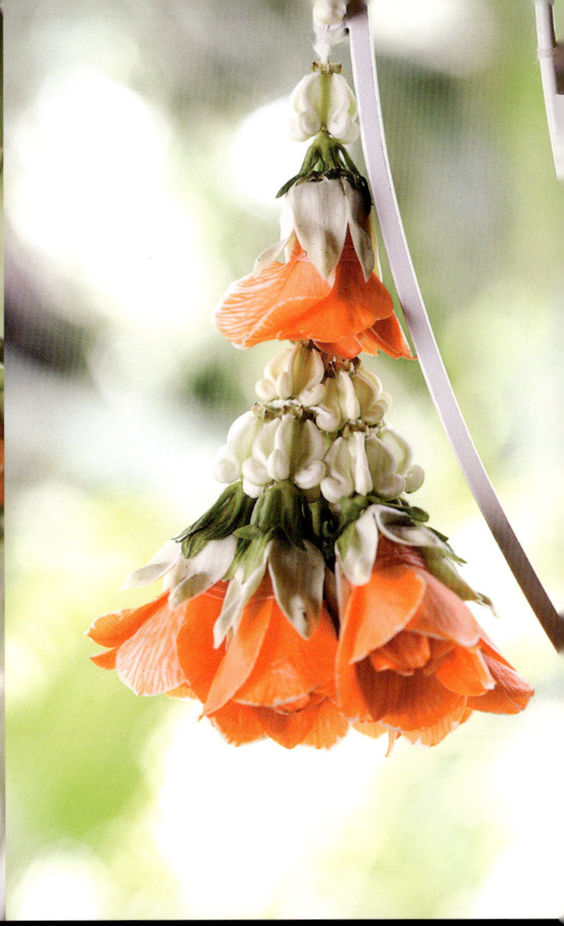
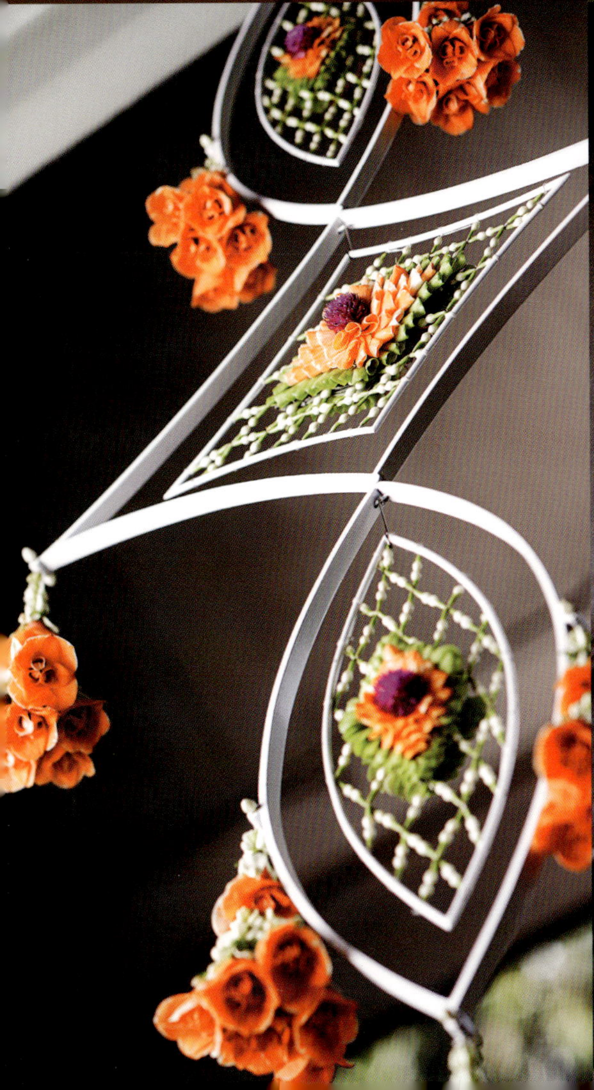
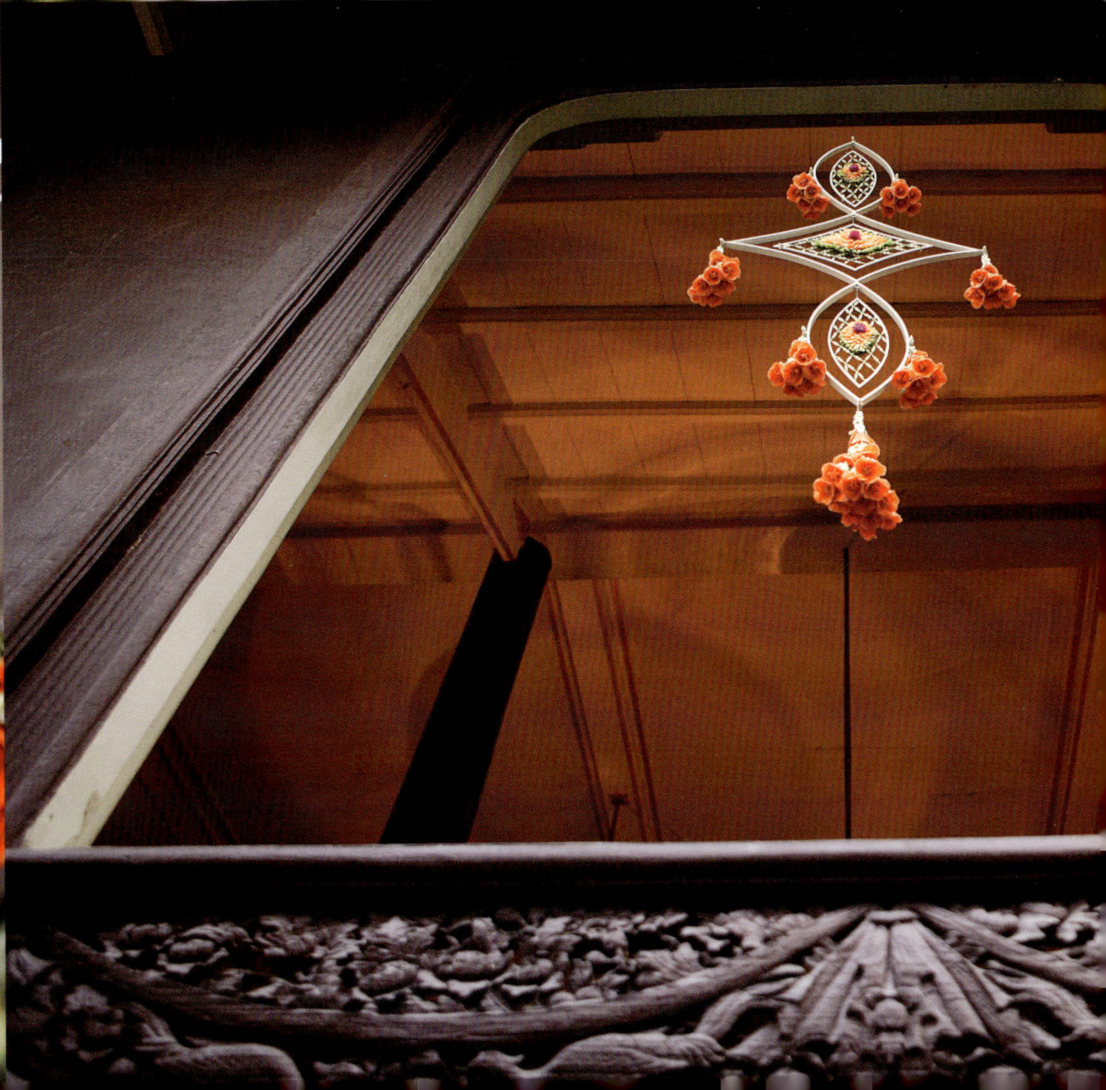

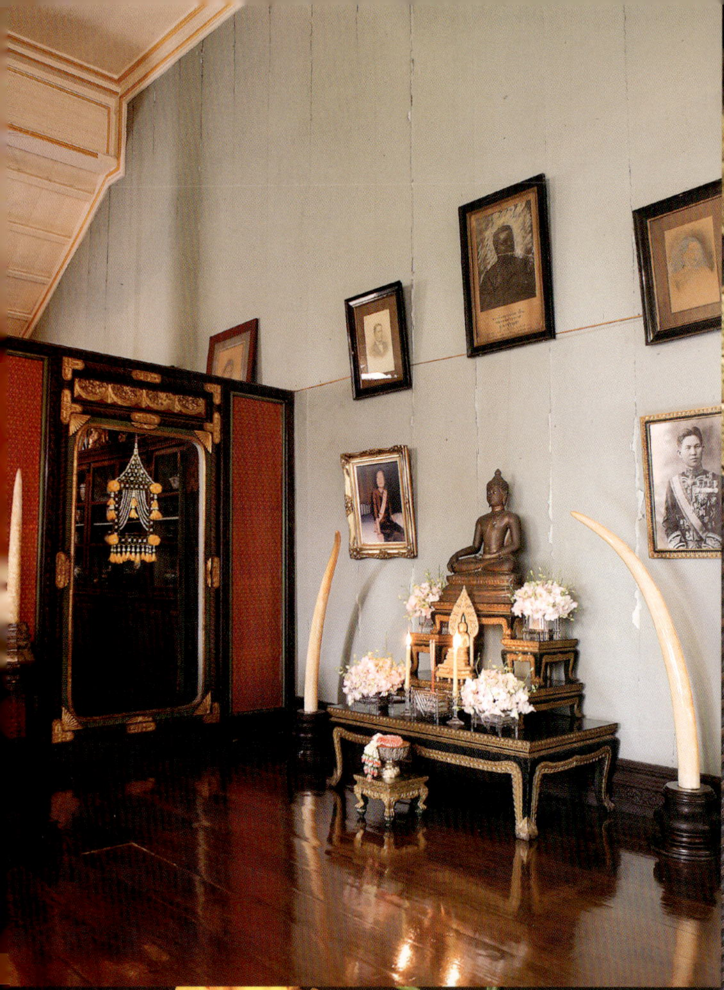
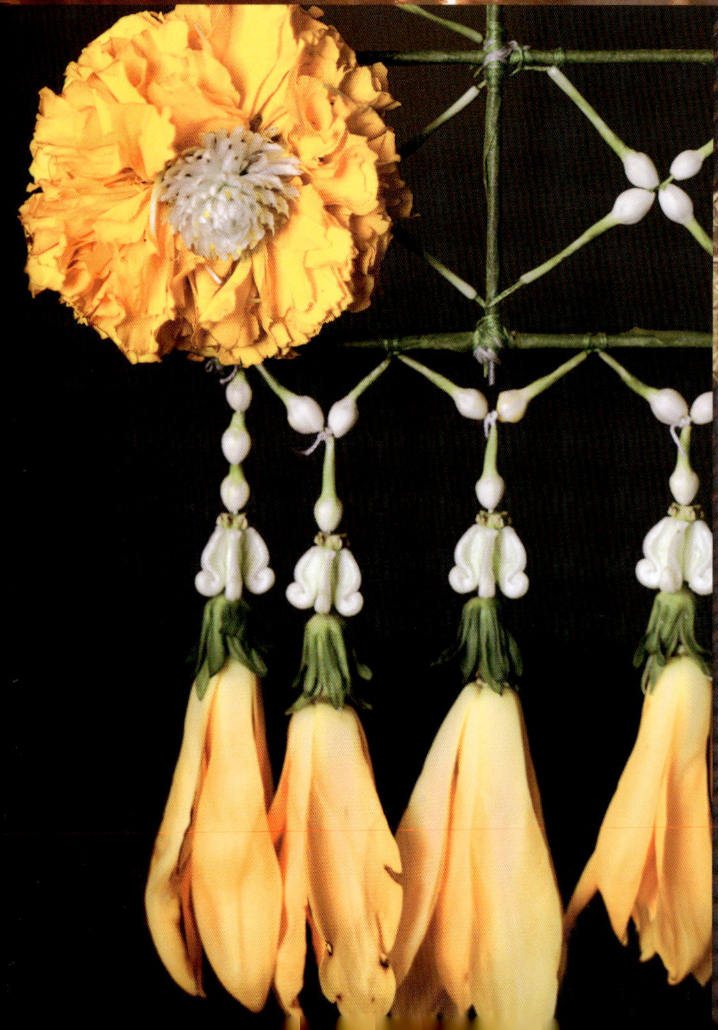
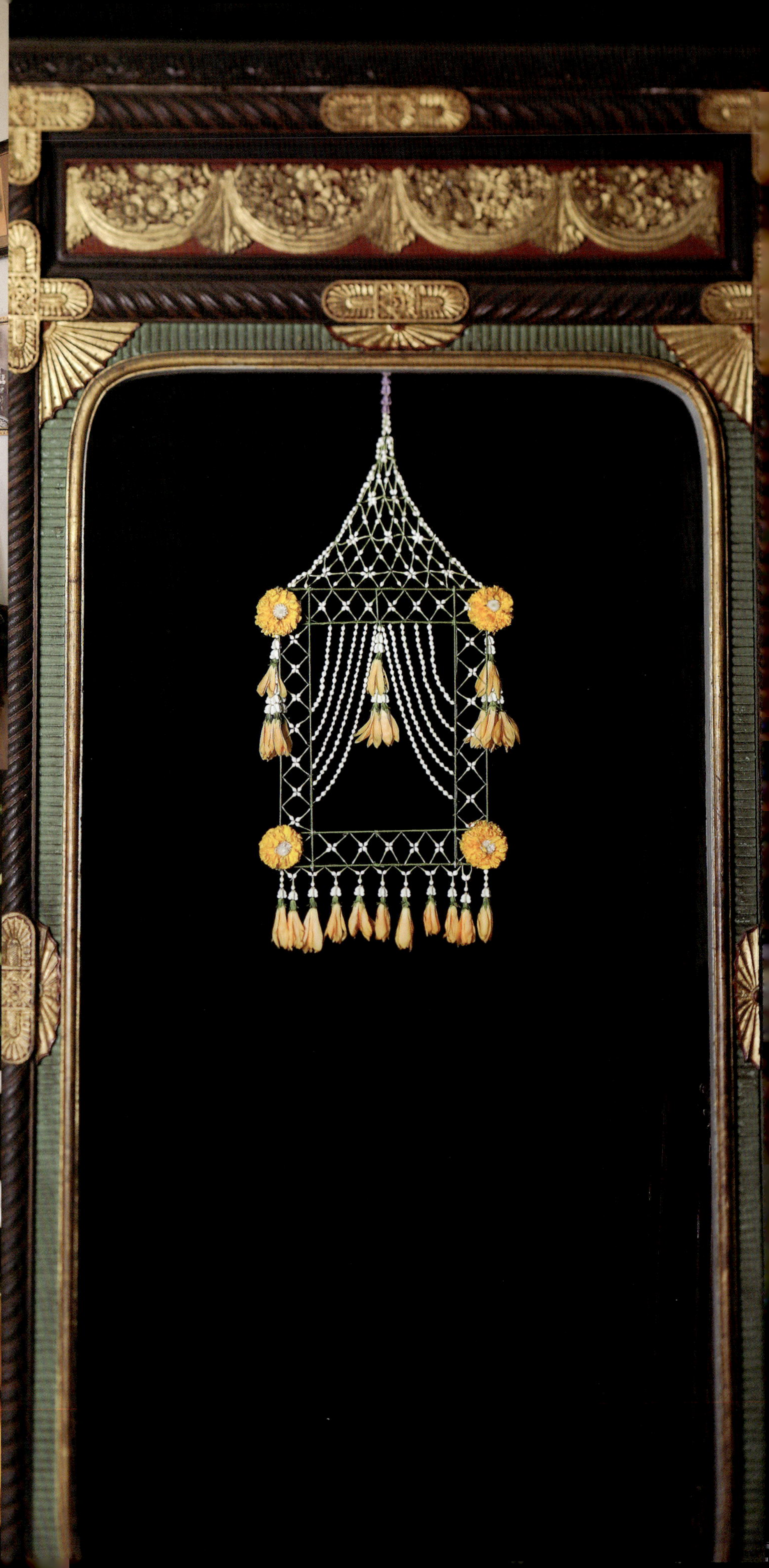

This Spread

The shape of this two-dimensional «*wiman thaen*» floral pendant was inspired by a traditional Thai architectural motif which depicts the celestial residence of the gods. All pictures were taken in the throne hall of Ban Moh Palace; built in the early Rattanakosin period, Ban Moh Palace is one of the oldest examples of traditional wooden architecture in Thailand.

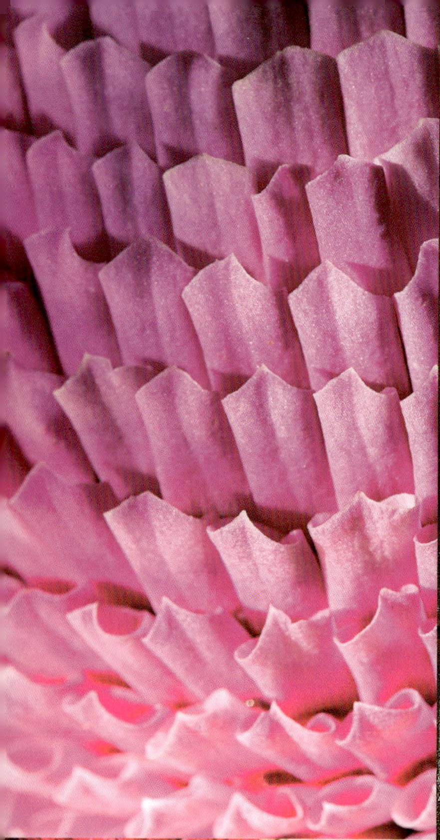
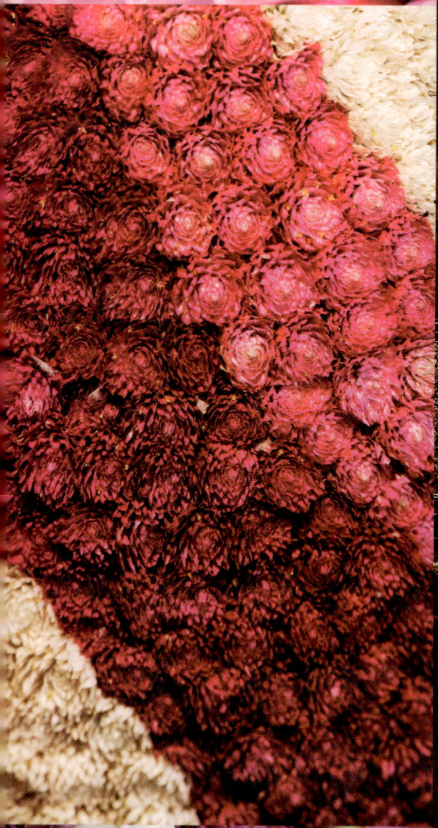
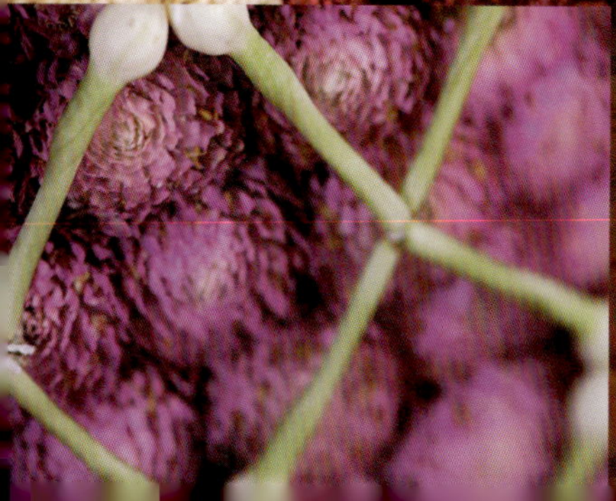
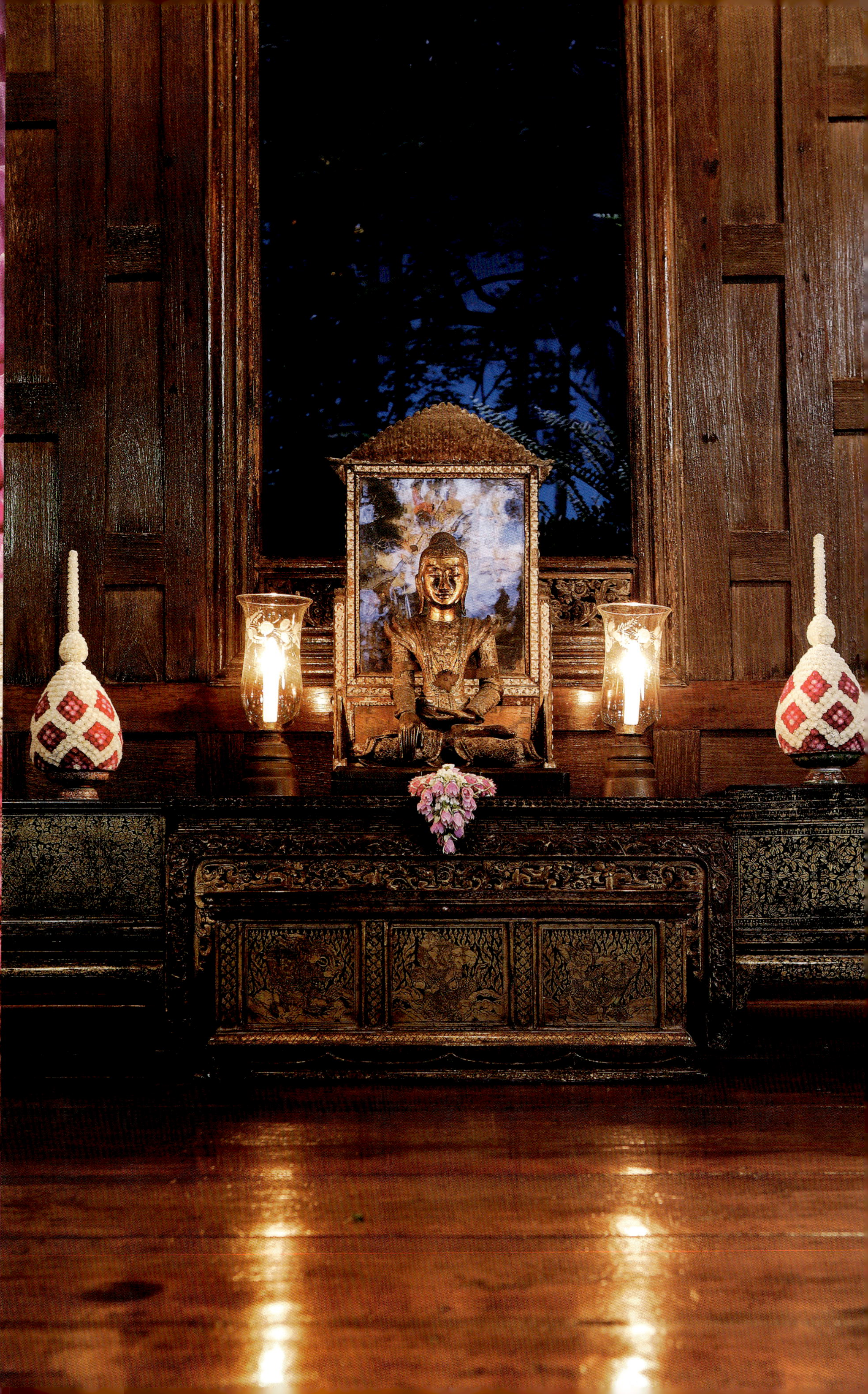

พานดอกไม้

Phan Dokmai
Floral Arrangements on Pedestal Trays

After the three-month summer holidays, which end in May, Thai schools begin a new term. Students meet their new classmates and teachers; others must learn the ropes at a new institution. According to custom, an important ceremony for students to pay respect to their teachers, named «phithi wai khru», is held soon after the new year of study commences.

Conventionally, *phithi wai khru* is held on a Thursday, as this is «*wan khru*», or teachers' day, in Thailand. Thais therefore believe that holding the auspicious ceremony on this day will yield beneficial results for students' studies.

For *phithi wai khru*, students prepare intricate floral arrangements set symbolically on pedestal trays («*phan dokmai*»), and floral arrangements with incense sticks and candles also set on pedestal trays («*phan thup thian*»). Similar to the flower cultures of other East and Southeast-Asian countries, Thai floral culture often makes use of plant and flower symbolism in the selection of the plant materials to be incorporated into an arrangement.

Opening Spread
(clockwise from top left)

Folded orchid petals create the delicate texture of a contemporary «*phum dokmai*»; a pair of patterned «*phan phum*» are placed as an offering on either side of a Buddha image at The Jim Thompson House and Museum, Bangkok; a net of small gardenias covers a *phum dokmai* made from globe amaranths; and three different shades of globe amaranths form this striped *phum dokmai*.

This Spread

Pink, green, white and purple dendrobium orchid petals are folded and fastened to a foam base with pins to form *phum dokmai*. Placed upon a silk table runner, these arrangements serve as a charming centrepiece at The Jim Thompson House and Museum.

Phan Dokmai

54 *Phan Dokmai*

Phan dokmai in *phithi wai khru* traditionally present three kinds of plant materials; their positive symbolism pertaining to progress in the students' education: «*dok khem*» (flowers of the *Ixora* sp.); «*ya phraek*» (Bermuda grass of the *Cynodon* family); and «*dok makhuea*» (plate brush eggplant, *Solanum torvum*). *Dok khem*, or «needle flower», represents sharpness of mind. *Ya phraek*, a ground-covering grass that is given to branching out, symbolises the expansion of knowledge in every direction. *Dok makhuea*, which bears countless fruits on a single tip, signifies the abundance of knowledge, and thus the advancement of the student's life in the future.

This Spread

These small white «*phum dokmai*» are made from five flowers commonly used in Thai floral art: small gardenias, jasmine, crown flowers, orchids and globe amaranths. The spires are made from crown flowers and small gardenias.

This Spread

Together with vases of fresh orchids, candles and incense sticks, nine «*phan phum*» are placed as the offerings on the altar in front of the principal Buddha image in Wat Ratchabophit Sathitmahasi-maram's main temple. Nets of small gardenias complete the delicate design of these elaborate *phan phum*, which are made entirely from globe amaranths – secured to the inner clay structure with slivers of dry skin of salak palm.

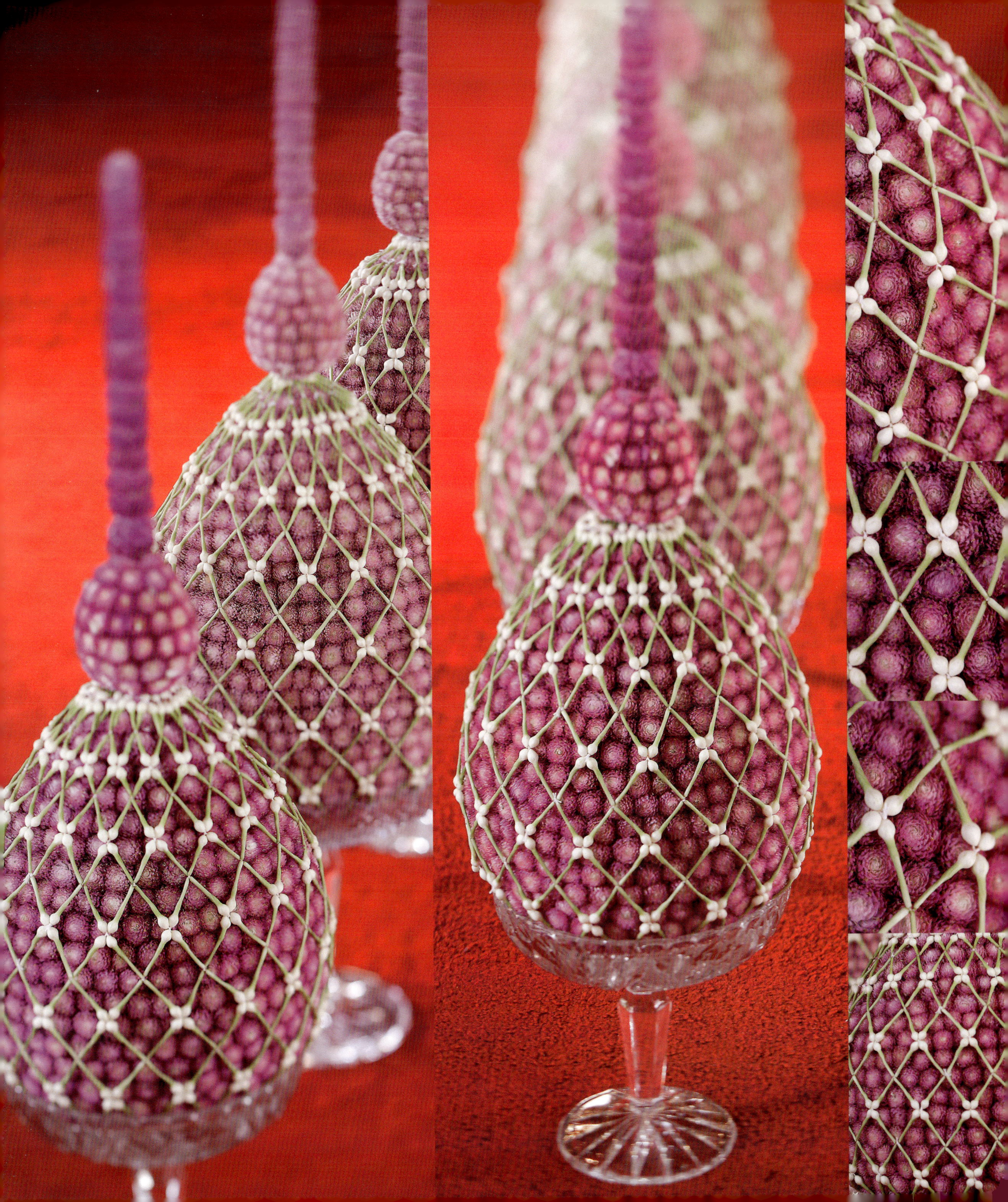

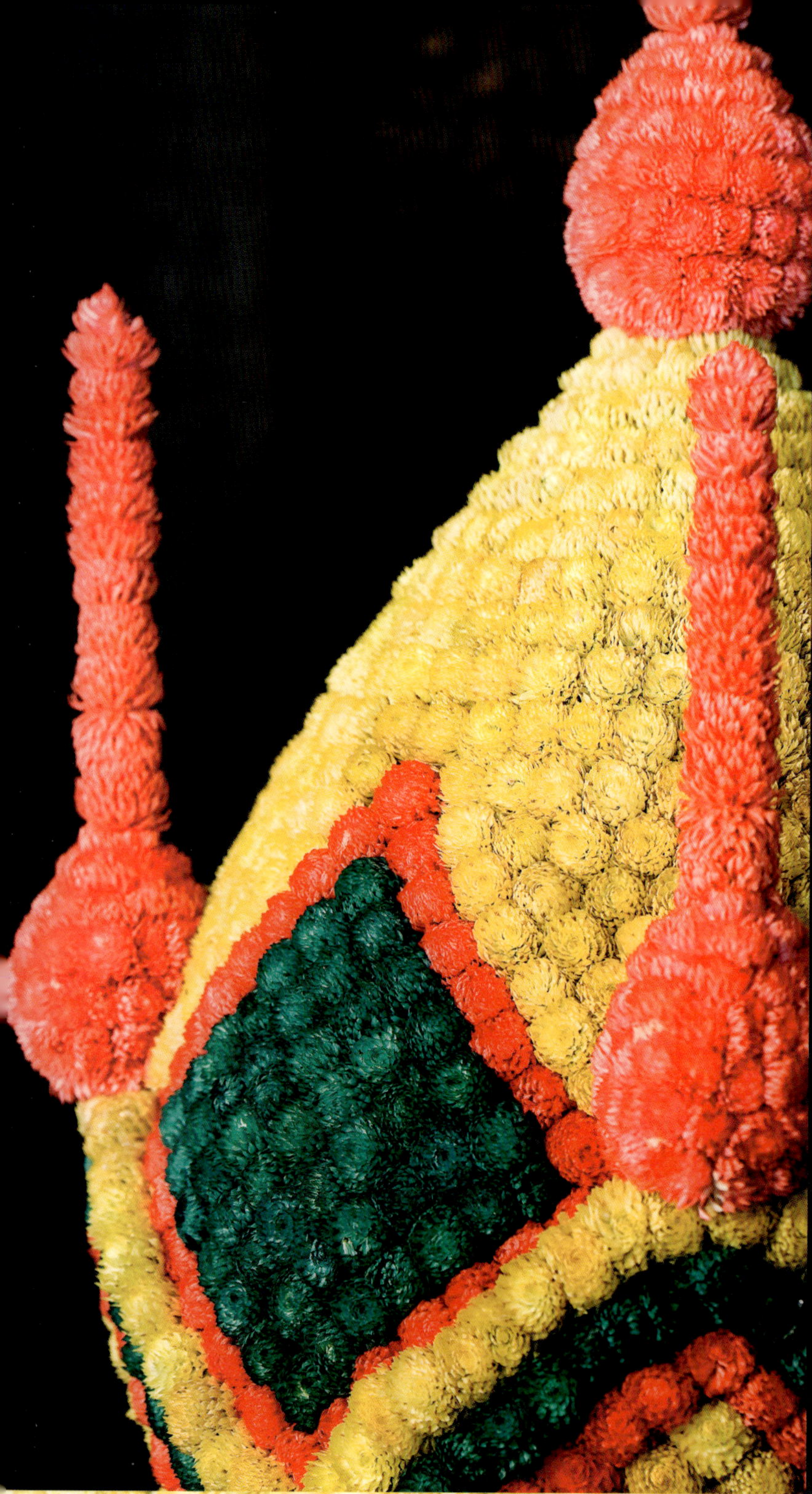

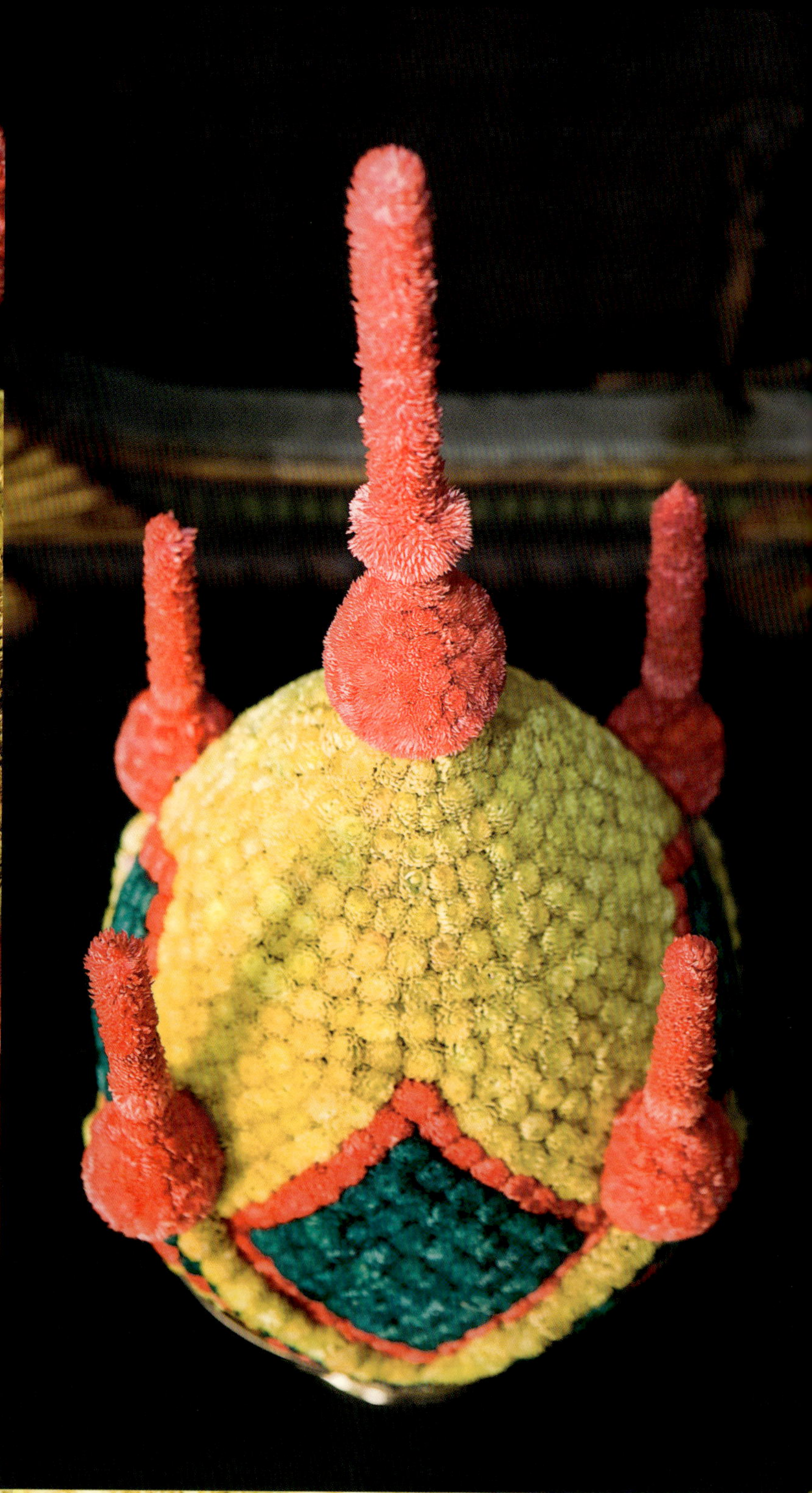

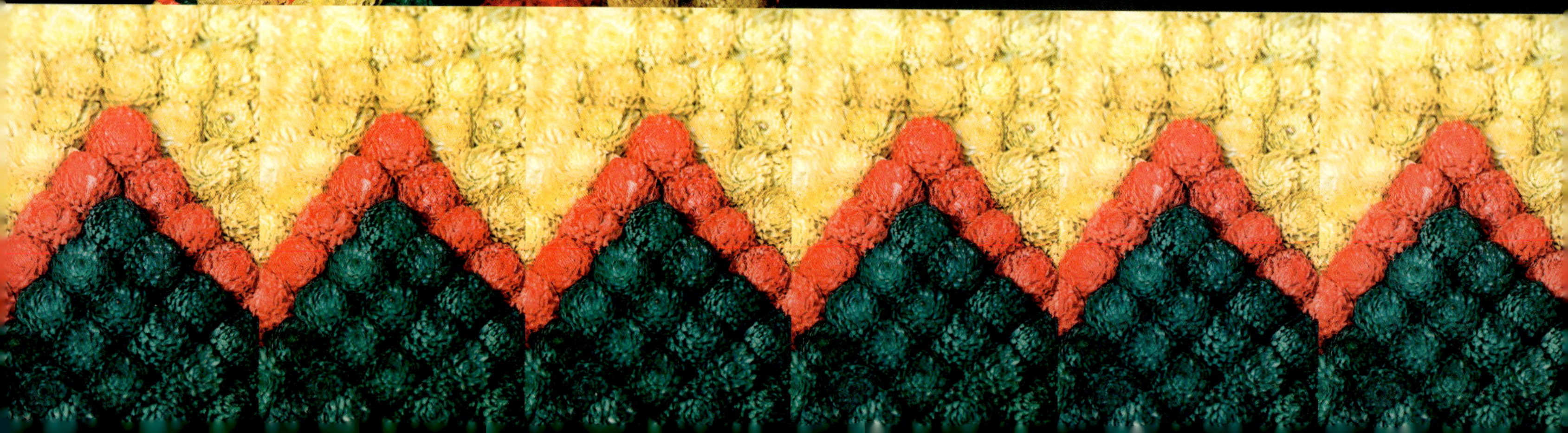

This Spread

Reminiscent of the spires in traditional Thai architecture, this ornate «*phum dokmai*» features five finials. Inspired by the interior-setting colours of Ban Moh Palace in Bangkok, yellow, green and red dyes were applied to white globe amaranths to create the vibrant arrangement.

Far Left

An old photograph found at the National Archives of Thailand reveals a «*malai thao*» (*left*), a set of garlands placed in size order on pedestal tray, and «*kruai upatcha*» (*right*), a «*phan dokmai*» for ordination ceremonies.

Main Image

Used in Buddhist ordination ceremonies, *kruai upatcha* (*left*) and *malai thao* (*right*) are presented to the officiating monk at the time of an ordination request. The yellow-green plant material at the *kruai upatcha's* centre hails from a coconut tree's young leaves.

Opposite Page (top)

Malai thao, complete with festoons of small gardenias and tassels of purple crown flowers tied with orange champak flowers.

Opposite Page (bottom)

Details of *kruai upatcha* and *malai thao*.

«*Toh mu bucha*», an altar of Buddha images, has been a significant feature of the Thai house since time immemorial. This domestic altar traditionally comprises a group of small wooden tables of different heights – five, seven or nine in number – arranged symmetrically in descending order from the centre. The main Buddha image is placed upon the tallest table, which is set in the centre behind the others. Offerings of candles, incense sticks and flowers are positioned on the smaller tables. Generally, the flowers are beautifully arranged, both in vases («*chaekan dokmai*») and on a pedestal tray. The latter are traditionally arranged in a globular design. Special *phan dokmai* in the form of a stupa, or «*phra kieo*» (a top-knot ornament for royalty), are especially splendid examples of Thai-floral-art creativity. Nowadays, *phan dokmai* are more commonly seen in a no-less-exquisite lotus-bud shape, named «*phan phum*».

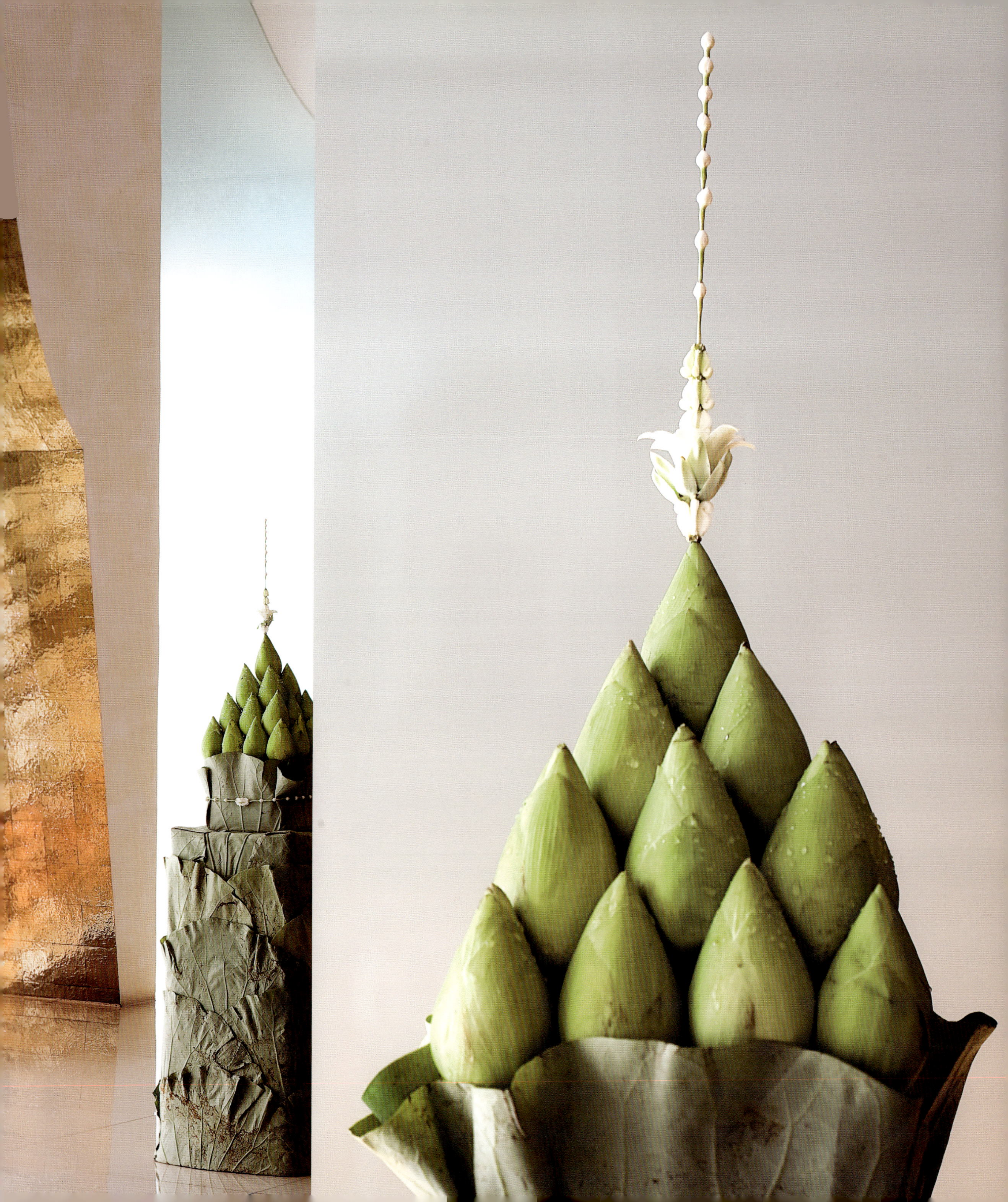

In the design of a contemporary Thai house, the architect normally includes a special room for the *toh mu bucha* in the blueprint. Named «*hong phra*», or Buddha image room, the room is used by Thais for prayer and meditation. Offerings of candles, incense sticks, *chaekan dokmai* and *phan dokmai* are made daily to aid the worship of Buddhism's three jewels: the Buddha, his teachings and the monk community.

Phan dokmai and *phan phum* are also used for decoration. *Phan phum*, for example, can be seen embellishing living chambers, and as the charming centrepiece for a dining table. Sakul Intakul's contemporary interpretations illustrated in this chapter also lend themselves as decorative interior features.

This Spread

Devarana Spa Bangkok's arrival area is decorated by Sakul Intakul's contemporary interpretations of «*phum dokmai*». These refreshing creations are made from white lotus flowers; crown-flower finials, orchid petals and small gardenias provide the finishing touch. The container is wrapped in a lotus leaf and then tied with a string of small gardenias and a pair of ornamental crown flowers.

This Spread

Sakul Intakul designed this pair of two-dimensional «phum dokmai», made from jasmine and crown flowers. Inspired by traditional arrangements on pedestal trays, the modern structures are constructed from brass.

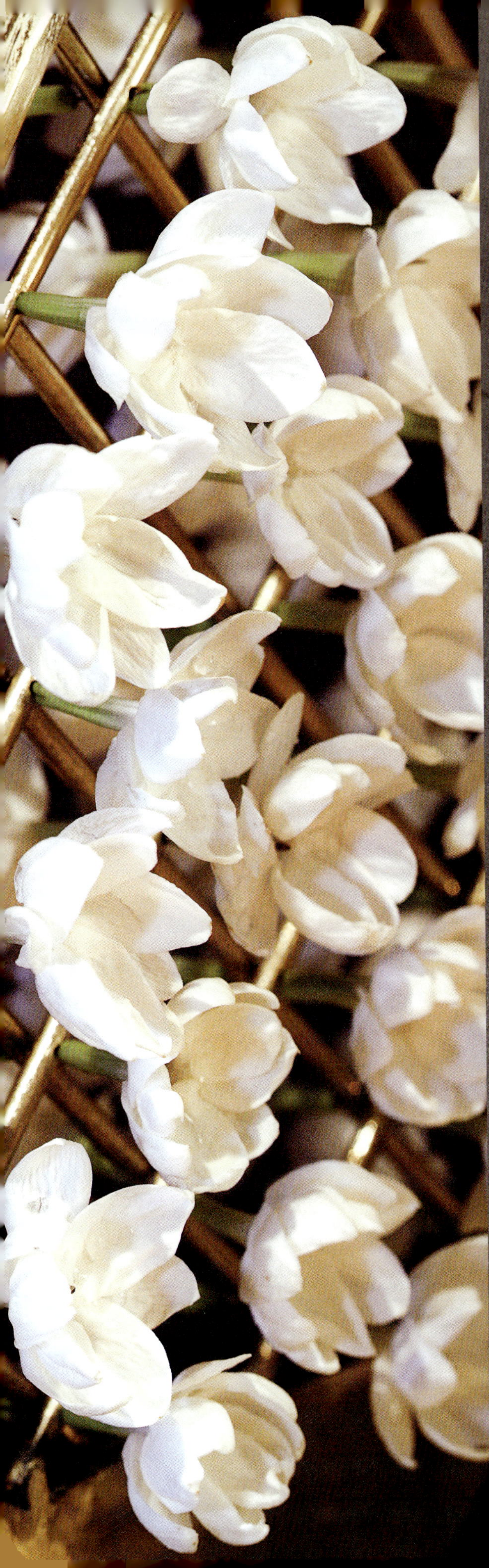

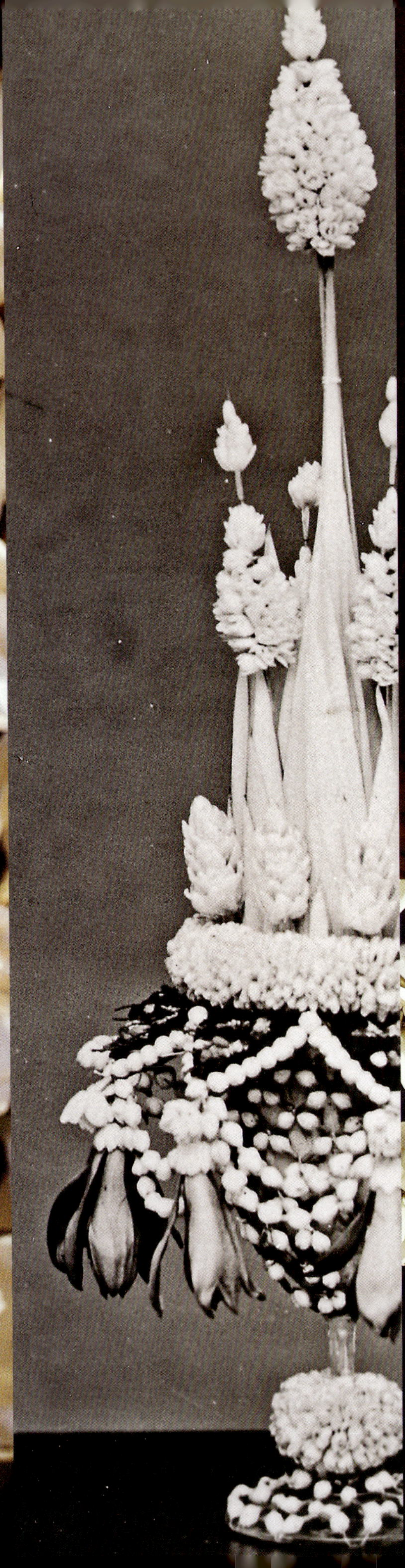

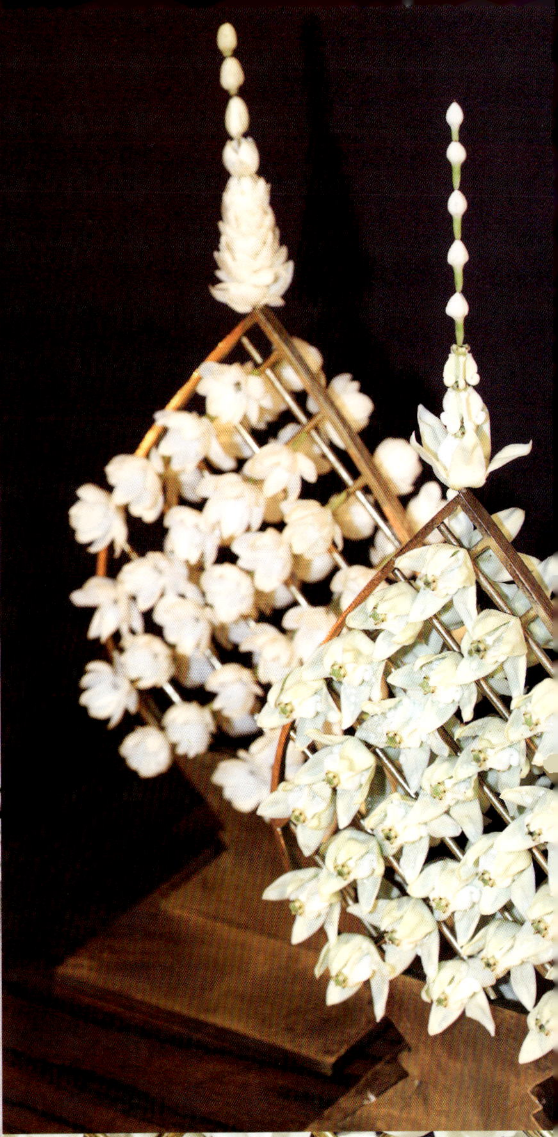

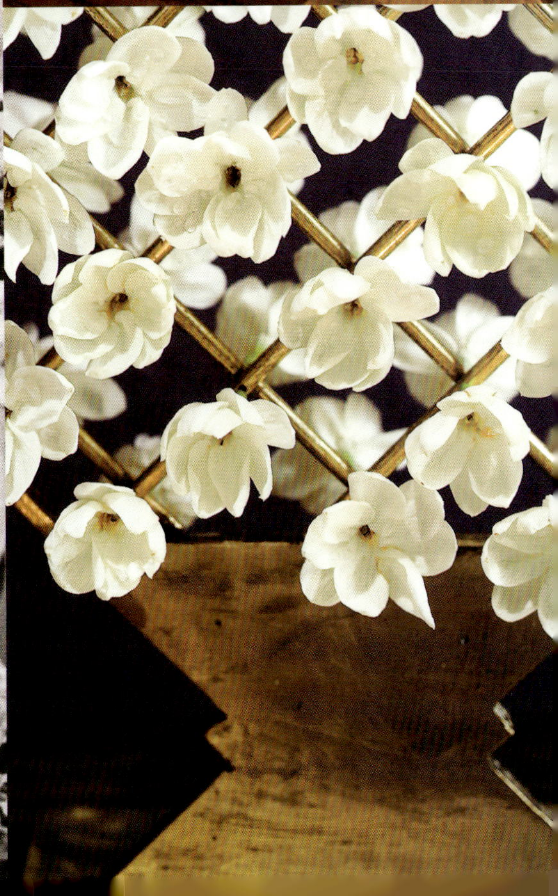

A day before *phithi wai khru*, students attentively prepare *phan dokmai* and *phan thup thian*; each classroom requires a set of two. These pedestal trays are then presented as offerings to the teachers the following day. Students are free to design the floral creations as they see fit and, after the ceremony, their *phan dokmai* and *phan thup thian* are judged, with awards and recognition for the most creative ones. The process allows students to work together and get to know one another before the new semester formally begins and a new chapter of their life unfolds. ♠

This Spread

A contemporary interpretation of «*phan phum*» by Sakul Intakul decorates a living room coffee table at The Sukhothai Residences, Bangkok. The traditional globe amaranths are here replaced by orange rose petals. Crowned with decorative finials of orange roses and small gardenias, the arrangements' bases employ complementary-colour combinations of orange, green and purple.

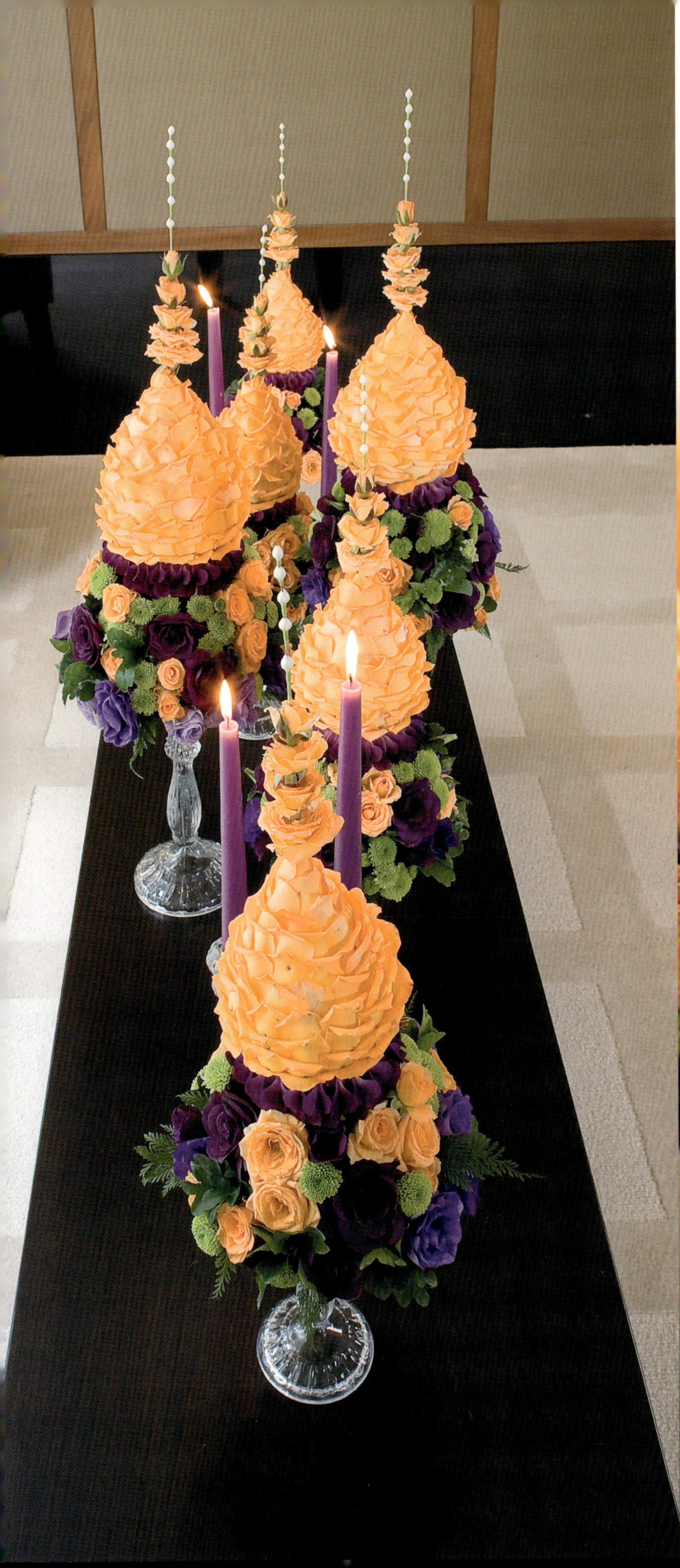

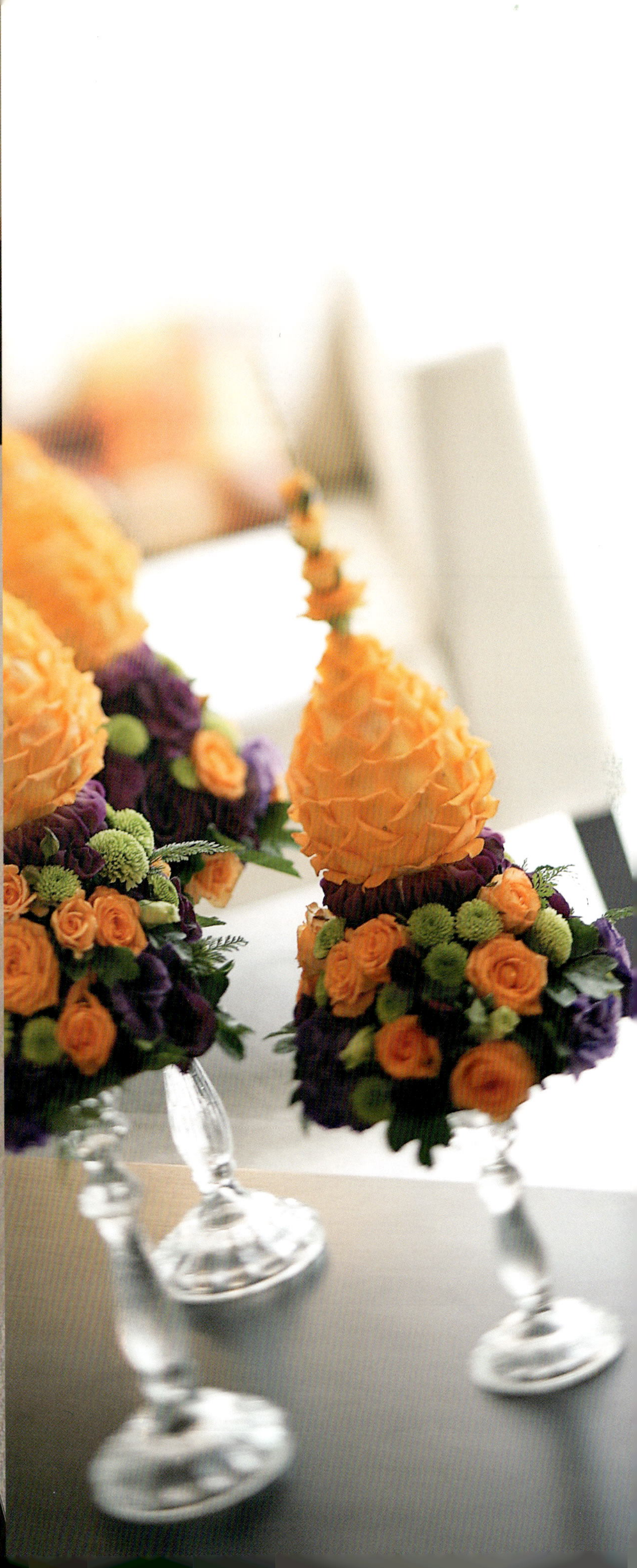

กระทง
และงานใบตอง

Krathong & Ngan Baitong
Floral Floats, Leaf Containers & Banana-Leaf Works

Full moon nights are simply magical in the tropics, especially when the moonlight is reflected upon the rivers, glistening along the waterways' gentle ripples. In Thailand one full moon night is more romantic than all the others. It falls on the 12th lunar month, in late November – the night of «Loy Krathong», or the festival of light.

In the days before *Loy Krathong*, local Thai markets heave with all the floral floats on display. Most of these floats are fashioned from slices of banana trunk; folded banana leaves of differing patterns are attached around them to form lotus-flower-like floral floats. To create distinctive styles, other leaves such as «*saonoi prapang*» or dumb cane, are also used, as they imitate lotus petals. Fresh flowers, candles and incense sticks are placed in the «*krathong*» – which literally means ‹a container made from leaves›. («*Loy*» translates as ‹to float›; *Loy Krathong*, therefore, is the ‹floating of leaf containers›.)

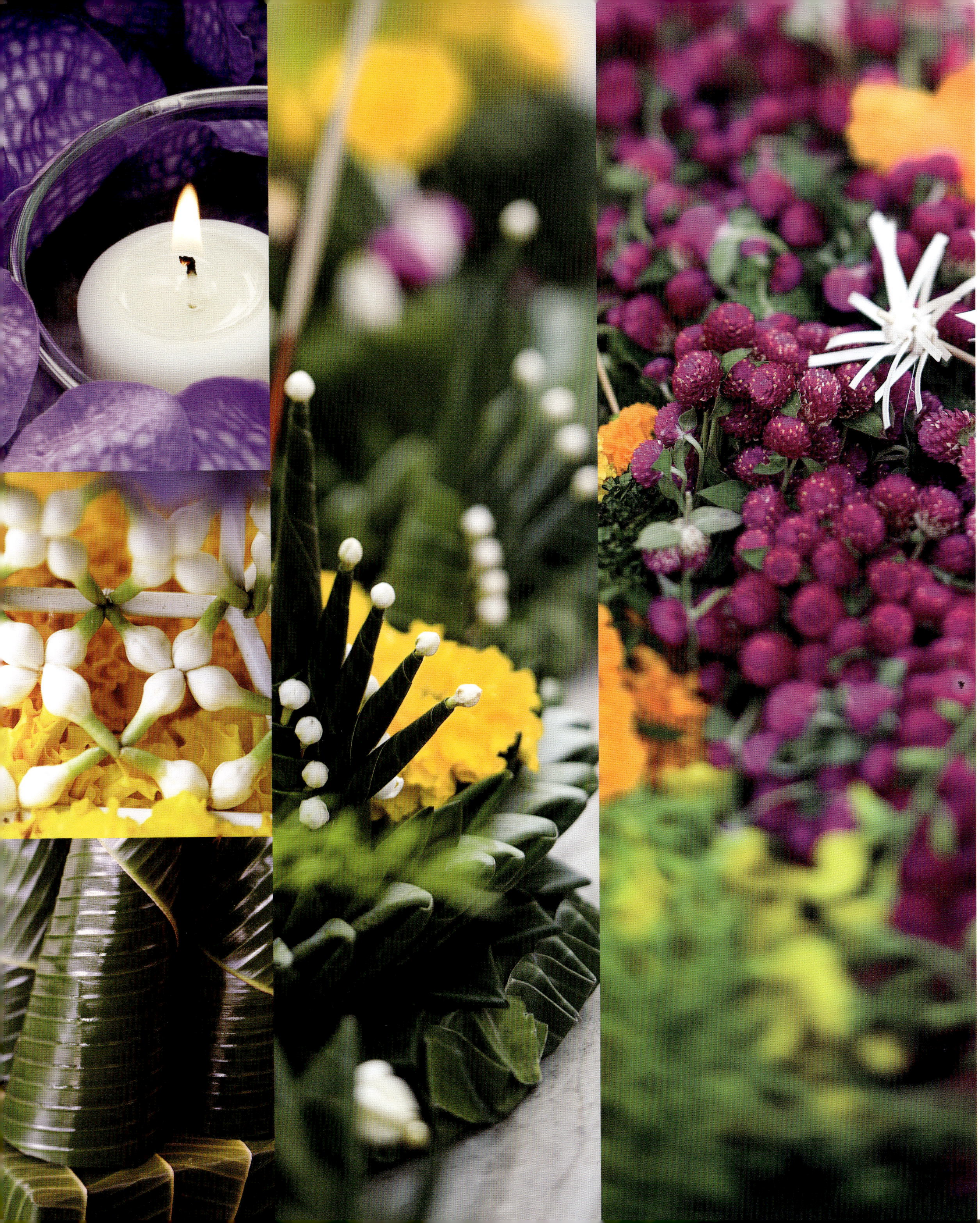

Opening Spread (left, top to bottom)

Vanda orchid flowers fill the central space of a contemporary floral float; a floral net of small gardenias embellishes an elaborate floral float; and cone-shaped banana leaves form the main feature of this contemporary floral float.

Centre

«*Krathong*», or floral floats, are normally created from folded banana leaves, forming an open, lotus-like container.

Right

Pink globe amaranths are prepared for use as decorative floral materials in floral floats.

This Spread

In Chiang Mai, these simple floral floats are made from banana leaves in a variety of styles. Local crown flowers, globe amaranths and African marigolds add splashes of colour and a mood of gaiety to the «*Loy Krathong*» festival (celebrated on the 12th lunar month's full moon night throughout the Kingdom). Flowers, candles and incense sticks are integral components of these floats.

The word *krathong*, however, is not only used in a *Loy Krathong* context. *Krathong*, commonly made from «*baitong*», or banana leaf, can range from the simplest to the most sophisticated forms imaginable. Simple *krathong baitong* are widely used as containers, mostly for food, while the more sophisticated versions are used in ceremonies and festivals. Another type, «*krathong dokmai*», a flower container with a conical lid, is made entirely from banana leaf. *Krathong dokmai* are generally used as an offering, in conjunction with a bundle of incense sticks and candles on a pedestal tray.

The 12th lunar month is a special time of year in Thailand. The rainy season is over; the cool, dry wind from the South China Sea sweeps across the north-eastern highlands to the country's central plains, bringing the fair weather with it. The dampness of the rains is gone and the skies are bright and clear once again. Meanwhile, water from the mountainous north arrives in the lowlands, flooding rivers and canals – some overflowing their banks. For country folk, after the strenuous labour of ploughing and planting rice from dawn till dusk for the past three months, the hard toil has come to an end. They have only to wait a month or so for harvesting. It's time to rejoice. It is time for *Loy Krathong*.

72 *Krathong & Ngan Baitong*

This Spread

An elaborate floral float designed by Sakul Intakul sits in The Sukhothai Bangkok's central pond. The float is meticulously created from banana leaves, African marigolds, crown flowers and small gardenias. The white buds which tip the decorative folded banana leaves hail from small gardenias. Floral nets of small gardenias and festoons of purple crown flowers work as finishing details.

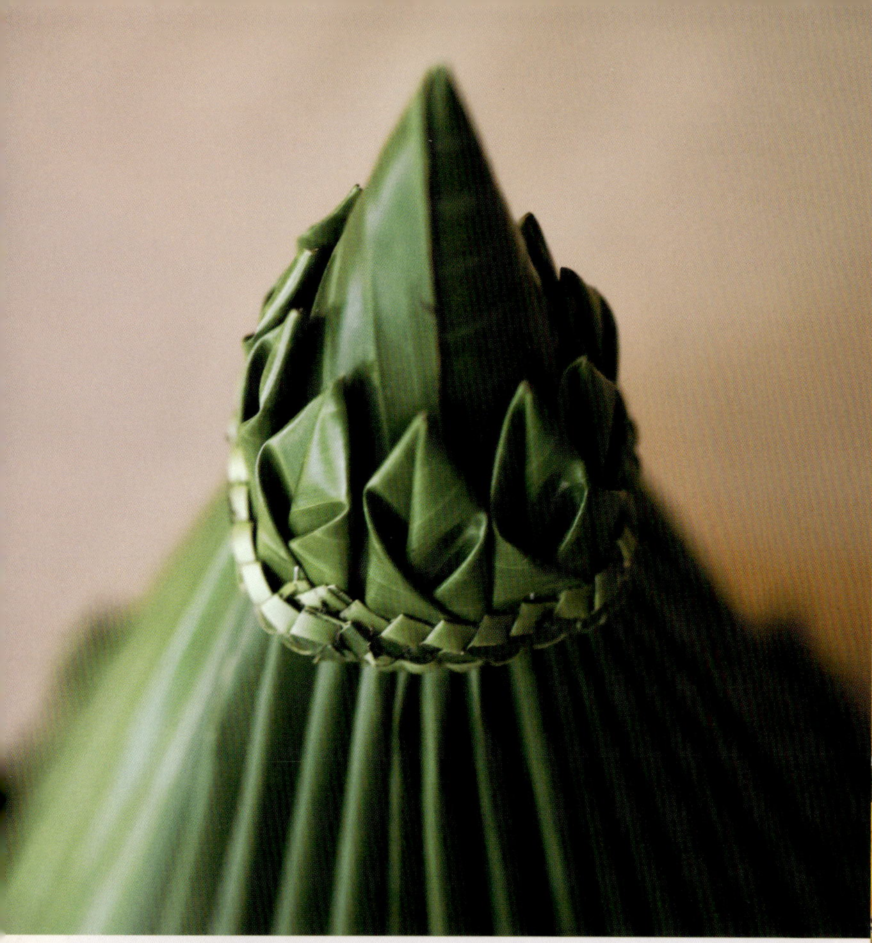

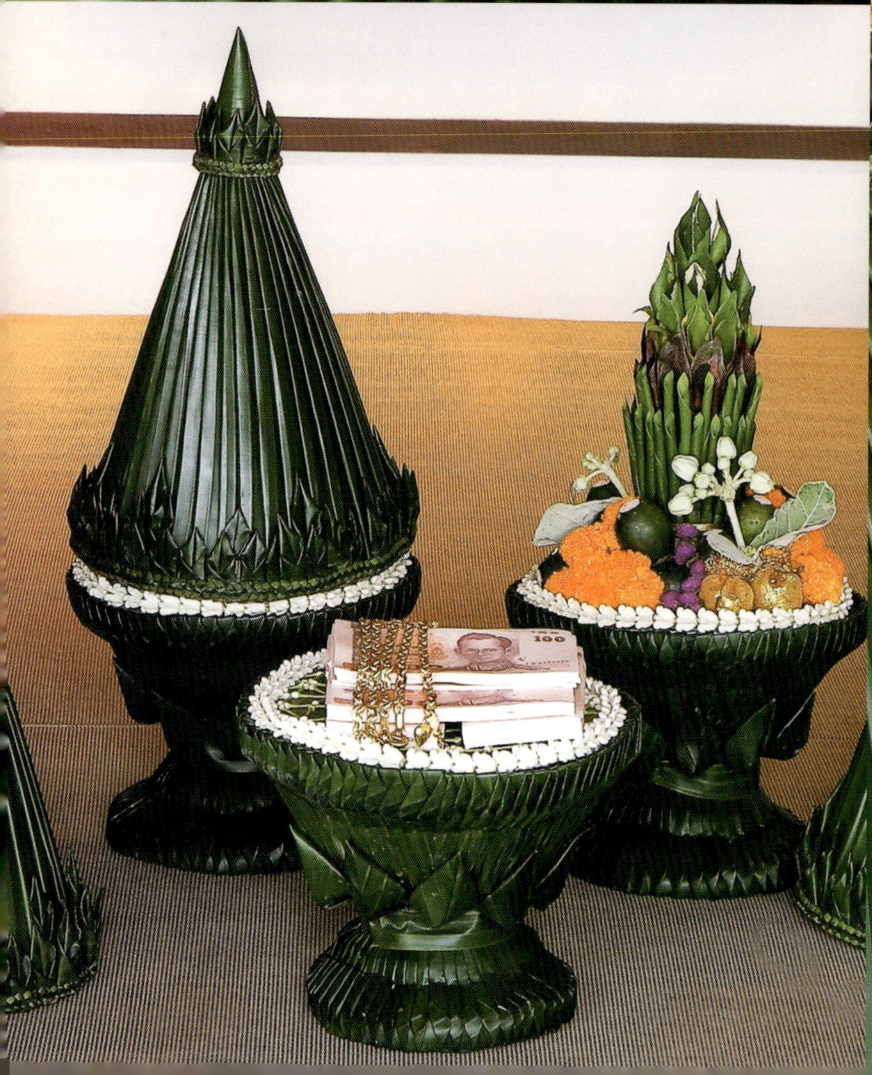

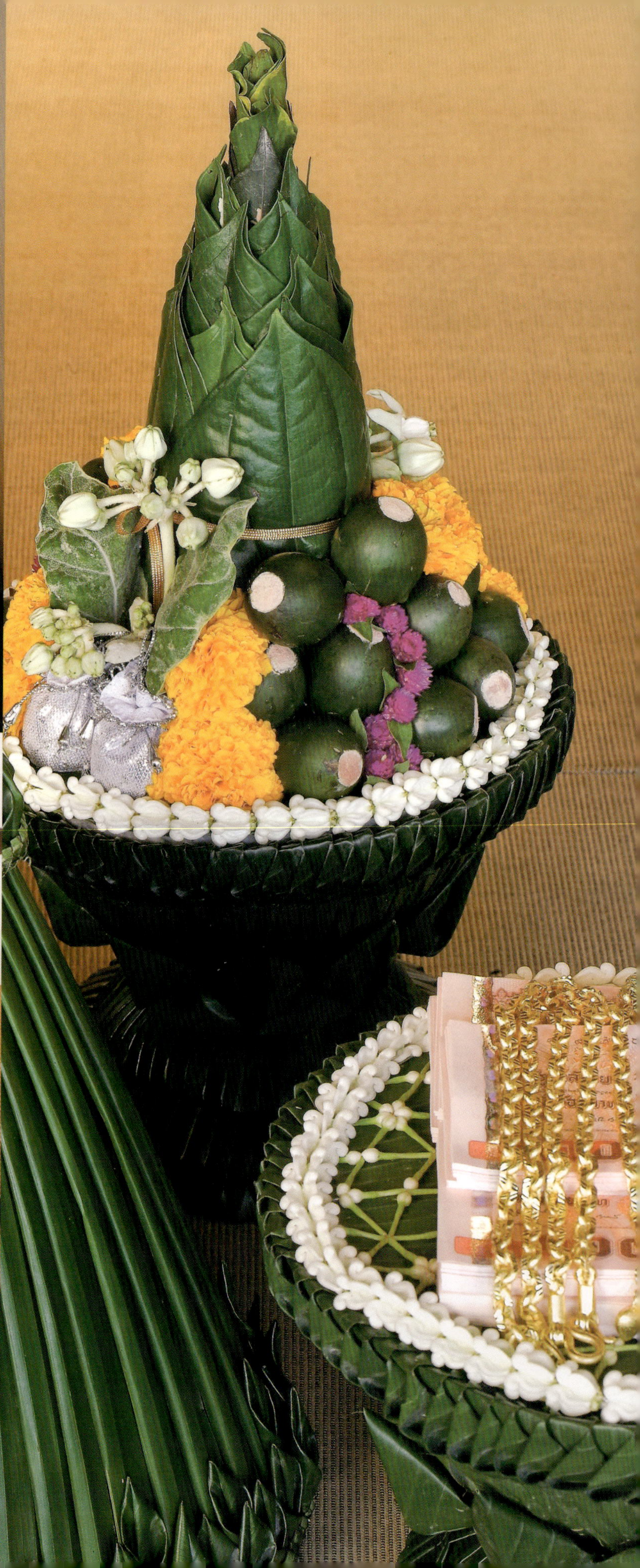

This Spread

These «*phan khan mak*», or wedding dowry trays, are made entirely from banana leaves; generic «*phan*» (pedestal trays) are constructed from metal. In the Thai tradition, *phan khan mak* are brought by a groom to his bride's family.

Top Right

In addition to «*mak*» (areca nuts) and «*phlu*» (betel leaves), *phan khan mak* makes use of other leaves and flowers for their auspicious symbolism: «*rak*» (crown flowers) for love; «*dao ruang*» (African marigolds) for prosperity; and «*ban mairurouy*» (globe amaranths) for everlasting love. Gold and silver bags are also essential components.

This Spread

Shown here, at The River by Raimon Land, are the finest, most complex, examples of «*krathong dokmai*» (banana leaf containers for flowers). *Krathong dokmai* are used in conjunction with bundles of incense sticks and candles on a pedestal tray as a Buddha offering, or an offering to one's spiritual guide at the beginning of Lent. They are also carried by young men when paying respect to their superiors just before entering the Order. A newly married couple brings *krathong dokmai* when paying respect to their elders.

Left Page (top right)

A crystal pedestal tray from Lotus Crystal International Company Limited

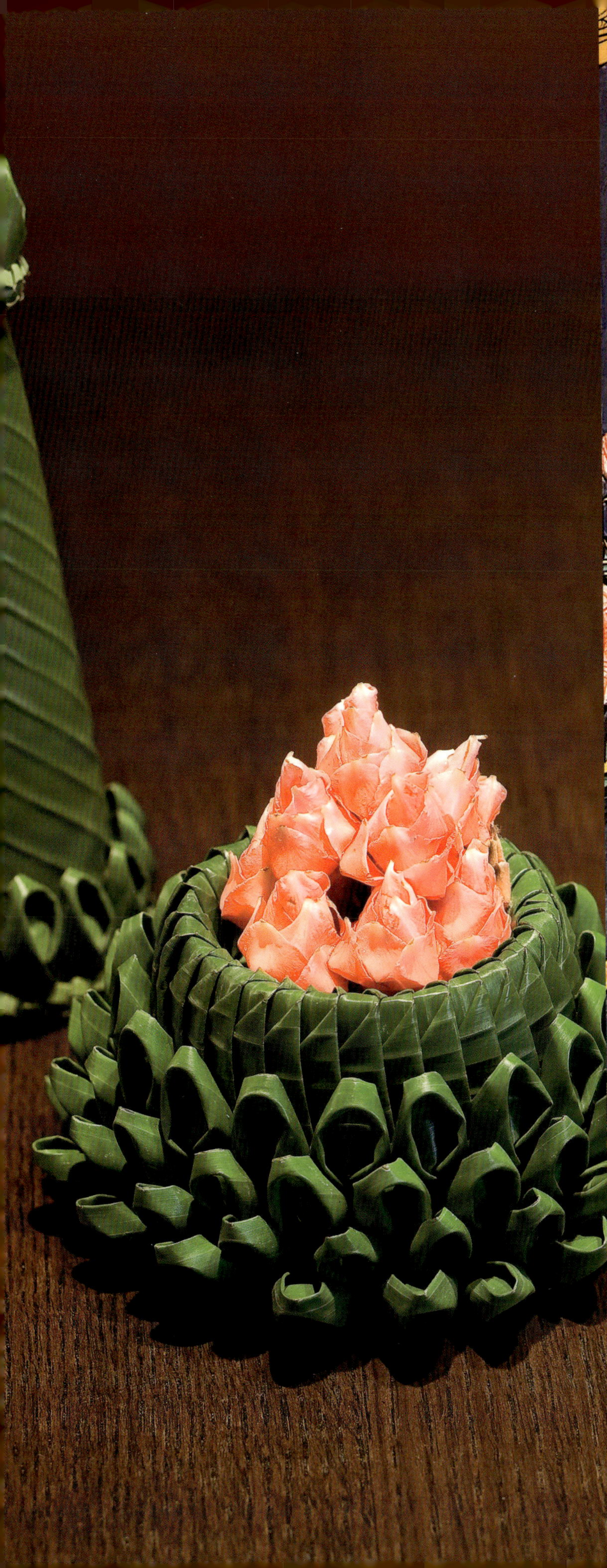
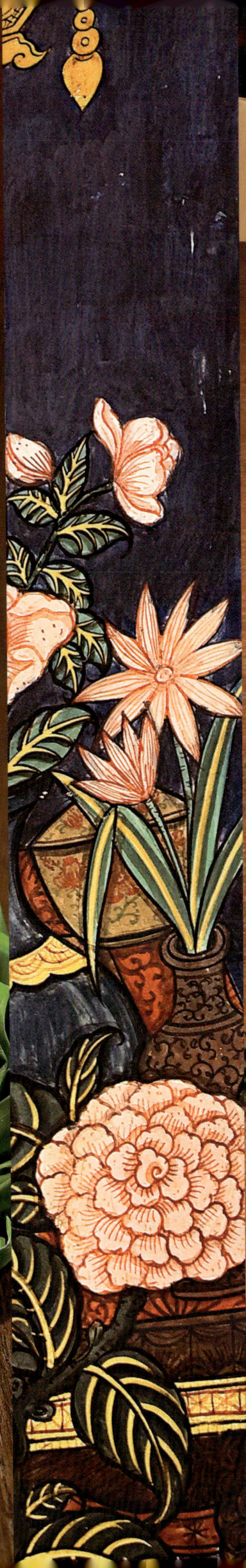
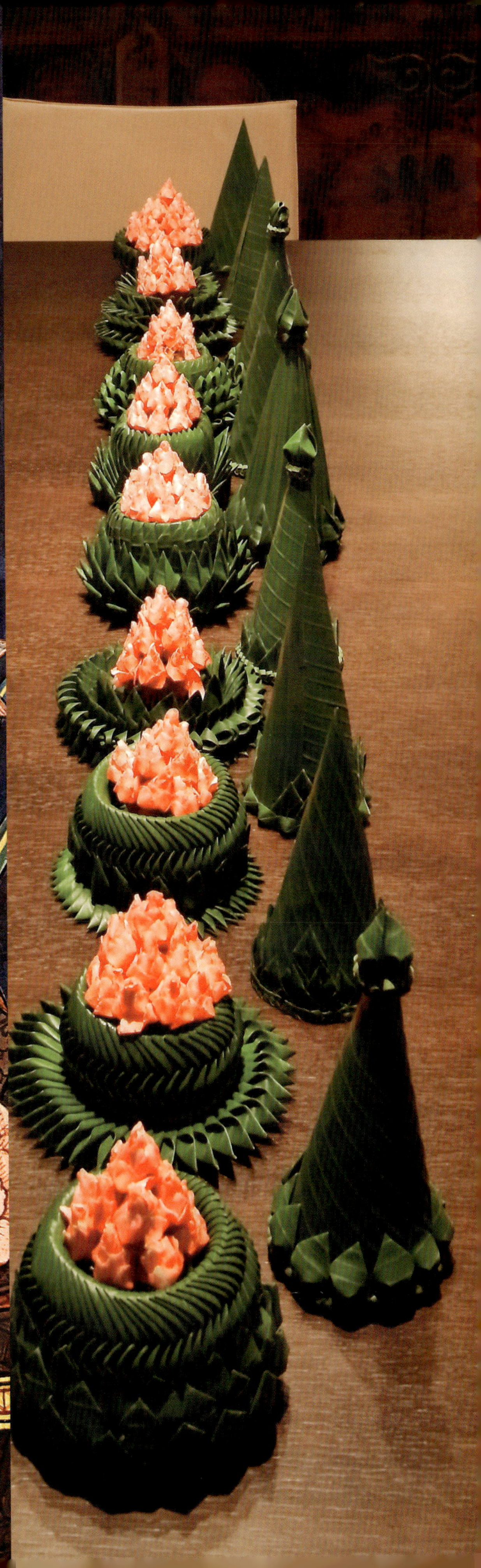

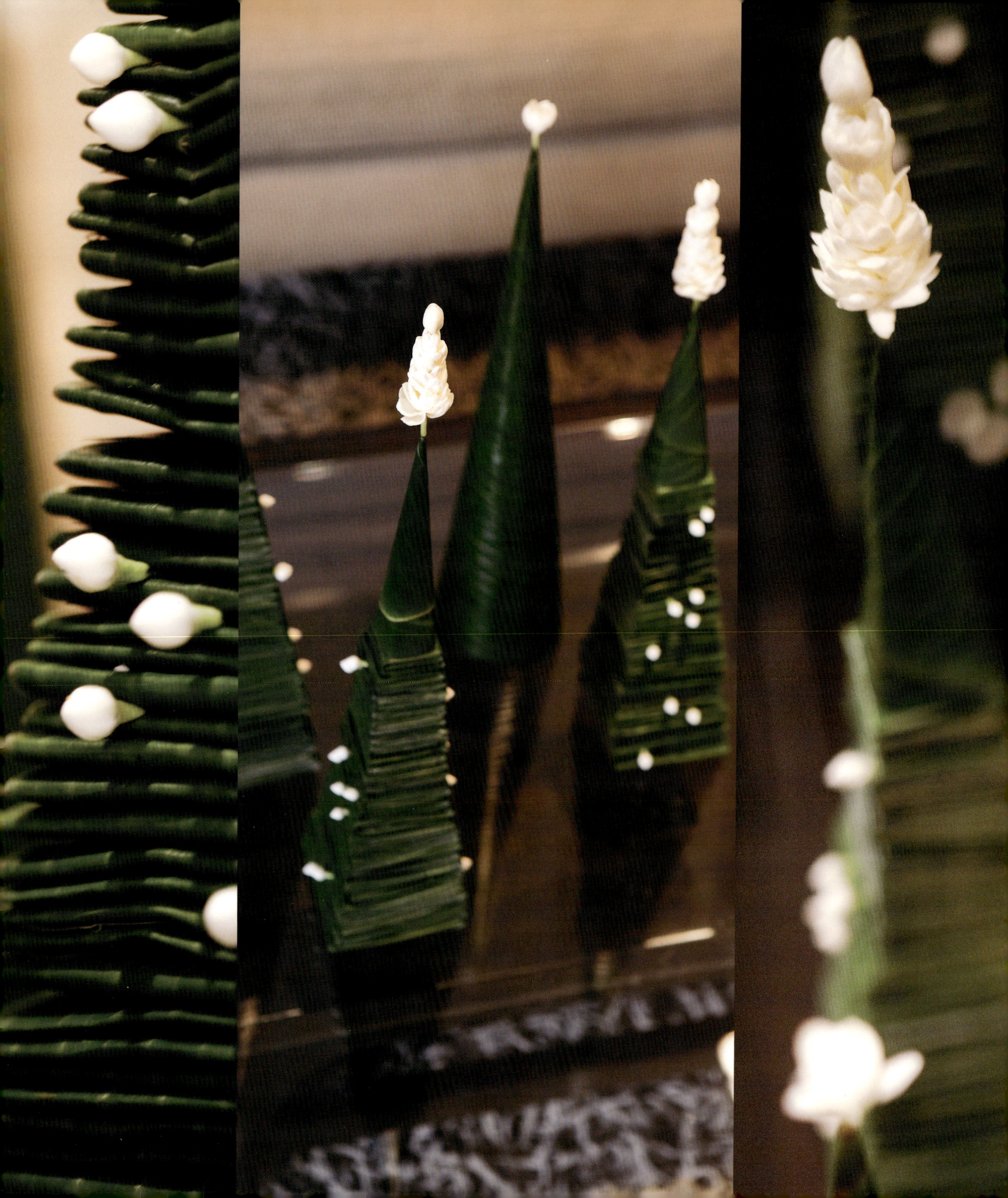

On the night of the festival, Thais carry their *krathongs* to the river's edge. After the candles and incense sticks are lit, the floats are gently cast into the placid water. Hundreds of *krathongs* streak down the river; the flickering lights of their innumerable candles reflecting upon the river. Fireworks light up the sky. The sweet smell of flowers drifts through the air as clouds float across the moon. Showered by moonlight, lovers wish for their *krathongs* to float away in pairs until they are far from sight. Thousands and thousands of fireflies dot the night with a poetic, mesmeric beauty. *Loy Krathong* is the most romantic night in tropical Asia.

This Spread

Inspired by the spires of traditional Thai architecture, this contemporary work by Sakul Intakul is constructed from banana leaves, small gardenias and jasmine. The seven banana-leaf cones are topped with fragrant jasmine, while the three pieces in the middle are made from small banana-leaf strips folded into squares of diminishing size, held together with long needles then finished with finials of jasmine. The tiny white dots are small gardenias. All pictures were taken at The River by Raimon Land.

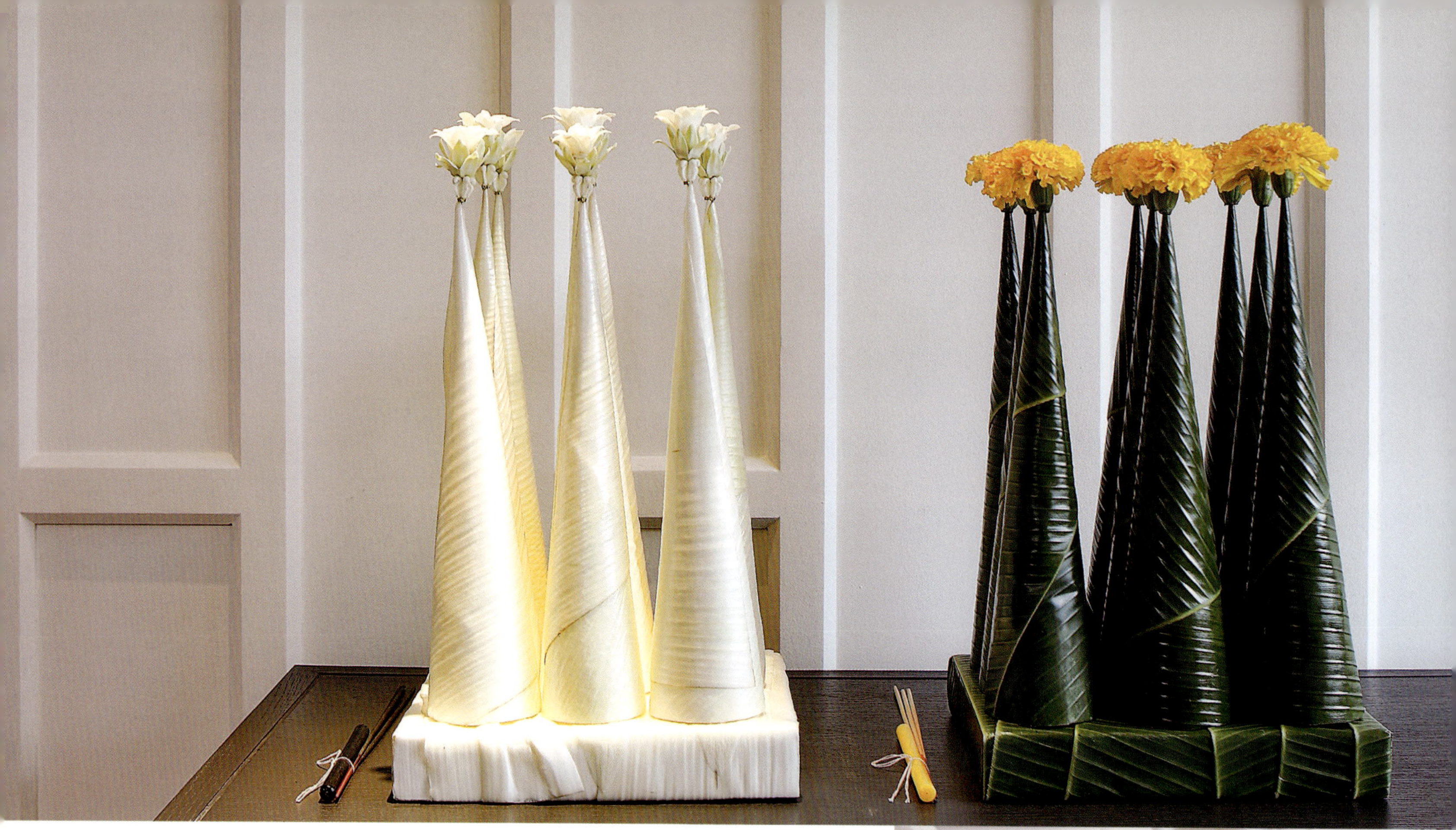
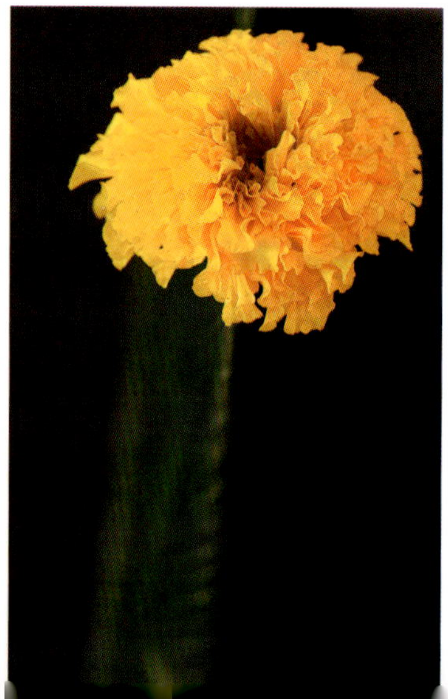
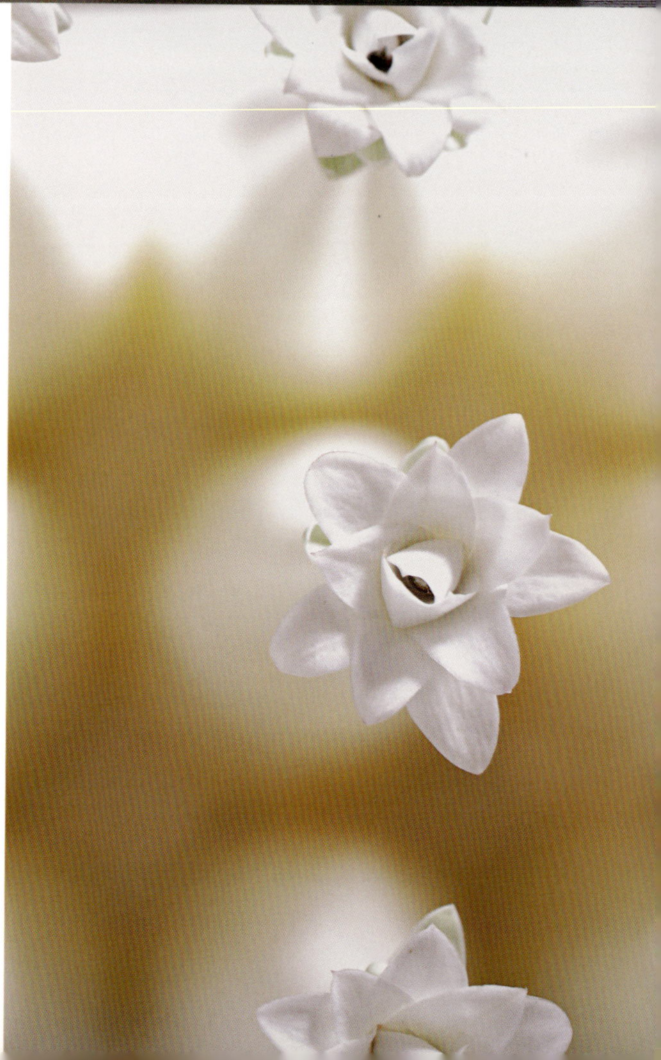

This Spread

The crinum lily's trunk produces white sheets of paper-like natural fibre; these are used to produce Sakul Intakul's contemporary interpretation of white floral floats. Banana leaves create their green counterparts.

Top Right

These white «*dokkha*» (fabricated flowers) are made from individual white orchid petals held together by a long thin strand of cotton.

Bottom Left

African marigolds are placed atop the banana-leaf cones.

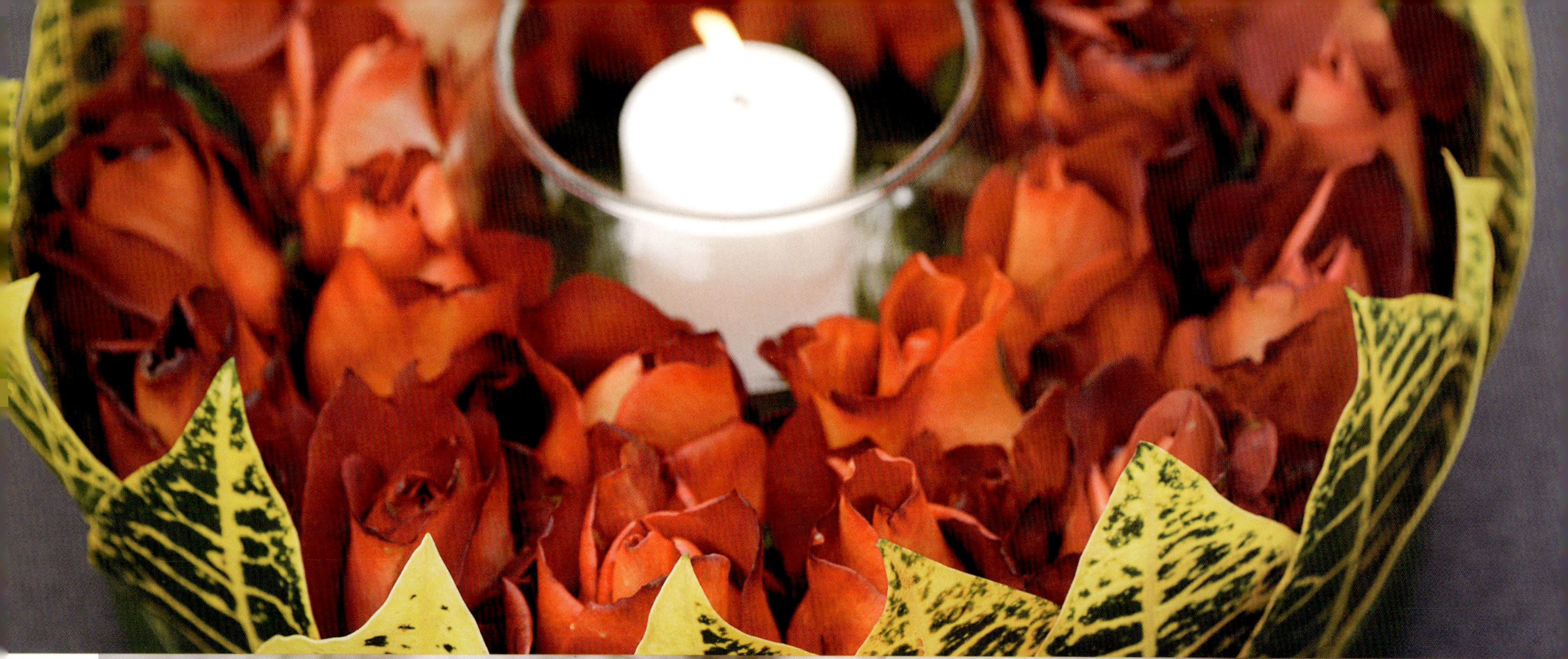
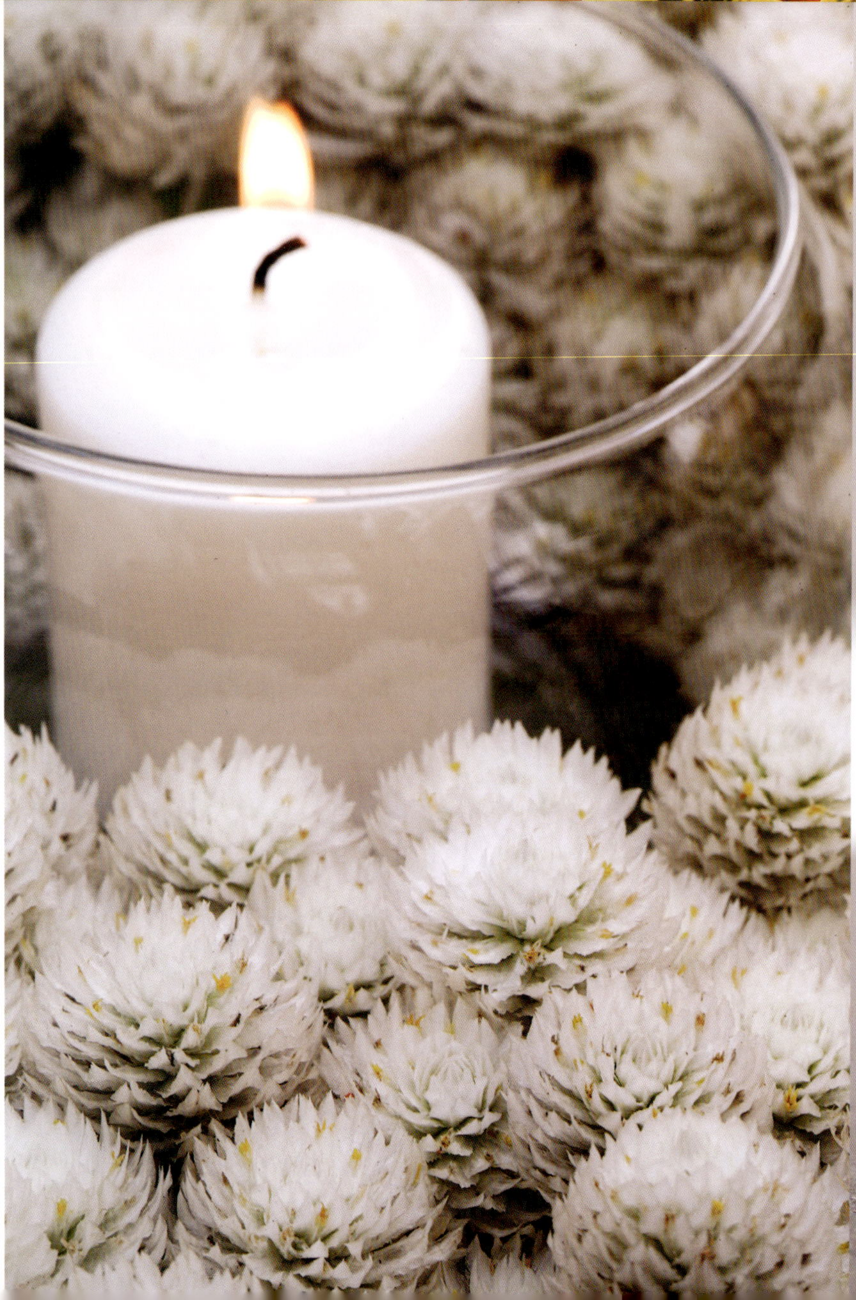
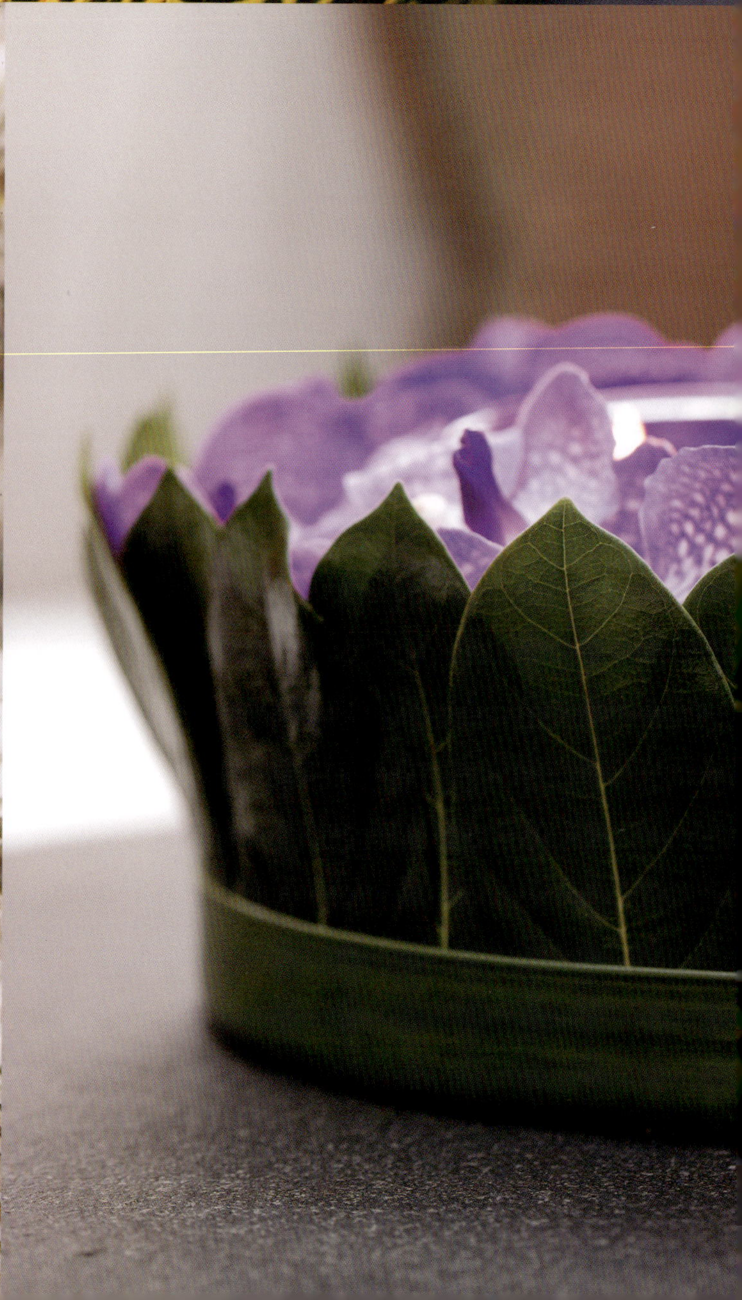

This Spread

A set of contemporary floral floats by Sakul Intakul decorates The Sukhothai Bangkok's Zuk Bar. The floats are made from five types of leaves, which match five kinds of flowers.

Clockwise From Top Left

Croton leaves with roses; Zuk Bar's outdoor conservatory space; ruffled fan palm leaves with roses; variegated screw pine leaves with African marigolds; jackfruit leaves with blue Vandas; and white globe amaranths fill the frangipani-leaf container.

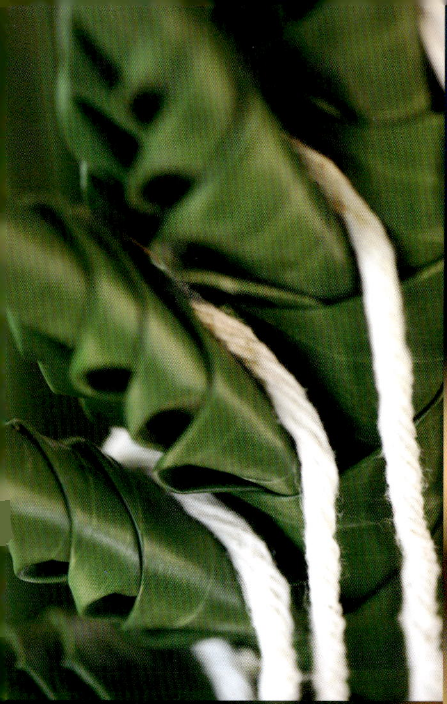
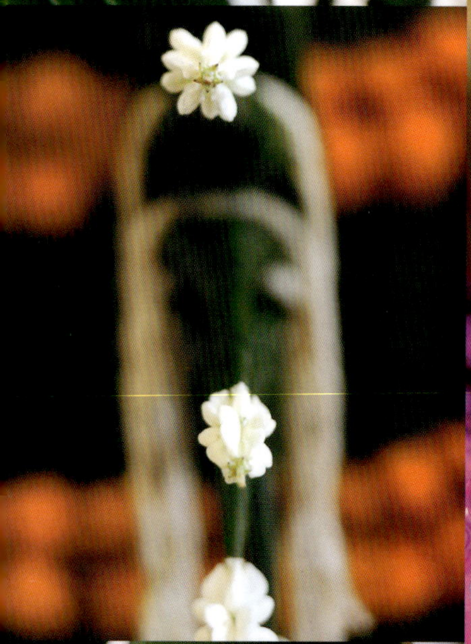
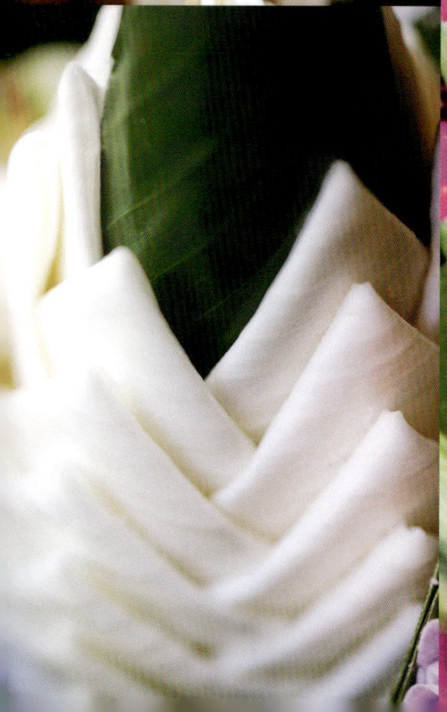
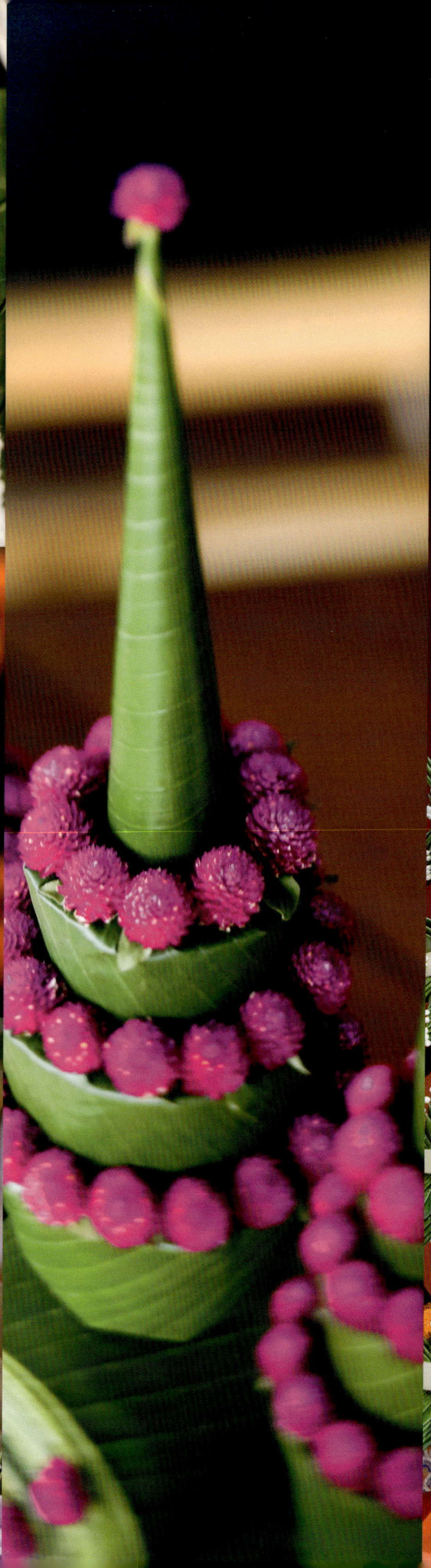
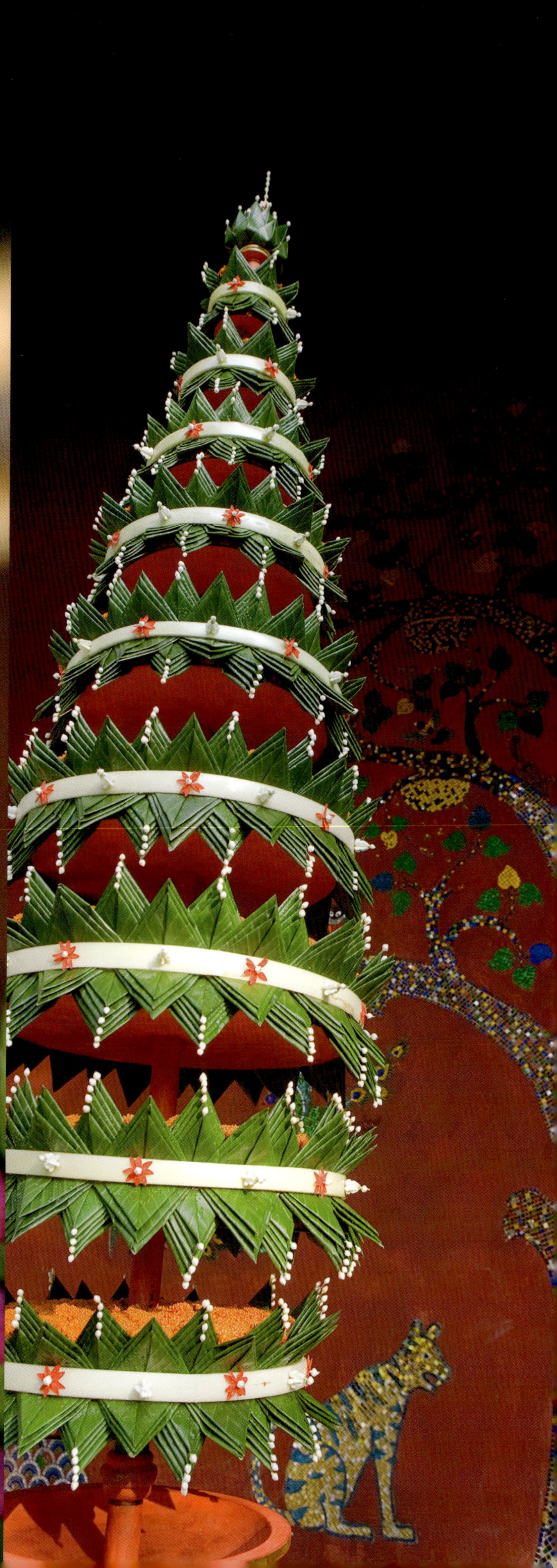

บายศรี

✤ Baisri ✤
Offerings to Divinities

At eight o'clock on the morning of January 6, 1927, in the second year of his reign, HM King Prajadhipok (King Rama VII) and HM Queen Rambhai Barni arrived at the Chitralada Royal Train Station to board the special locomotive bound for the north of Thailand.

This marked the first ever visit by a monarch of the Chakri Dynasty to the kingdom's northern territory. At ten past eight, the royal train left the station.

The royal itinerary's designated stops were northern cities Phrae, Lampang, Chiang Rai, Chiang Mai and Lampoon. Given that this was to be the first royal event in the north for 21 years – since «monton phayap» (the northern region) received HRH Crown Prince Mahavachiravuth in 1905 – careful preparations for the welcoming ceremony were busily underway in each destination.

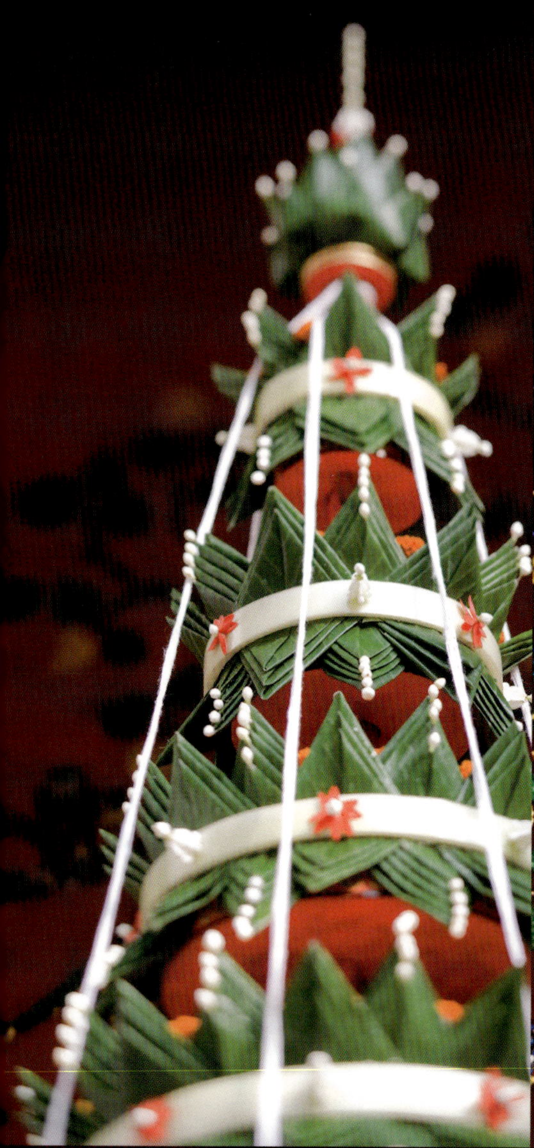
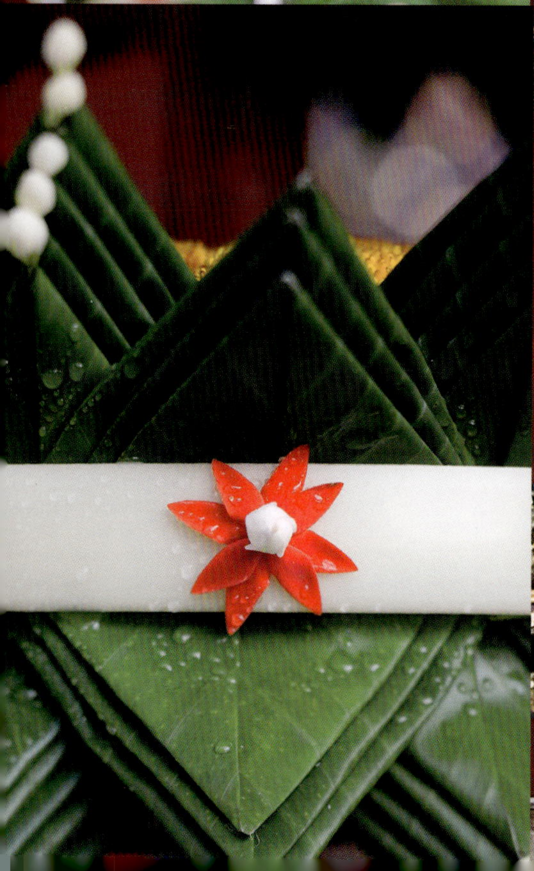
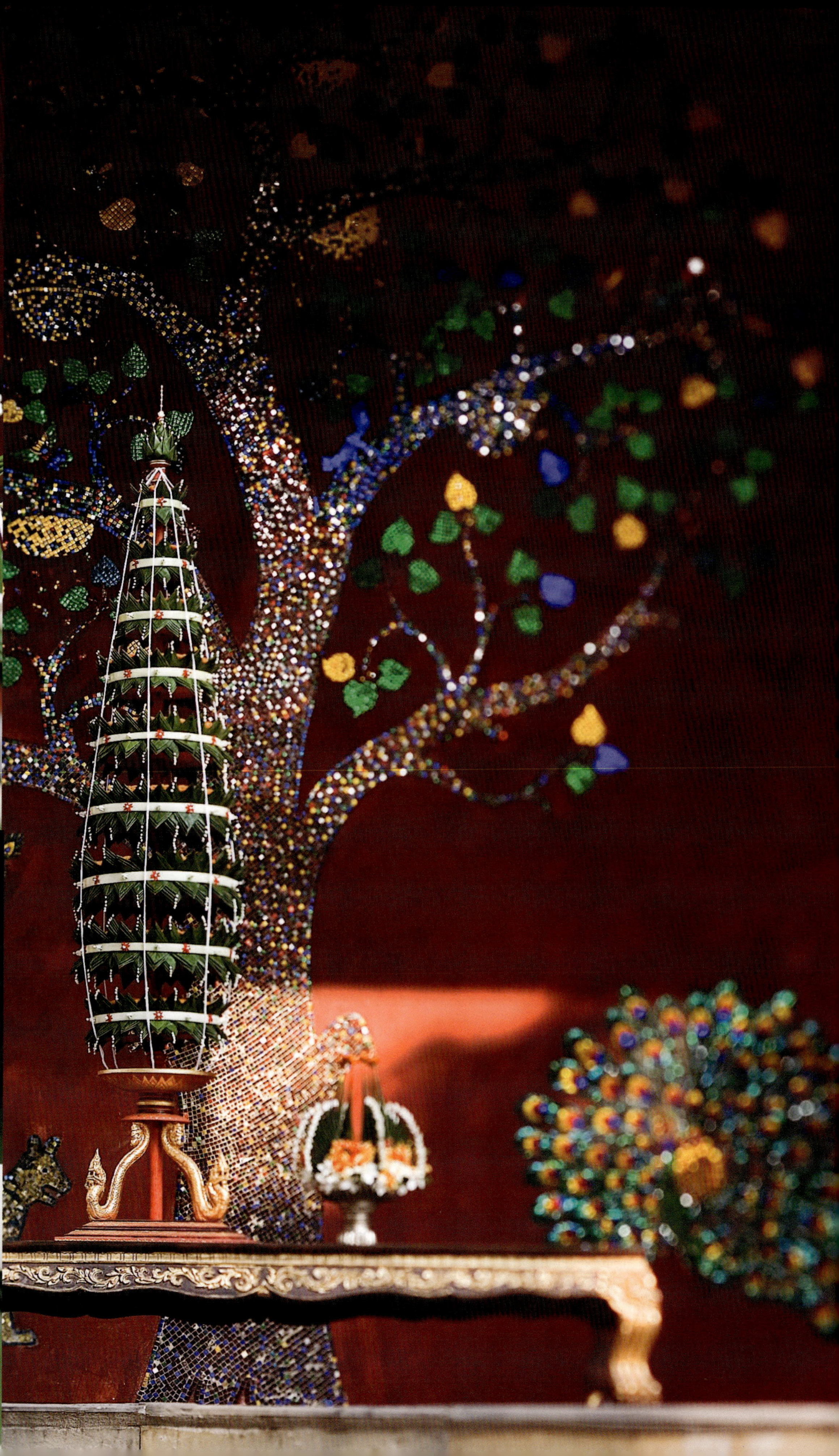

According to records of the time, of all the welcoming ceremonies, none were more spectacular than in Chiang Mai – the governing centre of the northern region, and the Lanna Kingdom's ancient capital. By royal train, HM King Prajadhipok and HM Queen Rambhai Barni arrived in Chiang Mai on January 17, 1927.

The royal procession, which comprised of 84 elephants, members of Lanna royal families and thousands of officials, transported the royal couple from Chiang Mai train station to the royal residence in the city centre. The procession passed through ten elaborate victory gates constructed in Their Majesties' honour. Chiang Mai residents of all ethnic backgrounds waited to welcome the royal couple from their respective pavilions on both sides of the procession's pathway.

This Spread

Reconstruction of a nine-tiered «*baisri*», this «*baisri ton*» has a wooden structure with nine wooden platforms of diminishing size attached to its central formation. Each wooden platform is decorated with folded banana leaves and flowers.

Right Page (top left)

1927 photograph of the original nine-tiered royal *baisri*.

Right Page (top right)

«*Baisri nom maew*» is used with *baisri ton* in «*phithi baisri thoon phra khwan*» – the royal ceremony to call back the soul, details of which are described in this chapter.

On January 23, another important ceremony, «*phithi baisri thoon phra khwan*», was organised for Their Majesties by members of the Lanna royal families, according to local – and Siamese – custom. It was believed that when people travelled (or became sick or frightened), their souls wandered elsewhere. When the journey ended, or upon recovery from the illness, a ceremony was then arranged to call back their wandering souls. For commoners, this ceremony was called «*phithi baisri suu khwan*».

Opening Spread
(clockwise from top left)

Strings of holy cord are hung between the banana-leaf structures of a «*baisri*» in preparation for the «*tham khwan*» ceremony (the calling back of the soul); inspired by the headdress of an «*apsara*» (celestial nymph), this contemporary *baisri* is made from banana leaves and decorated with globe amaranths; a reconstruction of a nine-tiered *baisri*, originally erected by the Lanna royal families to welcome King Rama VII to the north of Thailand in 1927; the white layer of a crinum lily's trunk is used to emblazon the central cone of a «*baisri pak cham*»; and crown flowers embellish the tips of «*tua baisri*» (banana leaf folded into triangular shapes).

This Spread

Baisri pak cham is used as an offering to divinities in Brahminical ceremonies, like the setting up of a shrine for «*phra phum*» (the guardian of the land) and the *tham khwan* ceremony (calling back of the soul). Around the centre cone of banana leaves are three pieces of *tua baisri* (banana leaves folded into triangular shapes). Between the *tua baisri* are three «*maengda*» (banana leaves cut in the shape of a horseshoe crab). The offering comprises cooked rice, a boiled egg, bananas, cucumbers and flowers. The container used here is from The Jim Thompson House and Museum's private collection.

Right Page (top middle)

The *maengda* of this *baisri* is elaborately decorated with folded orchid petals and small gardenias.

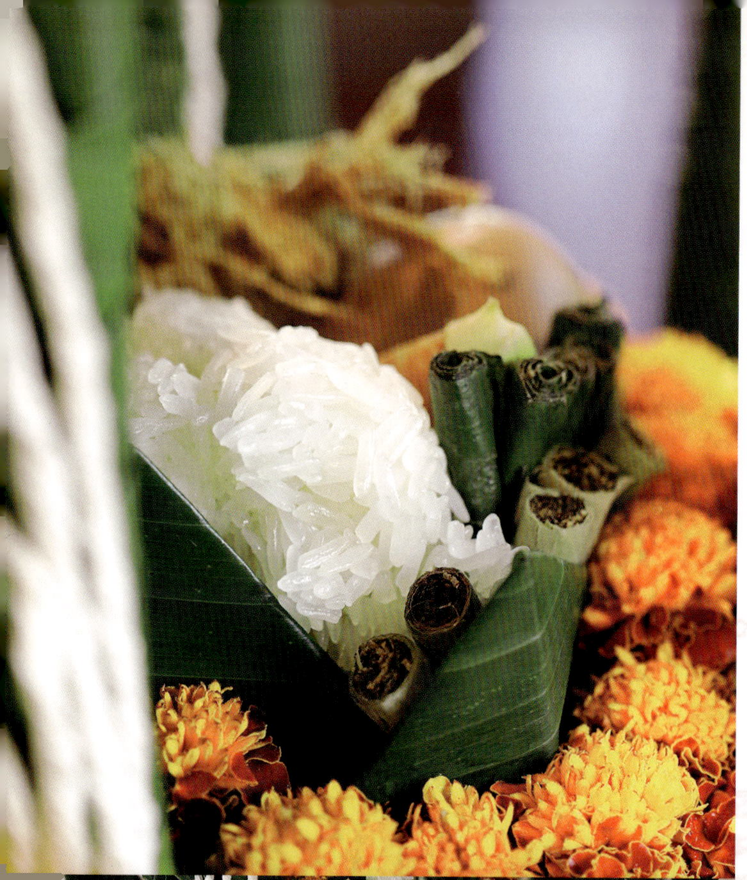
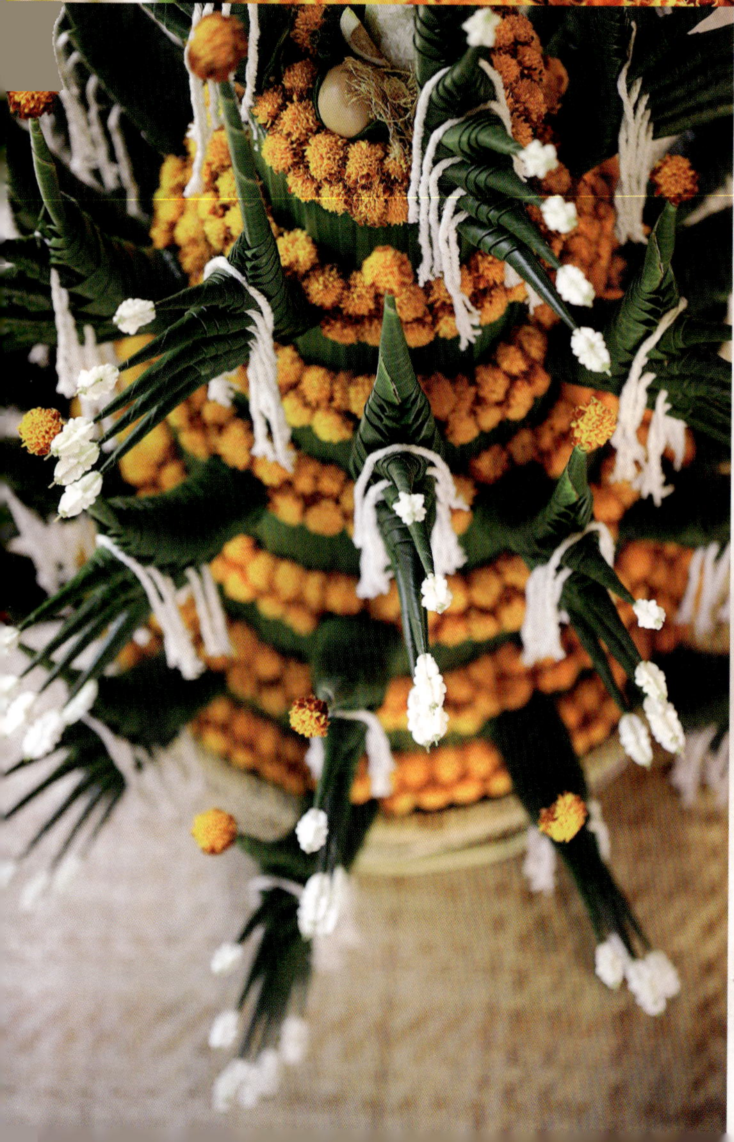
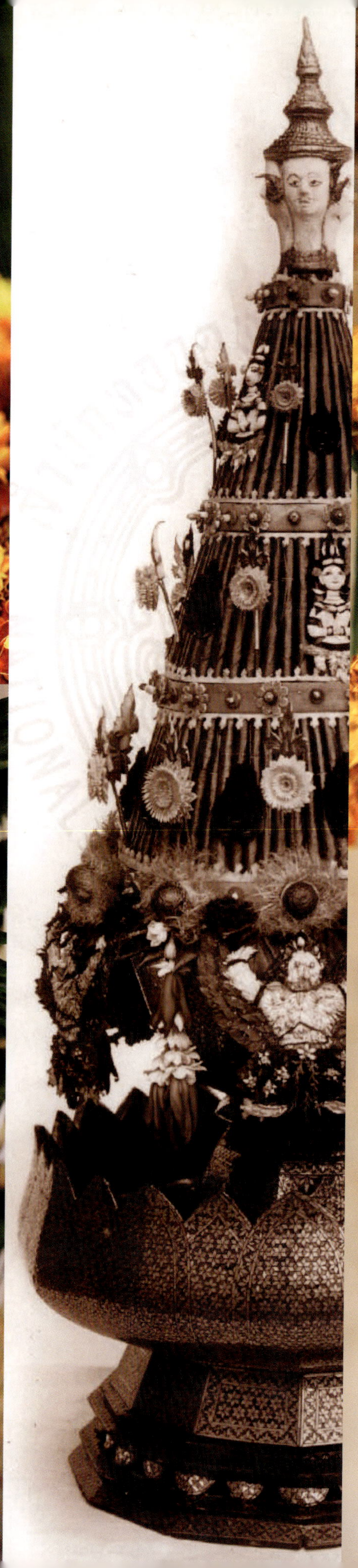
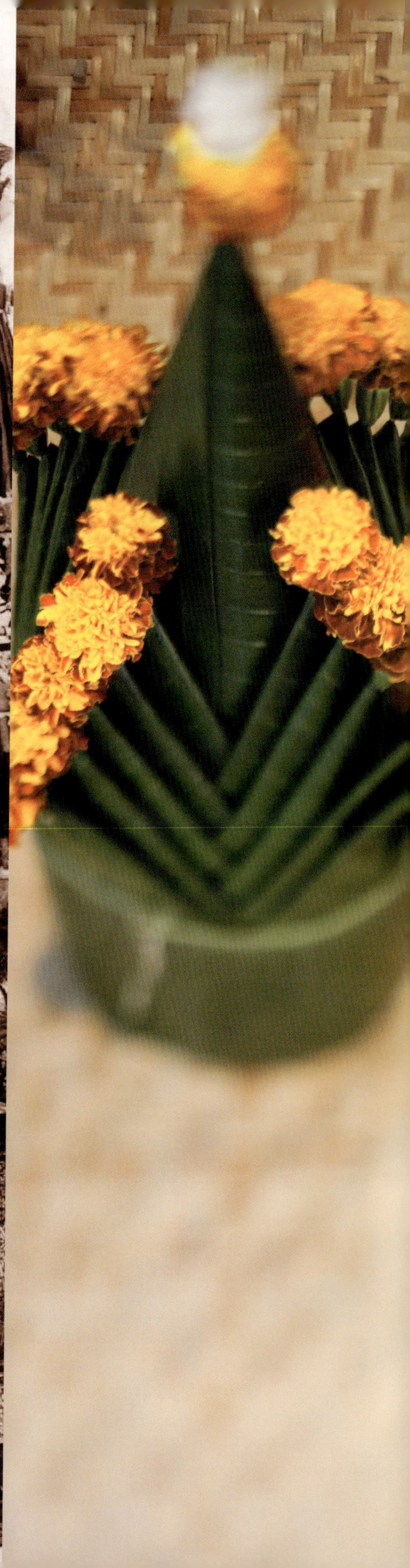

For the royal ceremony, two «*baisri*» offerings were elaborately made under the close supervision of Princess Dara Rasami of the Chiang Mai royal family, famed for her royal patronage of Lanna art and crafts. The princess was also a favourite royal consort of HM King Chulalongkorn the Great (King Rama V). The King's *baisri* had nine tiers, the highest rank, while the Queen's had seven. The term *baisri* is of Khmer origin; «*bai*» meaning rice and «*sri*», prosperity or auspiciousness. Combined, the two words denote an auspicious nutritional offering to the divinities.

Previous Spread

Belonging to the people of «*Isaan Nua*» (northern part of Thailand's northeastern region), the «*phan baisri*» (or «*pha khwan*») is used in the «*tham khwan*» ceremony, held to welcome guests upon their arrival.

Previous Spread (centre)

As part of the *tham khwan* ceremony, this «*mak beng*» made from banana leaves decorated with orange marigolds and crown flowers is used as a Buddha offering.

Previous Spread (far right)

A holy cord is tied around a guest's wrist in the *tham khwan* ceremony.

At half-past ten, HM King Prajadhipok and HM Queen Rambhai Barni arrived at the ceremonial pavilion. After the processions of students and various ethnic groups had run their course, «*krabuan khruang phra khwan*» – the procession of royal *baisri* – soon followed. The King's procession was led by seven pairs of dancers and princes of Lanna royal families, while the Queen's was comprised of princesses.

This Spread

The «*Isaan Tai*» (southern part of Thailand's northeastern region) version of «*baisri ton*» is made from banana tree trunks. Fruit and sweet offerings are secured in basket-like platforms made from bamboo slivers. «*Tua baisri*» decorate each layer of the platforms, and young coconuts top the *baisri ton* as part of the offering.

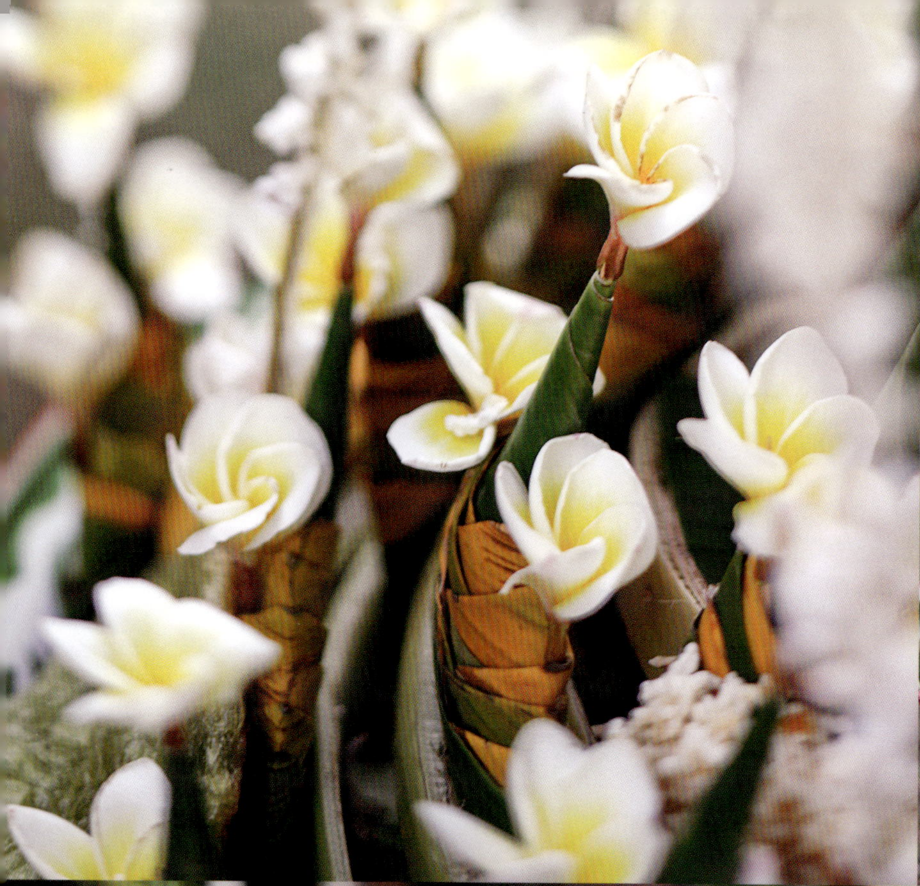
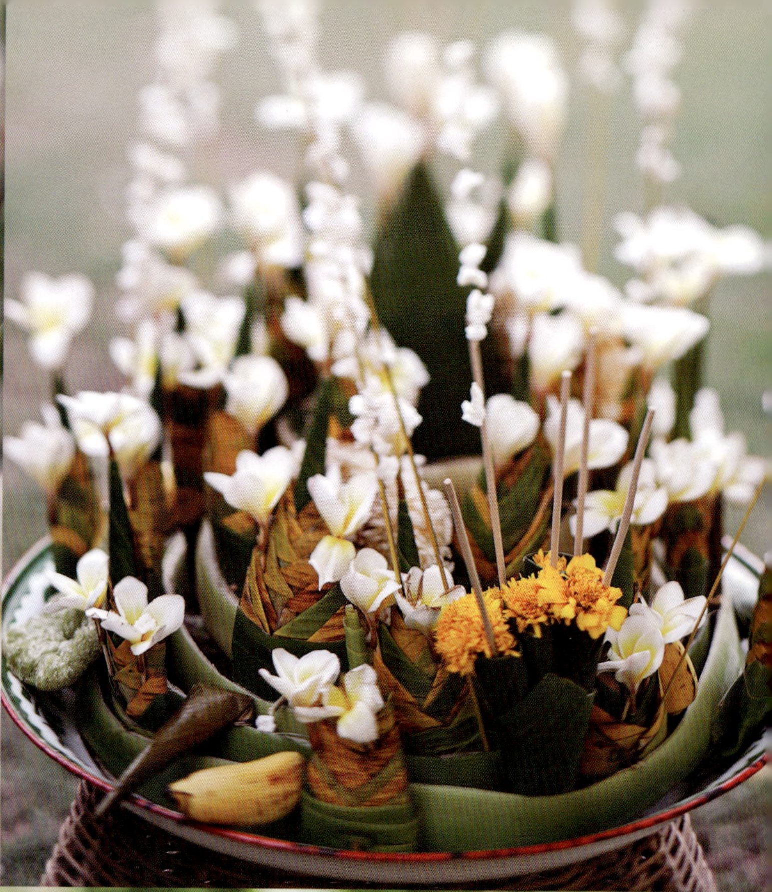
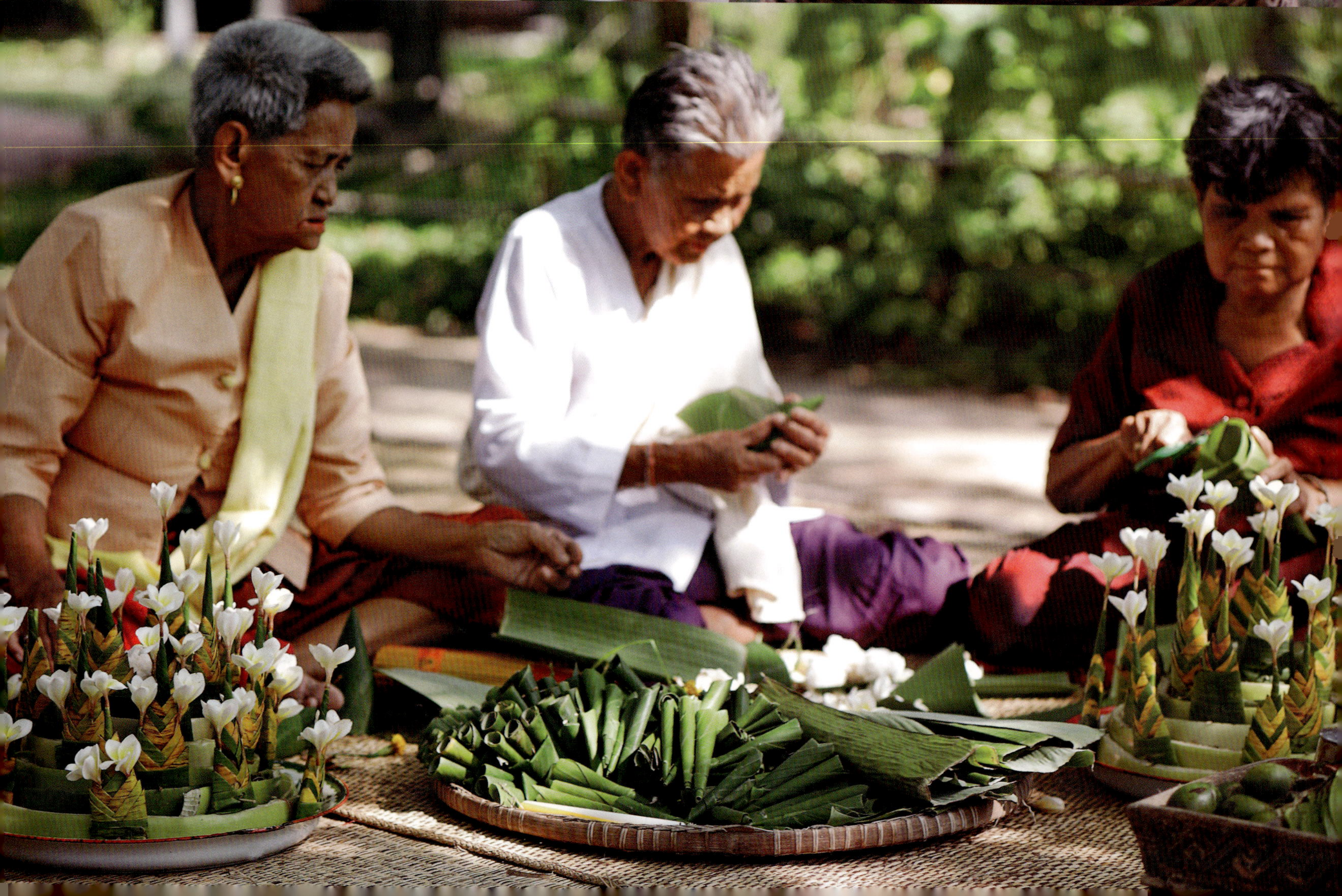

This Spread

«*Baisri thad*» (a *baisri* offering on a tray) is found only in the Thai-Khmer community of «*Isaan Tai*». Constructed in the form of Mount Meru, the centre of the universe in Hindu cosmology, cooked rice covered with a cone of banana leaves is *baisri thad's* central feature. Offering elements include flowers, sweets, fruits and, indispensably, popped rice glued on dry coconut frond spines.

At the front of the ceremonial pavilion, the processions were received by another troupe of royal dancers and the royal *baisri* placed in front of the royal couple. Princess Dara Rasami, Chao Jamari, Chao Maha Brahmasurathada, Chao Kaewnawarat and Chao Chakkamkajornsak of the Lanna royal families conducted *phithi baisri thoon phra khwan*. After the ceremony, HM the King bestowed the royal sword to the city of Chiang Mai, symbolising his sovereignty over the land being visited.

Following the details gleaned from old photographs taken on that day, the nine-tiered *baisri* for HM King Prajadhipok was laboriously reconstructed and photographed in Chiang Mai especially for this book. Other types of *baisri* from northern, northeastern and central parts of Thailand, including contemporary versions, are also shown in this chapter.

This Spread

Inspired by the headdress of an «*apsara*» (celestial nymph), this contemporary «*baisri*» by Sakul Intakul is made from banana leaves and decorated with pink globe amaranths. The *baisri's* lower section features a bunch of tightly rolled banana leaves placed on a modern square base.

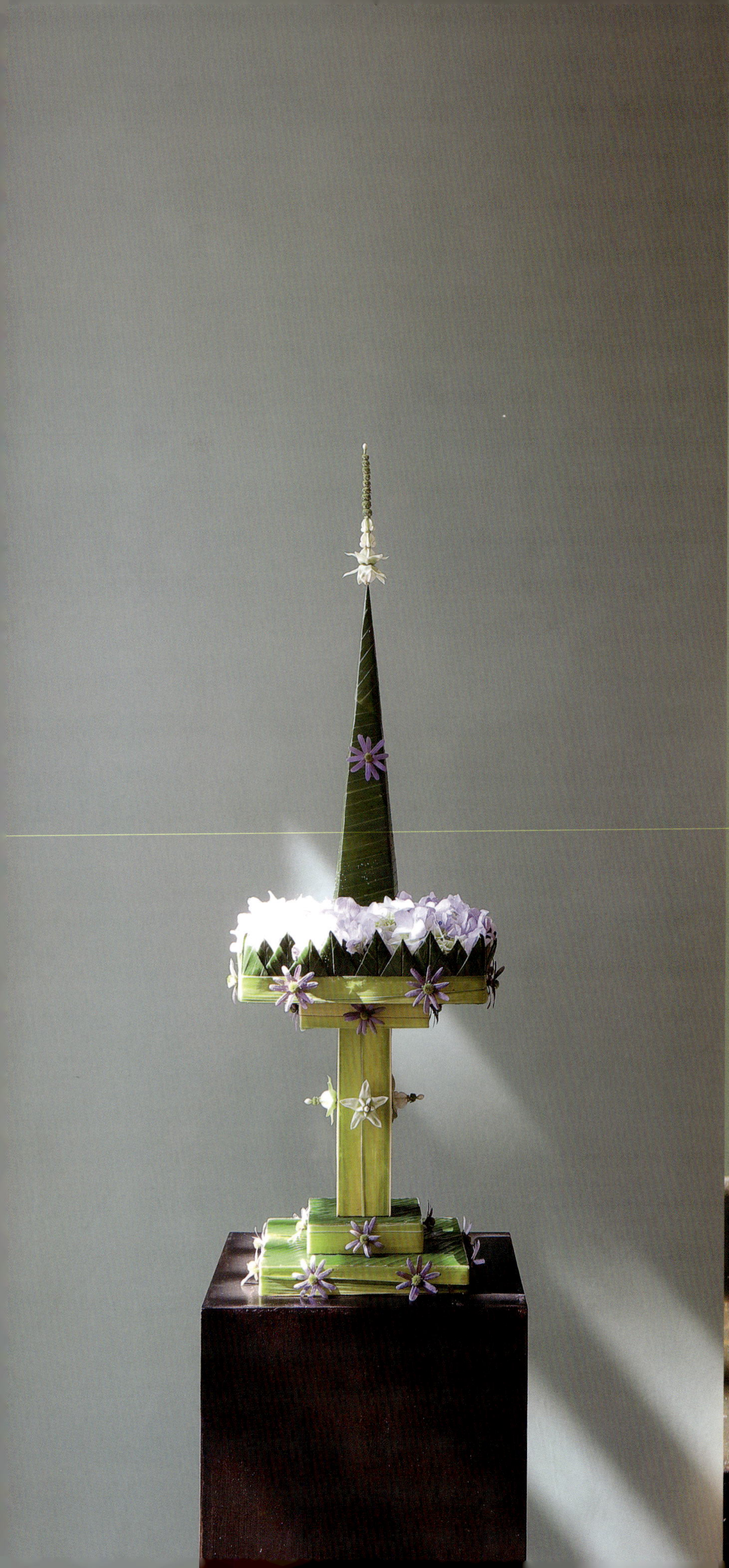
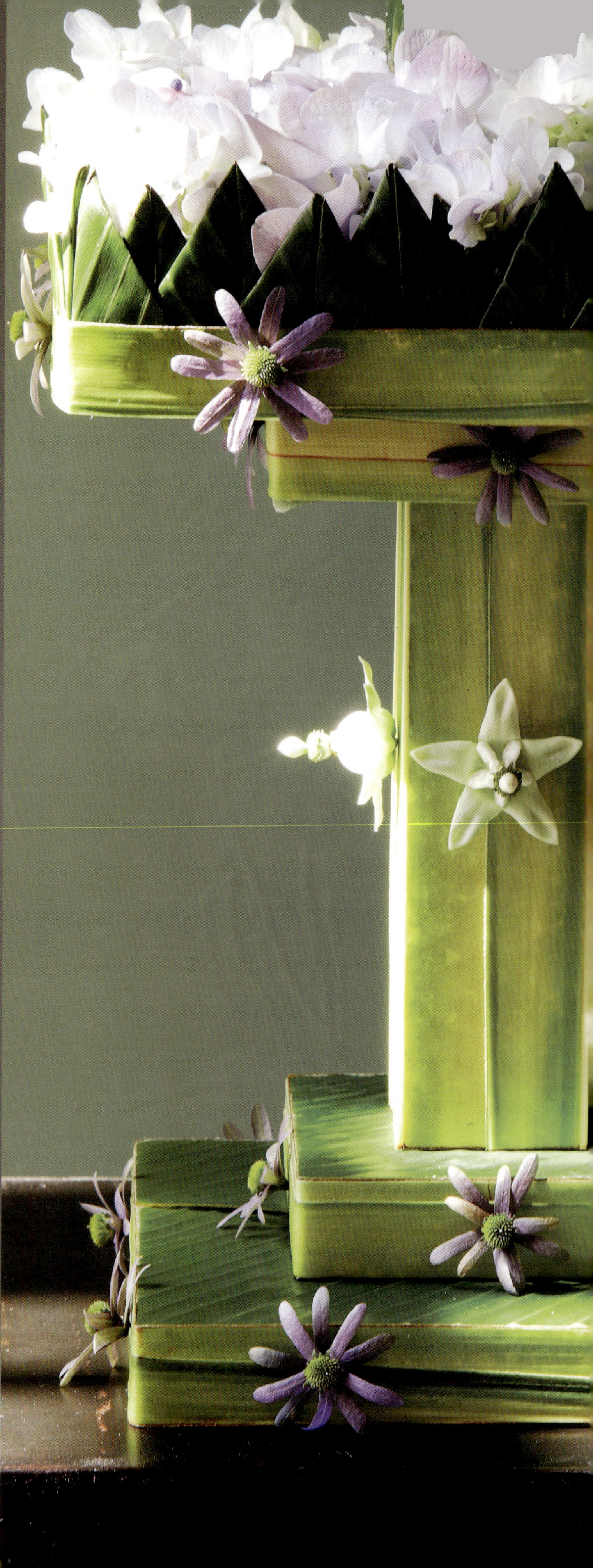

Three decades thereafter, in February 1958, Lanna royal families and the people of Chiang Mai once again prepared to welcome the reigning monarch – HM King Bhumibol Adulyadej (King Rama IX) and HM Queen Sirikit on their first royal visit to the region. Following the centuries-old Siamese tradition, a pair of royal *baisri* was erected for *phithi baisri thoon phra khwan* on March 5, 1958. ✽

This Spread

This contemporary «*baisri*» designed by Sakul Intakul was inspired by offerings on banana-tree trunks in the northern region of Thailand. The main sections of this *baisri* are made from banana and coconut leaves. It is then embellished with hydrangeas, purple wreath flowers (*Petrea volubilis* L.), crown flowers and small gardenias.

Far Right (top)

Lanna royal family members reveal their seven- and nine-tiered *baisri* to HM King Prajadhipok and HM Queen Rambhai Barni in 1927. Image courtesy of National Archives of Thailand.

This Spread

This set of three contemporary «*baisri*» by Sakul Intakul decorates the reception area of TENFACE Serviced Residence in Bangkok. Folded lotus leaves form and cover the base of these arrangements. Banana leaves, chrysanthemums, crown flowers and small gardenias are also employed.

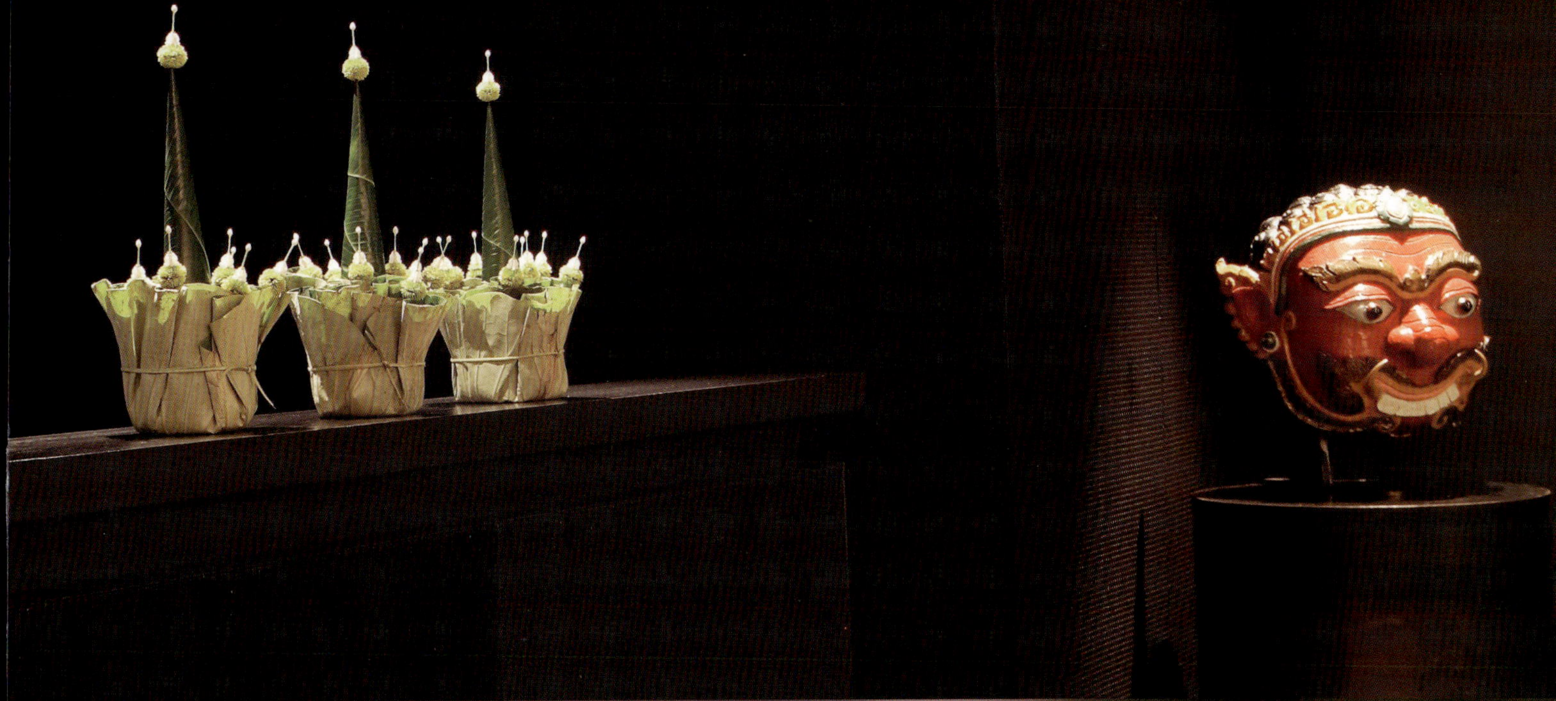

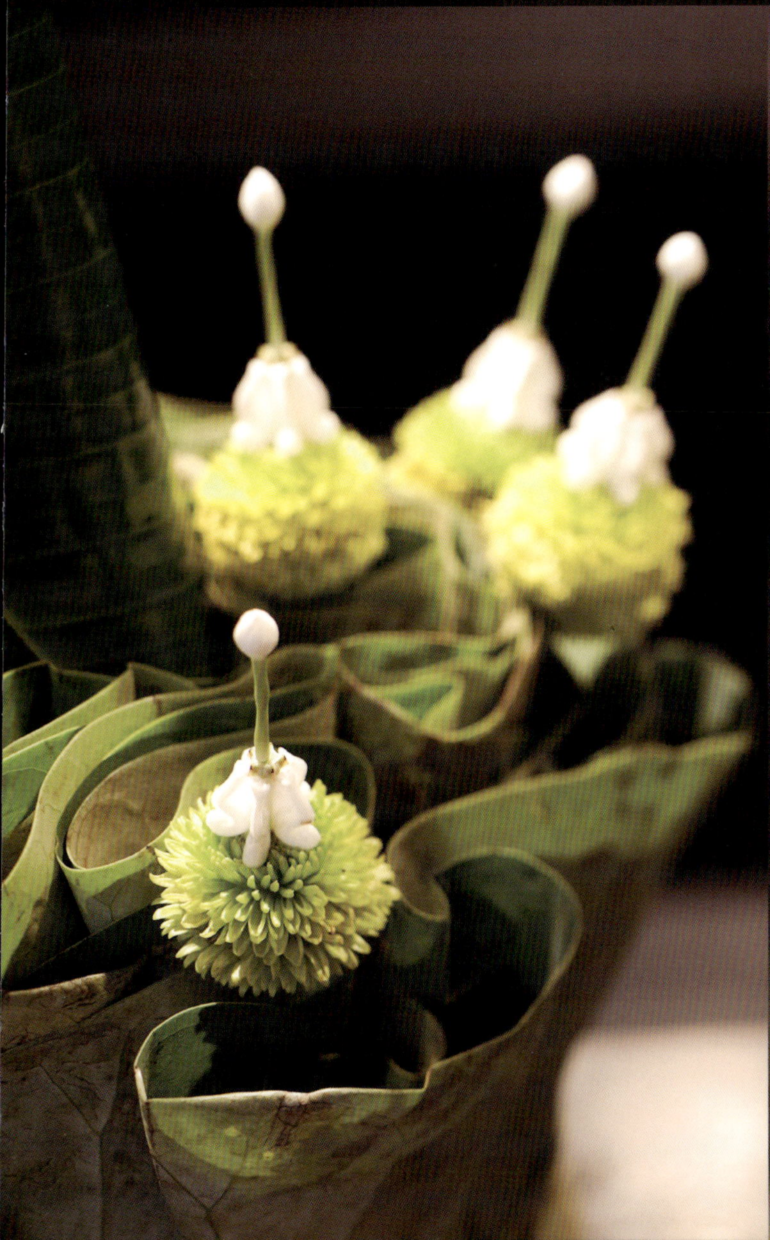

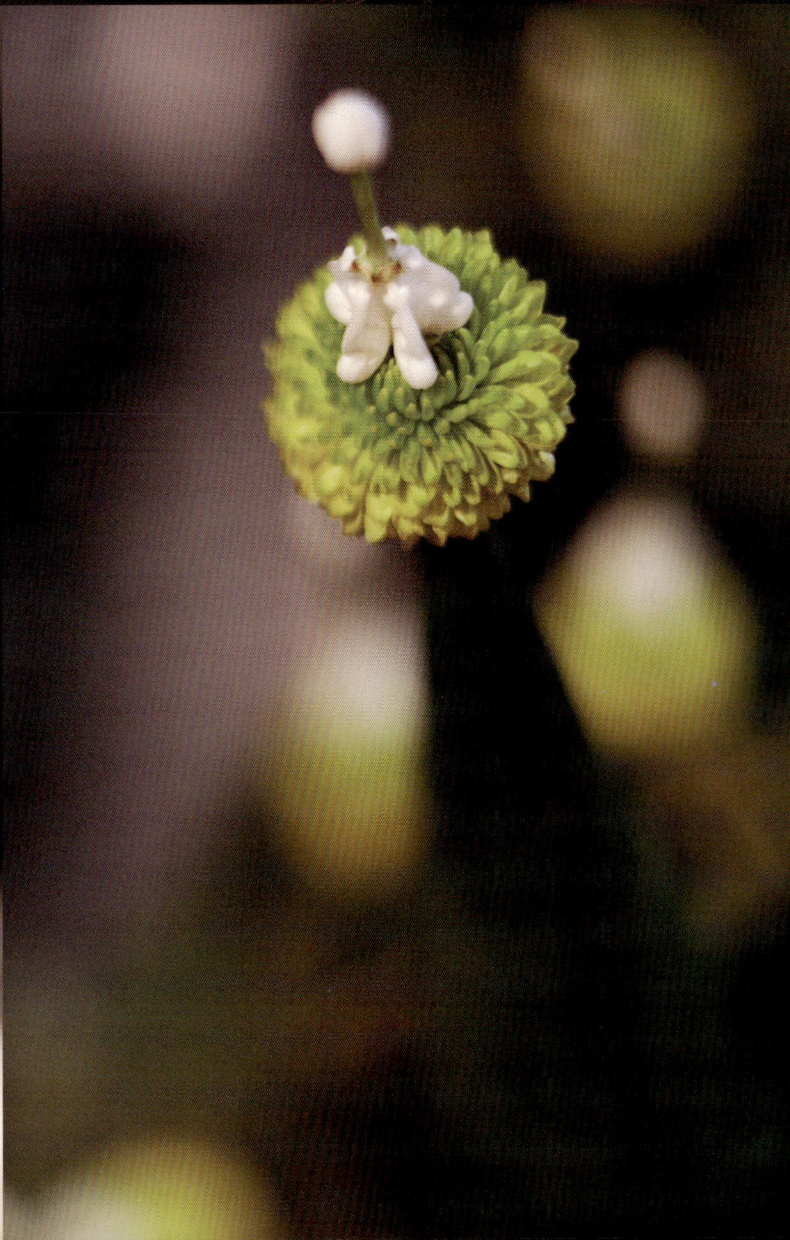

งานดอกไม้เล็ก

Ngan Dokmai Lek
Small Floral Works

"Chan aoey chan chao

Khor khao khor gang

Khor waen thongdaeng phook meu nong kha

Khor chang khor ma hai nong kha khii..."

An elder sister is singing a lullaby, asking the moon goddess for gifts for her little brother. A mobile of folded «bailan» (dry palm leaves) in the shape of «pla taphian» (Thai silver barb fish) gently swirls over the cradle to keep the little one amused. Responsibility begins at a young age in the land of smiles.

In extended families, where three generations live under one roof – or «share the kitchen» as Thai people say, age-old domestic customs pass down from one generation to the next via the watch-and-learn method. This holds true for the continuation of other forms of traditional Thai arts and crafts.

Children learn while they play. Uncles teach their nephews to make their own toys, such as horses from «*kankleuy*», the centre of banana leaves; insects from dry leaves; and «*takraw*», woven balls from coconut leaves. Little girls learn how to make dolls from lotus flowers, peacocks from crown flowers and fish from coconut leaves. Folding lotus petals into different patterns is a compulsory skill; girls later familiarise themselves with basic Thai florist's tools – long needles are essential – when they are taught how to make simple floral offerings such as «*malai mali*» (jasmine garlands) for everyday household use.

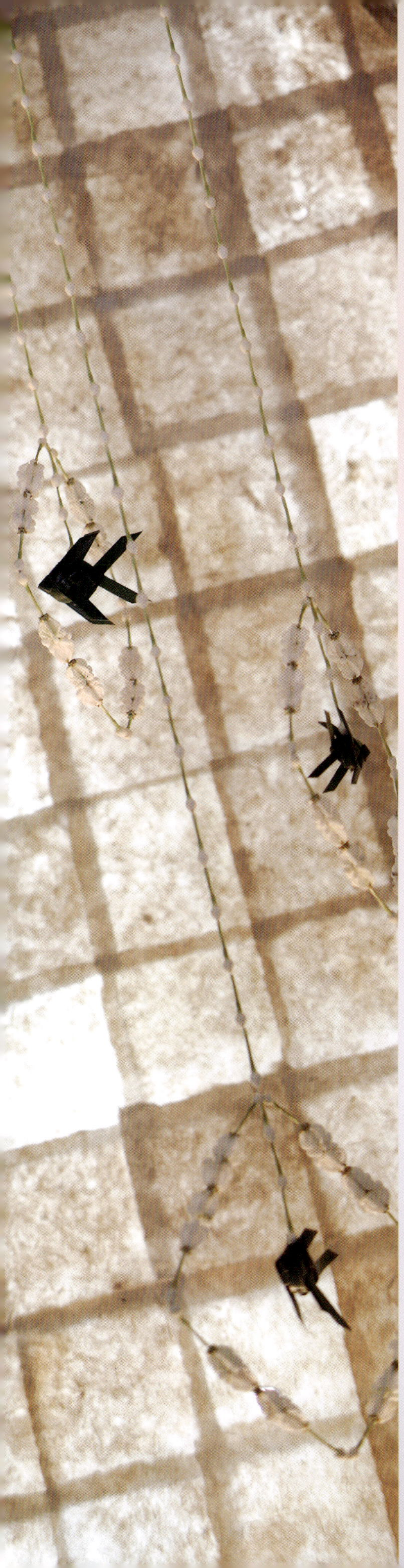
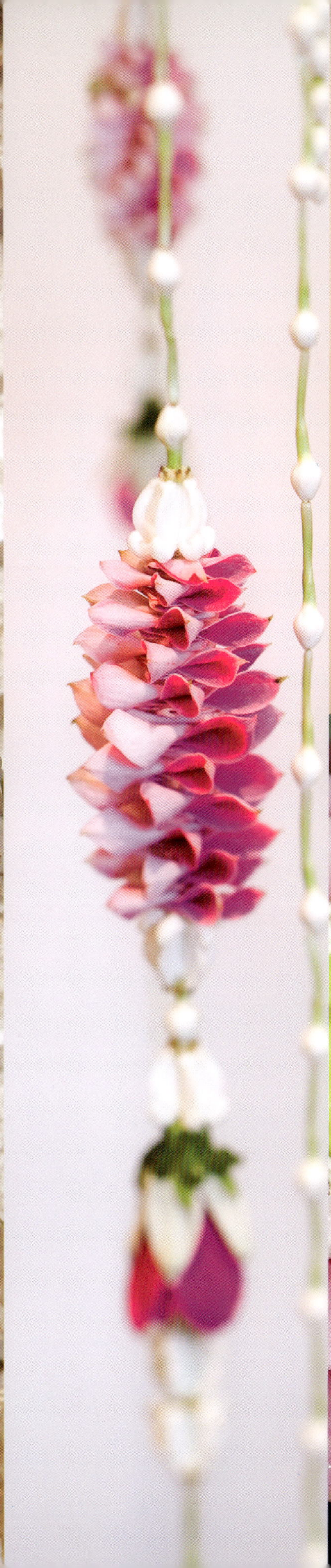
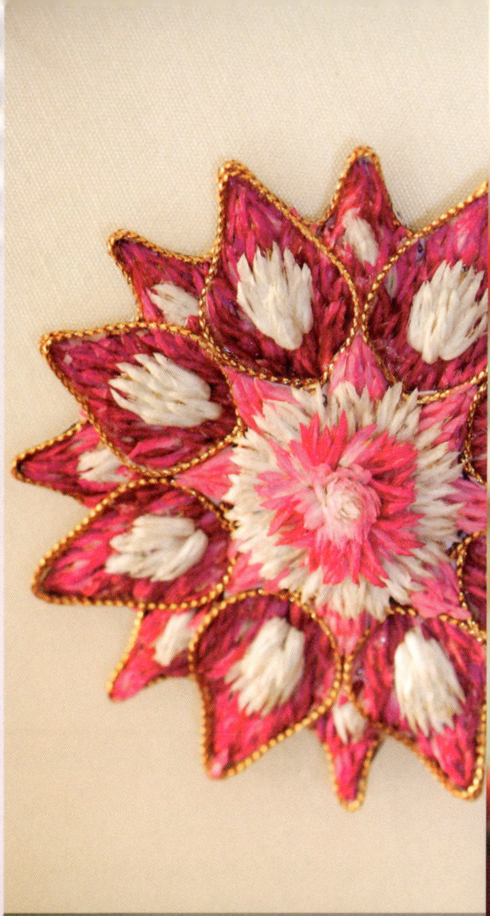
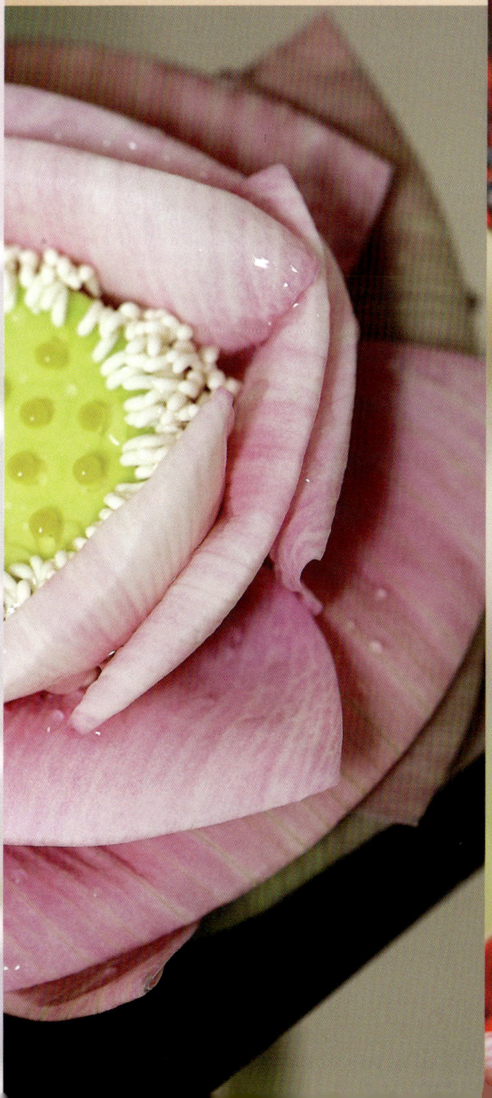
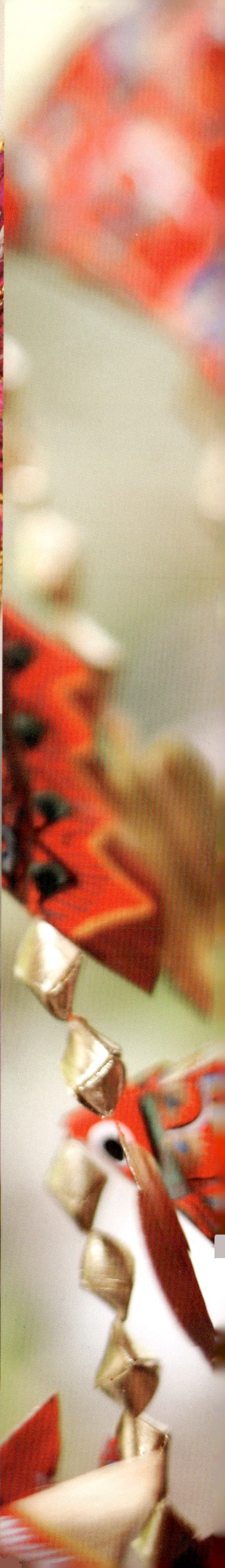

This Page

Silk flowers in dangling «*uba*» (floral tassels) decorate exquisite puppet headdresses during a puppet theatre rehearsal «*Taleng Phai*» by Chakrabhand Posayakrit and Company.

This Page

Floral Grace, a pastel painting by Thai national artist Chakrabhand Posayakrit. Made from small gardenias, a globe amaranth, crown flowers and white champaks, the model for the garland painted on the low table was designed by Sakul Intakul. All images on this spread courtesy of the Chakrabhand Posayakrit Foundation.

Opening Spread (clockwise from left)

Small floral pendants made from crown flowers and small gardenias feature folded, coconut-leaf fish hanging at their centre; a «*toom dokmai*» made from sewn orchid petals; this traditional Thai floral motif is made from tiny globe amaranth petals pasted on patterned paper; dry palm leaves are folded and painted to make a fish mobile; and mature lotus-bud petals are folded out as if the flower is in full bloom.

This Spread

«*Kratae*» is a special type of floral garland made from flowers, petals, or leaves sewn to mimic the shape of squirrels (*kratae* in Thai). All *kratae* pictured here are made from different coloured orchid petals, except the *upper-left* version, which sports orange jessamine leaves. The tails are made from globe amaranths sewn onto metal wires. *Kratae* are typically used as party favours in Thailand and are a particular favourite with children.

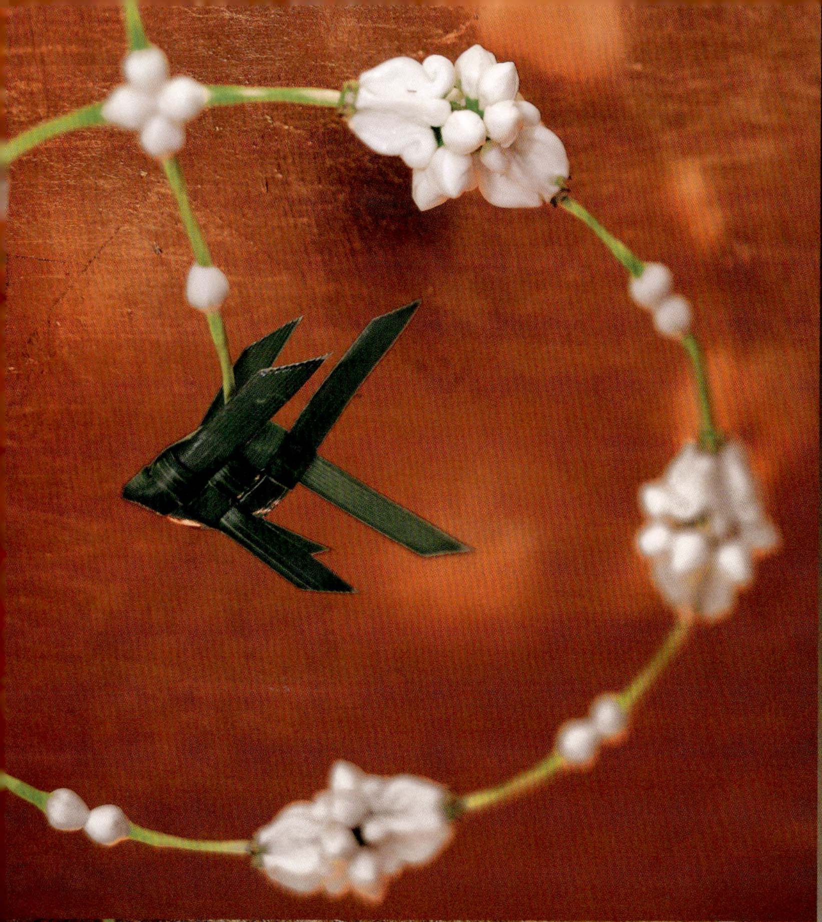
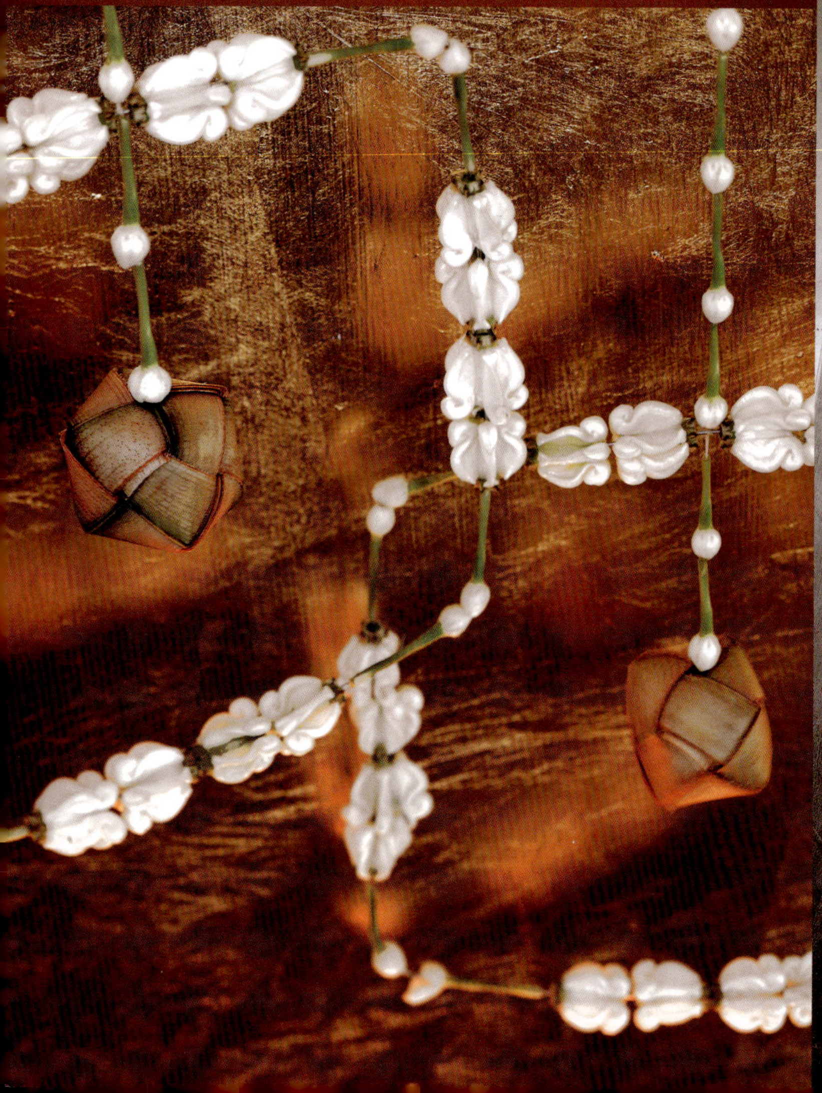
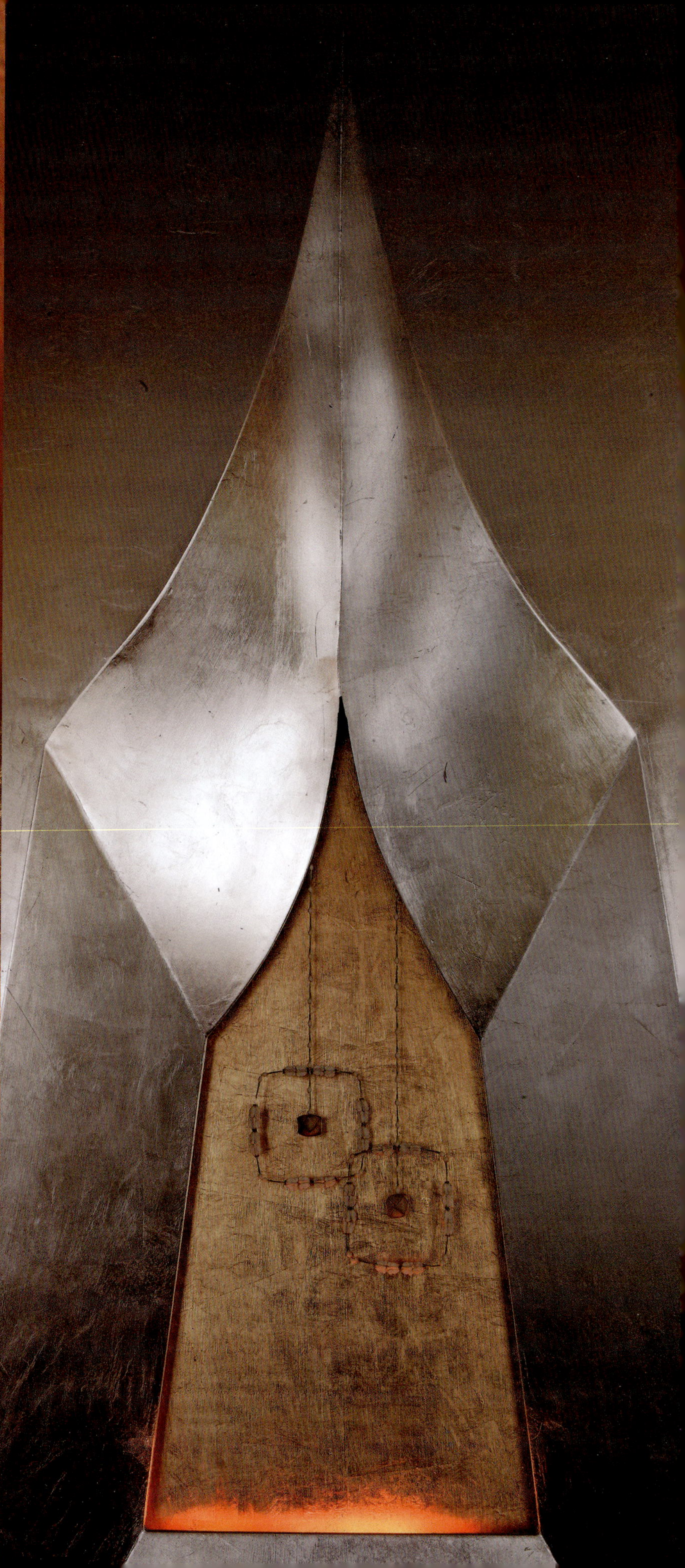

In the not-so-distant past, boys would be sent to temples for their education, while noblemen and government officials would send their daughters to the palace. The girls would learn how to read and write, run a household, and conduct and carry themselves as ladies. The Grand Palace's inner court became the girls' new home. Queens, princesses, «*chaochom*» (royal wives), their attendants, court ladies and female government officials resided here. It was like a small, female-only town, with its own laws, customs and practises, and a unique style of life that has formed the model for Rattanakosin-era culture.

This Spread

These small floral pendants, round and square, are made from crown flowers and small gardenias. At the centre of the pendants hang fish folded from coconut leaves, and cubes from young coconut leaves. Globe amaranths are used in the piece pictured *bottom right*.

Each mansion in the inner court was a royal lady's private home, with its own distinctive character. Some were famed for their scents and perfumes, some for their sweets, others for their embroidery or garlands. The ladies spent many hours a day to create and develop their chosen art.

The reign of HM King Rama V (King Chulalongkorn the Great) witnessed great developments in Siamese arts and crafts at the same time as the court welcomed ever more royal guests from the Western world. With foreign guests to entertain and impress, each royal residence in the inner court took immense pride in their art, and made every effort to excel through fine-tuning their designs and refining their craftsmanship.

Ngan Dokmai Lek 111

This Spread

In contrast to the traditional upright design of «*toom dokmai*» (a traditional Thai floral accessory made from flowers or petals sewn in pointed oval shapes), these contemporary adaptations are hung upside-down in strings of small gardenias – forming decorative hanging floral jewels on this Sakul Intakul-designed floor lamp. All pictures were taken at The River by Raimon Land.

↑ Sukhothai Gallery

Each royal lady would, according to custom, teach her art to her ladies-in-waiting, as well as to the young girls who came to live in the palace under her royal patronage. For floral art, this might have started with the simplest garlands and progressed to the most intricate ones. With no written text to guide them, the young ladies had to be extra attentive to what was being taught and handed down to them. They had to remember everything by heart – using the self-same skills they had acquired since infancy. Perfecting these skills was accomplished only through continuous practice.

This Spread

Acquired by Thai ladies at a young age, folding lotus petals into different designs is a basic skill in Thai floral art. Traditionally, these blossoms are placed in vases in front of a Buddha image as an offering. The lotus blossoms on this spread are the major plant material in this floral installation by Sakul Intakul for The Sukhothai Residences in Bangkok. Also illustrated here are the different ways in which to fold lotus petals.

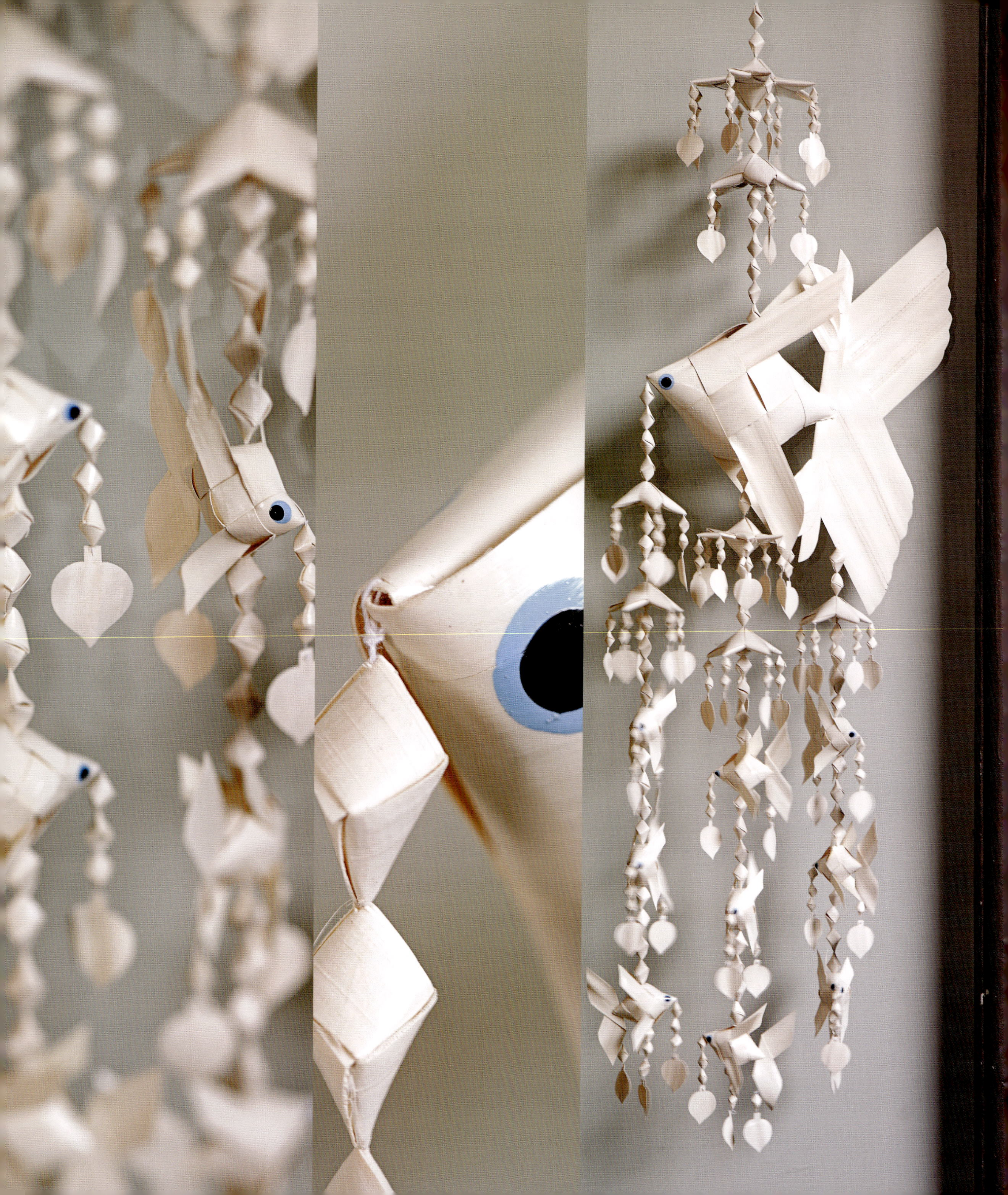

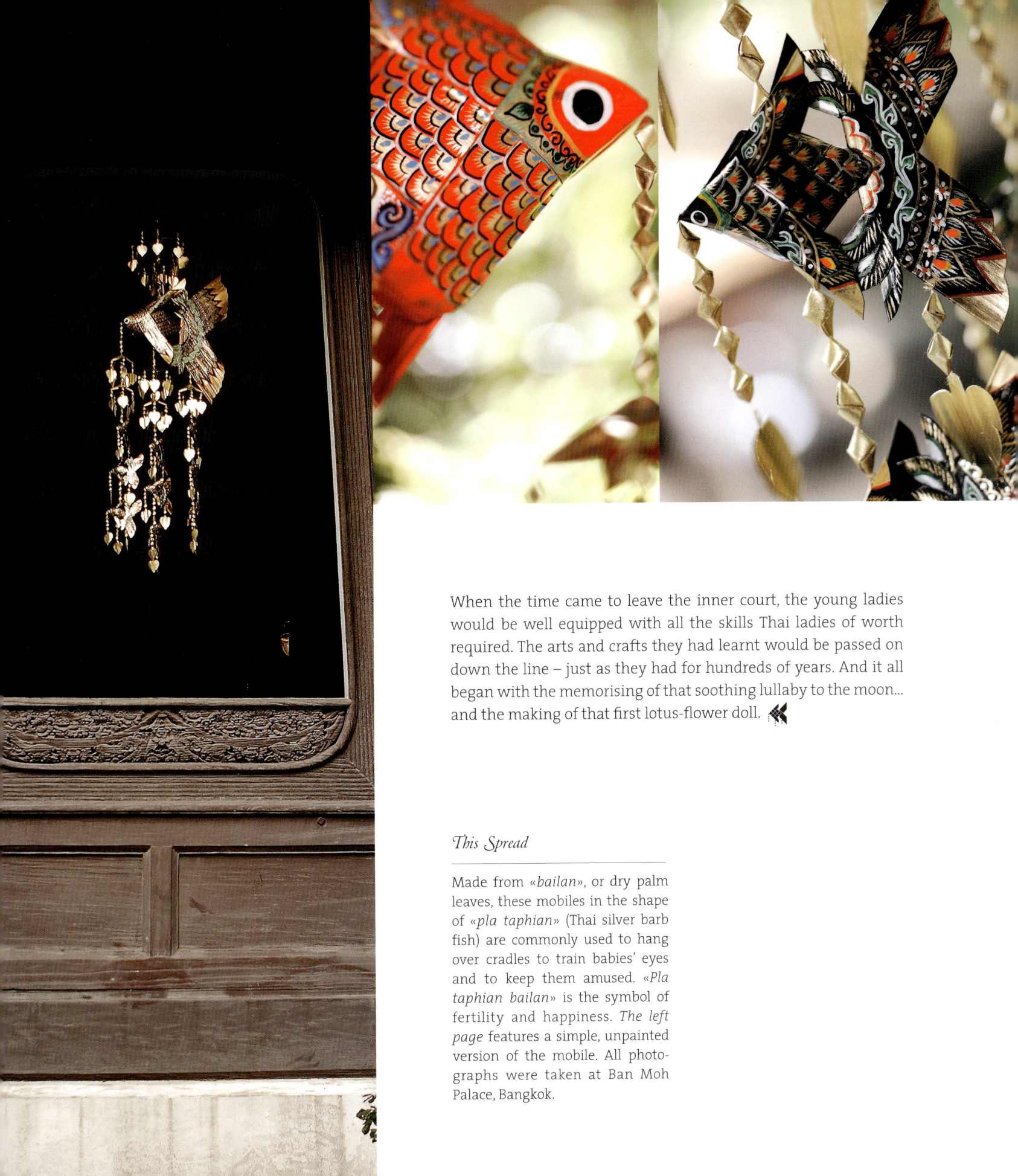

When the time came to leave the inner court, the young ladies would be well equipped with all the skills Thai ladies of worth required. The arts and crafts they had learnt would be passed on down the line – just as they had for hundreds of years. And it all began with the memorising of that soothing lullaby to the moon… and the making of that first lotus-flower doll.

This Spread

Made from «*bailan*», or dry palm leaves, these mobiles in the shape of «*pla taphian*» (Thai silver barb fish) are commonly used to hang over cradles to train babies' eyes and to keep them amused. «*Pla taphian bailan*» is the symbol of fertility and happiness. *The left page* features a simple, unpainted version of the mobile. All photographs were taken at Ban Moh Palace, Bangkok.

This Spread (from left to right)

A scarecrow set up at the rice fields of Mandarin Oriental Dhara Dhevi, Chiang Mai; toys for the children in northern Thailand – thin bamboo strips are woven to create animal figures like lizards, frogs, fish and birds; and these crickets, ants, mantises and beetles modelled from dry leaves are in their natural element at the farmers' hut at Mandarin Oriental Dhara Dhevi, Chiang Mai.

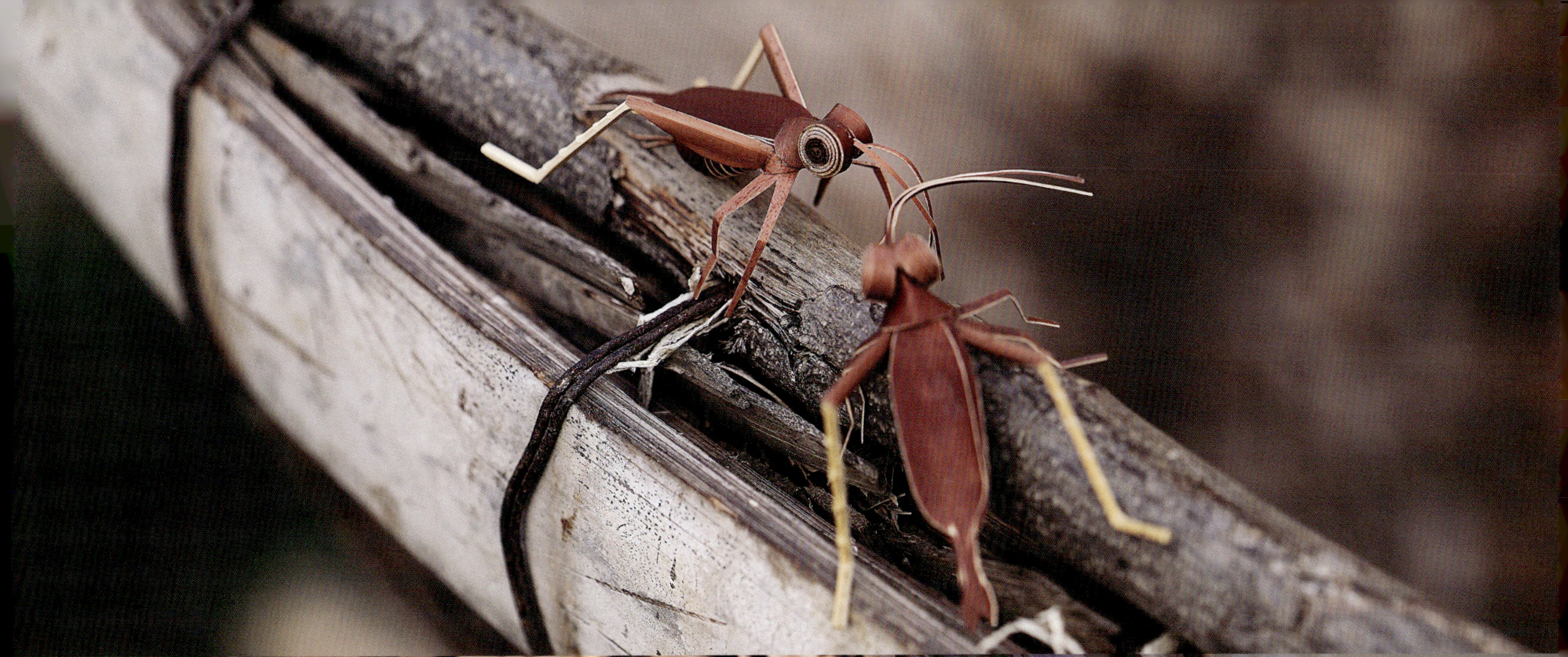
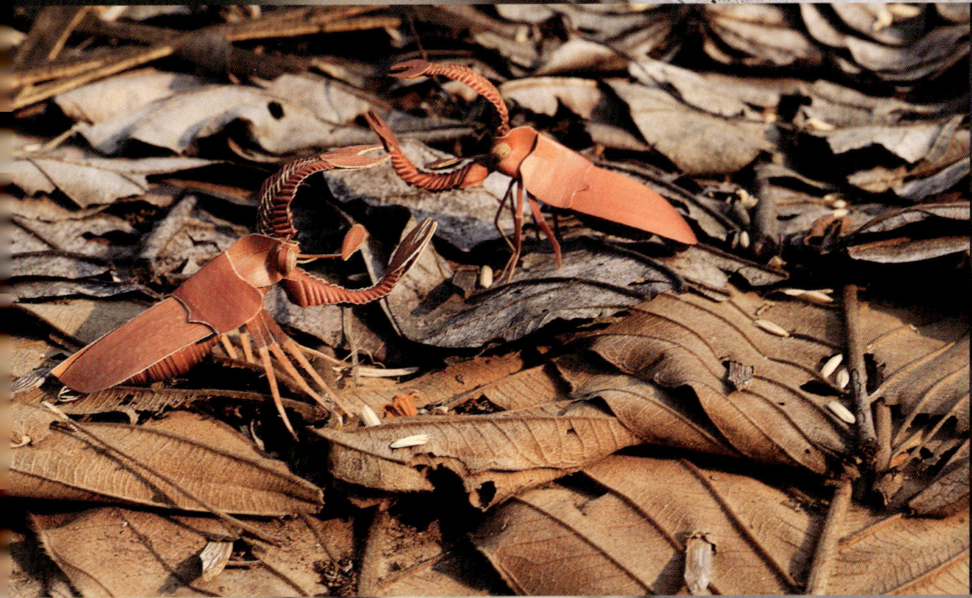
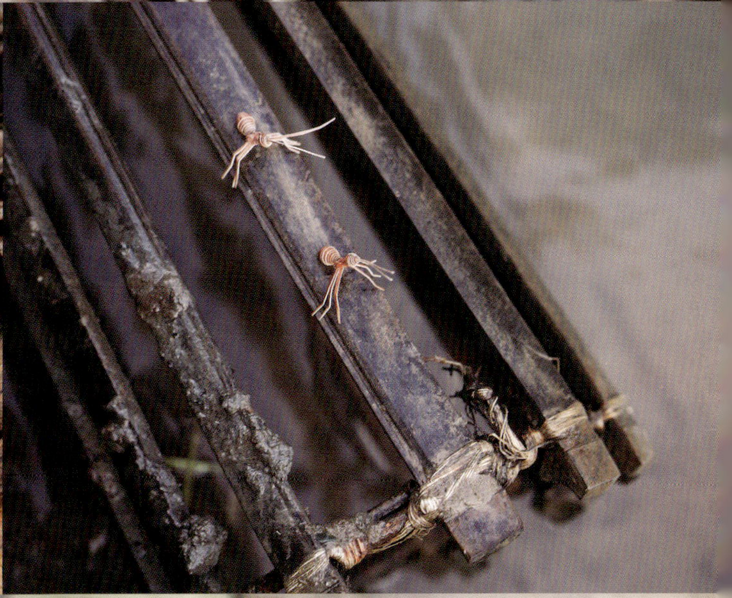
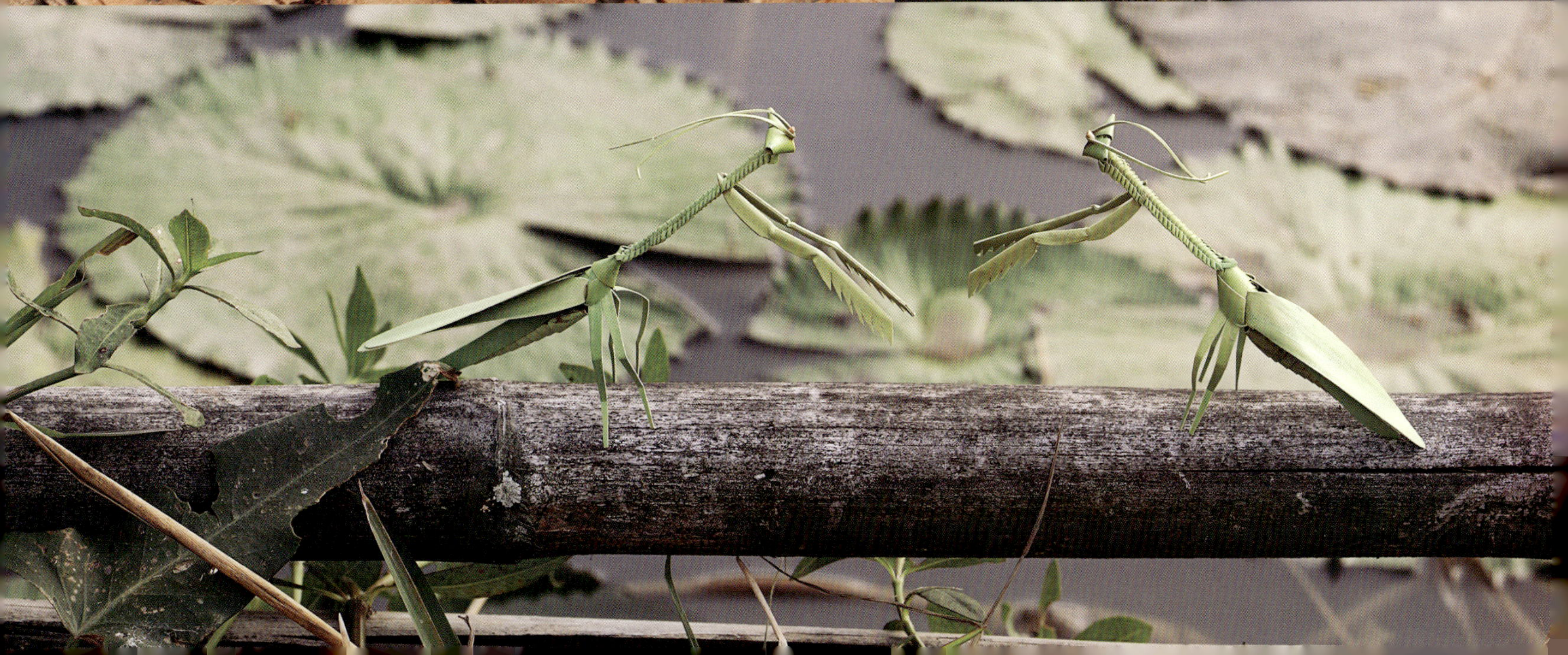

เครื่องแต่งตัว

Khruang Tangtua
Floral Accessories

In the Grand Palace's inner court, the ladies' lives have stepped up apace. Next Monday evening, a week from now, a state banquet is to be held at Boromrajasathitmaholan Hall by Their Majesties the King and Queen of Thailand to honour Their Majesties the King and Queen of Malaysia on their state visit to Thailand.

A state banquet is a national event. Everyone who has a part to play puts on their best gloves and performs their appointed duty to ensure everything is taken care of down to the most minute detail. Chakri Maha Prasat Throne Hall and its complex of adjacent halls (where the banquets used to be held) must be ready for the royal gathering. The new Boromrajasathitmaholan Hall (where banquets have been held for the past three years) is rigorously prepared to host yet another historical feast.

Royal dining tables and chairs are set out and straightened with rope so as to be in perfect alignment. Immaculate white tablecloths embossed with the royal insignia are laid, and laden with spotless royal crockery and cutlery. Piece by piece, the royal crystal collection is held up to the light to check for blemishes. And then it is time to organise the flowers.

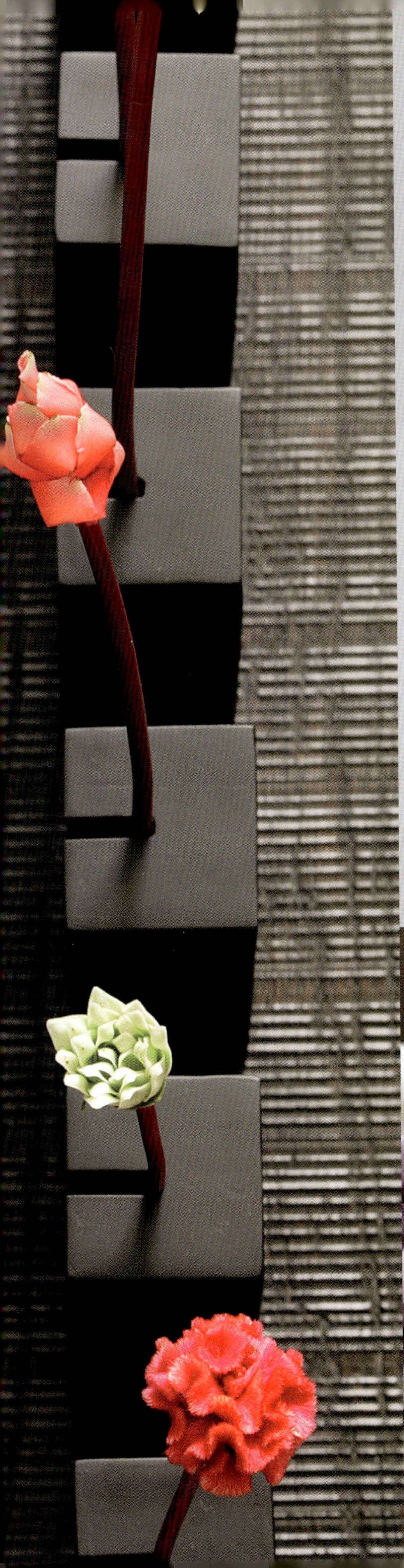
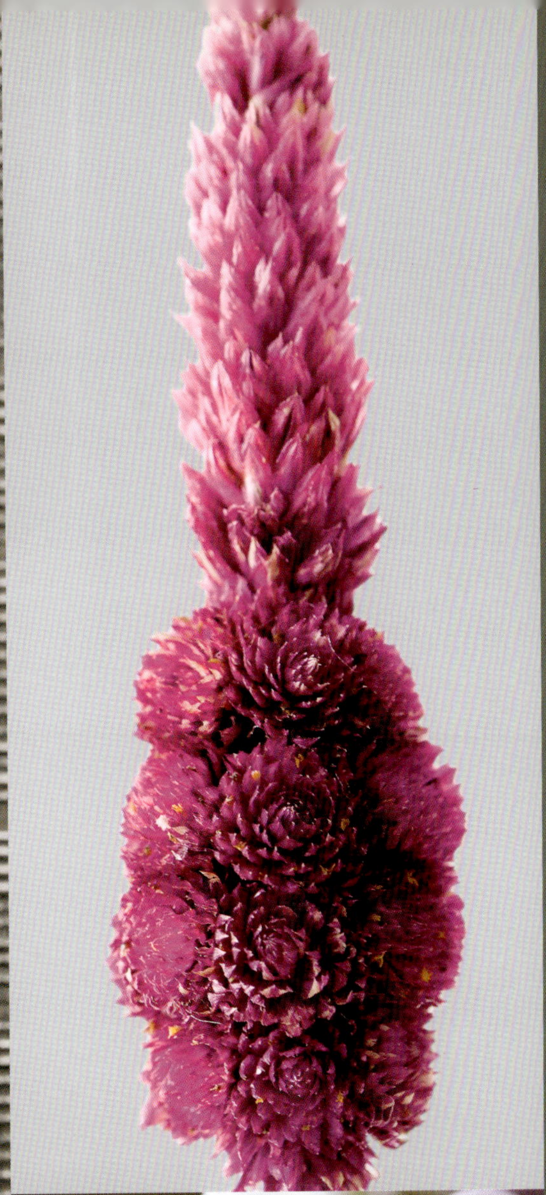
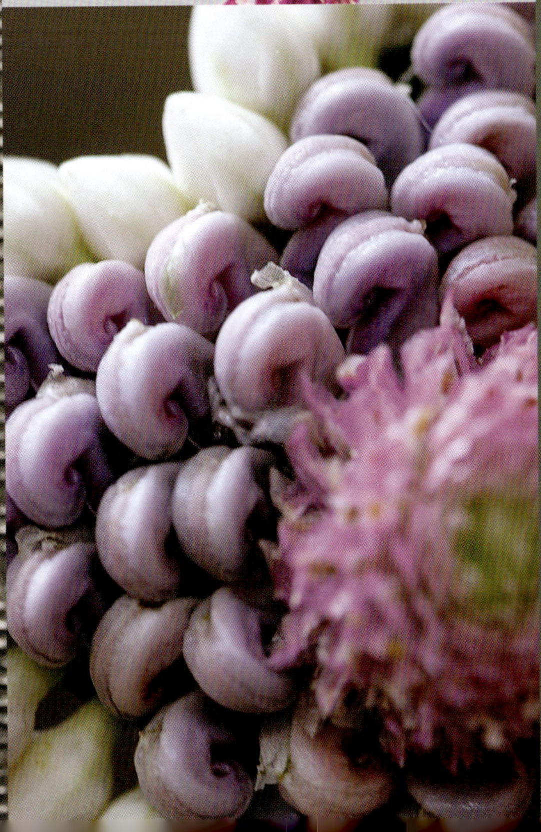
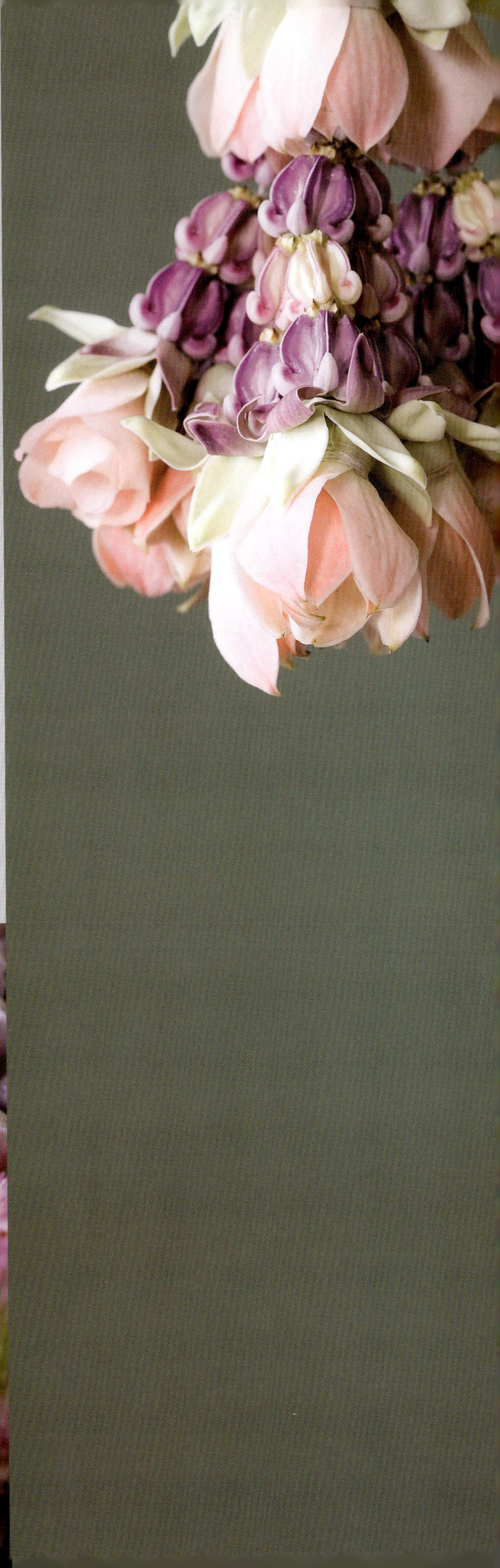

Opening Spread (clockwise from left)

These fabricated flowers named «*dokkha*» are made from individual petals held together by long thin strands of cotton; globe amaranth flowers sewn on a long needle to form a «*toom dokmai*», the finial of a «*phum dokmai*», or floral dome; tassels made of purple crown flowers and pink orchid petals; and detail of a «*thad hu*» made from small white gardenias, purple crown flower petals and a pink globe amaranth.

To add a Siamese touch to the European-format state banquets, floral decoration combines «*khruang tangtua*», or traditional Thai floral accessories, with classical European styles. To accomplish this, the dexterous hands of the inner-court ladies are required, to weave and sew the accessories, and then incorporate them into the grand design.

This Spread

Toom dokmai are the decorative finials of *phum dokmai*, traditional Thai floral domes. Petals or leaves are sewn onto long thin needles to create a pointed oval shape, generally with a crown flower at the bottom, and topped off with crown flowers and small gardenias.

Top Left (from left to right)

Toom dokmai made with rose petals; crown flower sepals; pink orchid petals; small white gardenias; flowers of globe amaranth; leaves of *Excoecaria cochinchinensis* Lour.; and pink orchids.

Bottom Left (from left to right)

Toom dokmai made with green orchid petals; rose petals; and orange jessamine leaves.

At present, a group of 76 ladies work in the inner court. Their main task is to create floral works, both for general use and for special ceremonies. Interestingly, while engaged in their floral duties, they are stationed at gates, doors, or even at the inner-court's junction, doubling as royal guards – men are not allowed in this area of the palace. Divided into two 24-hour shifts that begin and end at 9am, 38 ladies work every other day. However, a few days before a state banquet is held, all 76 ‹flower ladies› are needed, as well as five clerks, to create all the required Thai flower accessories.

This Spread

«*Takhai dokmai*» (floral nets) on show at TENFACE Serviced Residence in Bangkok. These nets can be found in almost all categories of Thai floral art, such as «*malai*», «*khruang khwaen*», «*krathong*» and «*phum dokmai*». *Takhai dokmai* are normally made from small white gardenias linked with fine cotton threads. The gardenias are individually sewn onto the threads in corresponding directions; these are then tied together to create the desired pattern.

Top Right (from left to right)

«*Dao-lom-duan*», «*kaeo-ching-duang*» and «*sii-kan-sii-dok*» arrangements.

Khruang Tangtua

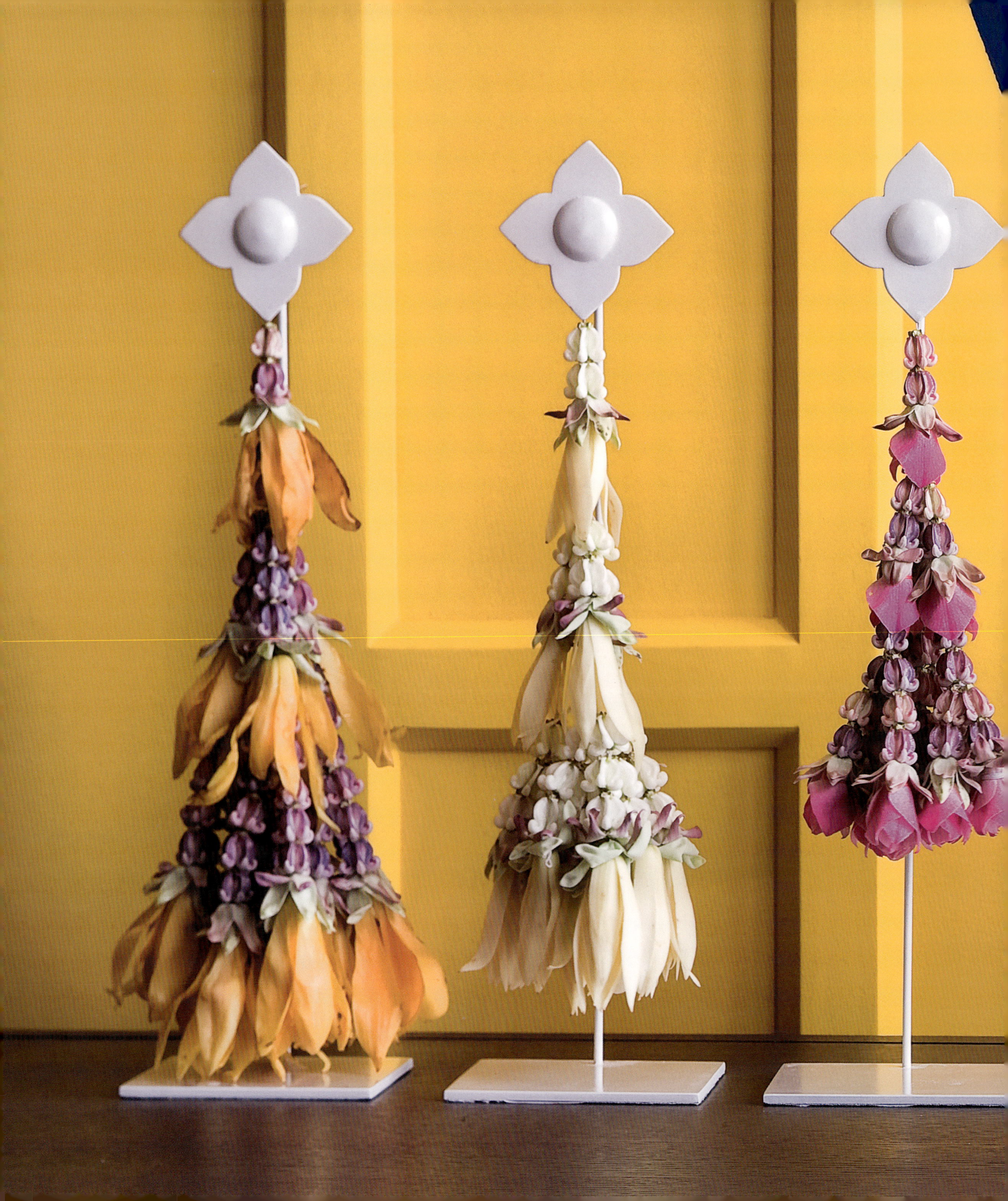

This Spread

«*Uba*» is a floral tassel used to decorate hand garlands, floral pendants, pedestal trays and elaborate floral floats. There are many types of *uba* with three pictured here, *from left to right*: «*uba song-khruang*» (elaborate floral tassels), two «*uba khaek*» (Indian-style floral tassels); and an «*uba sam-chun*» (three-stepped floral tassel).

This Page

Flowers and plant materials used as «*uba*» ending elements. *Clockwise from top left*: orange champaks; orange bougainvillea petals; orchid petals; and small gardenias.

Opposite Page (left)

These simple floral tassels are called «*uba look-lui*» and can be seen decorating floral pendants and «*phan dokmai*» pedestal tray rims.

Opposite Page (right)

An elaborate floral tassel named «*uba song-khruang*» is fabricated from crown flowers and orange champaks.

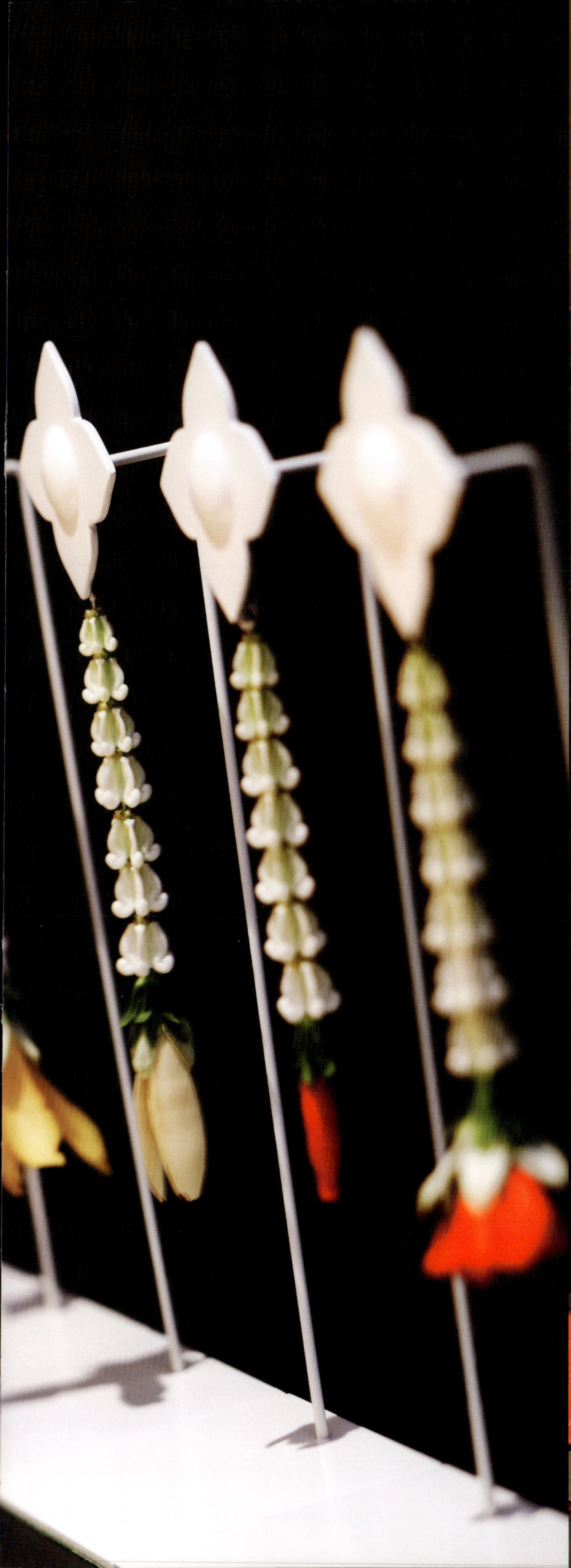

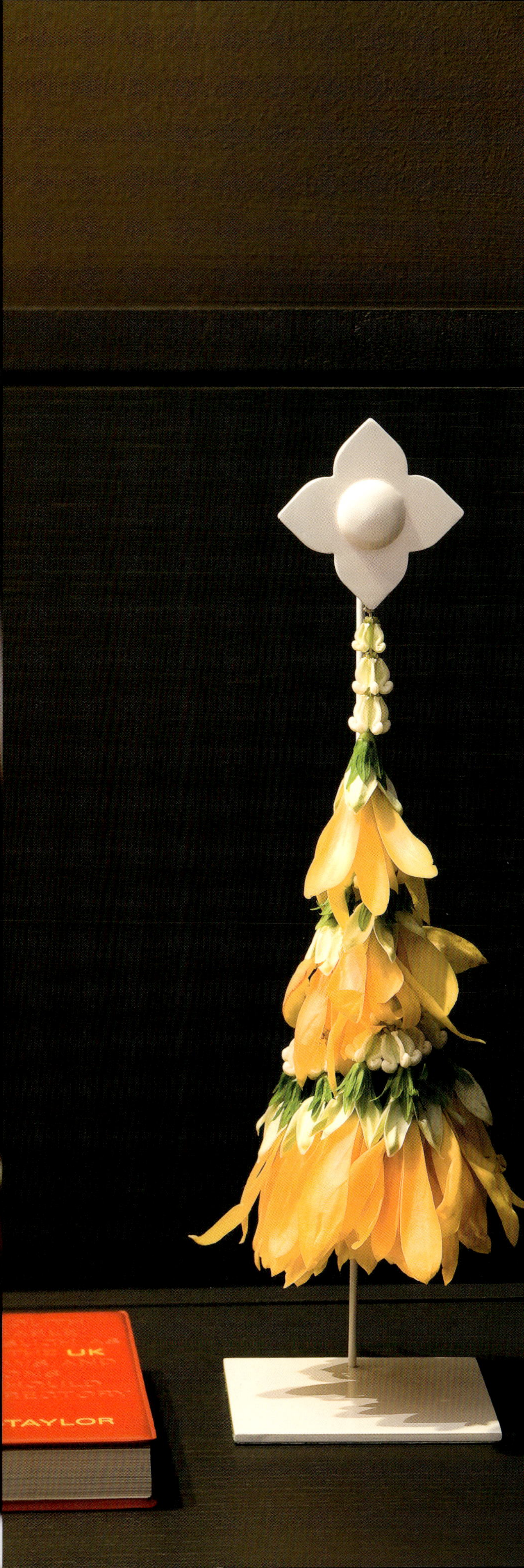
UK
TAYLOR

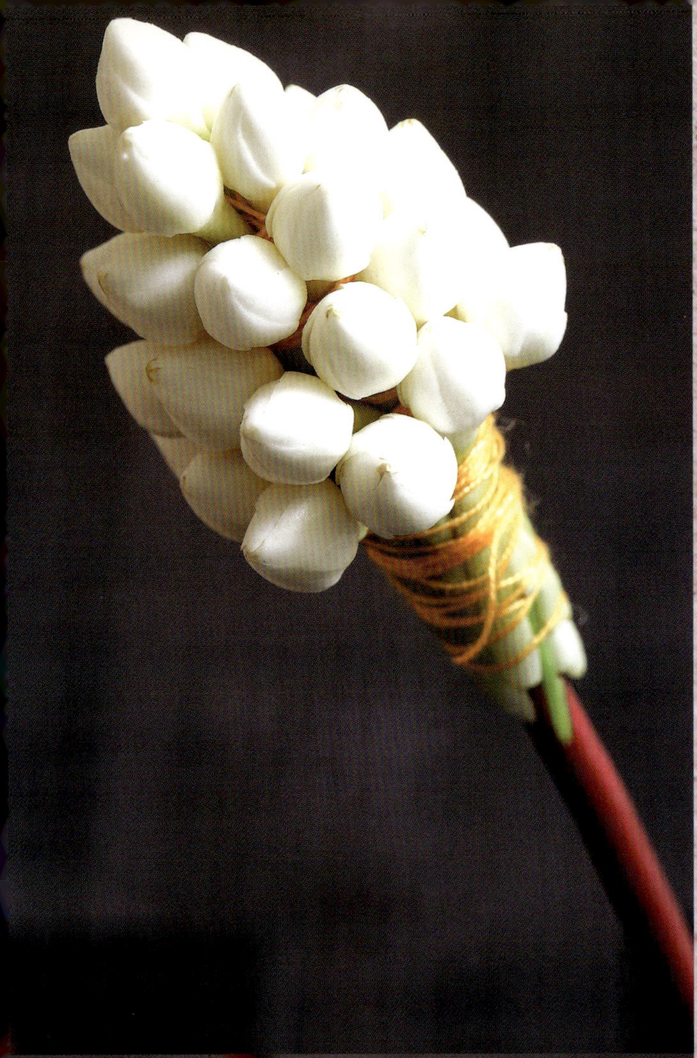

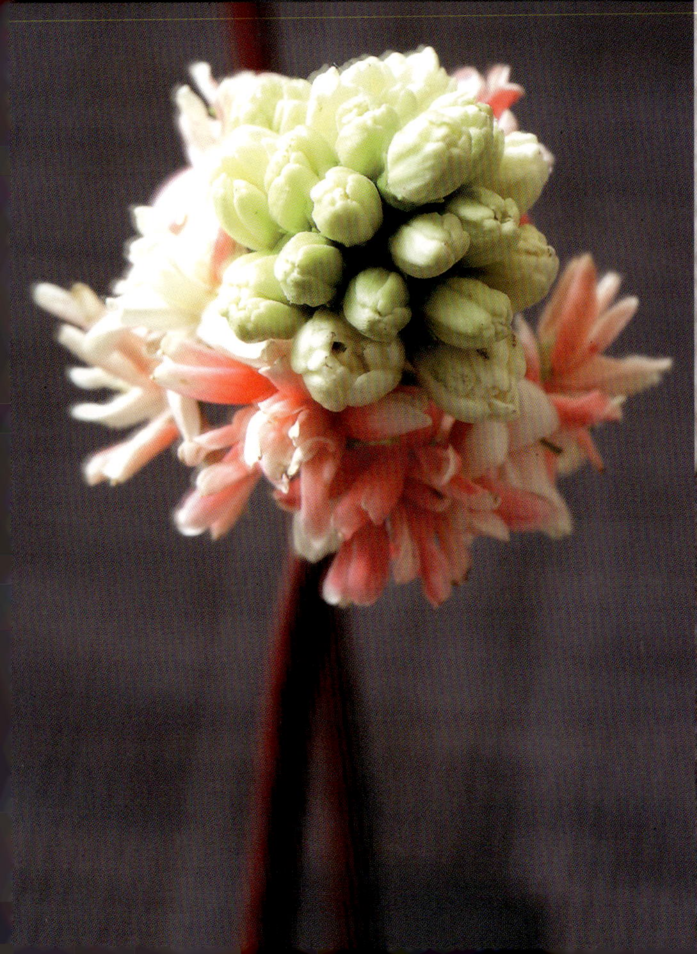

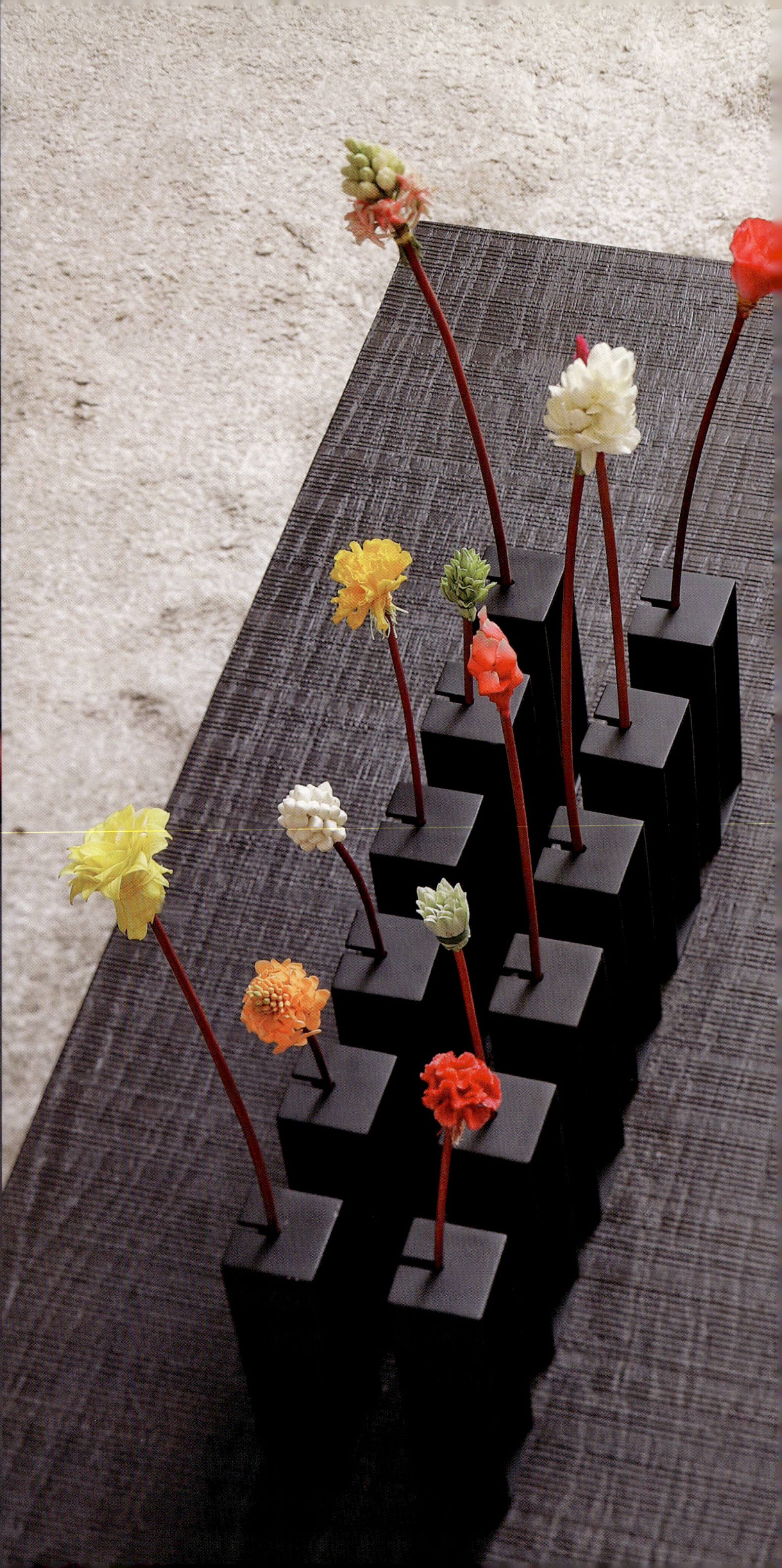

In addition to other flower works like «*phum dokmai*» (floral domes) and «*malai khor phra korn*» (hand garlands for royalty), the number of floral accessories to be crafted is calculated by one of the two chiefs on each shift, in accordance with the approved design. With a deadline set for midnight of the night prior to the banquet, the workload is allocated, and the team are told the size, the form, the colour, the length, the type of flower and the pattern of each accessory. These accessories include: «*takhai dokmai*», or floral nets; «*uba*», floral tassels; «*dokkha*», fabricated flowers made from petals; «*toom dokmai*», sewn floral finial of «*phum dokmai*»; «*thad hu*», petals sewn on layers of square- or round- patterned banana leaves; «*fuang*», floral garlands of sewn crown flowers or gardenias; and «*bab fuang*», petals sewn on layers of patterned banana leaves – made using the same technique as *thad hu*, but in the form of *fuang*.

Opposite Page

Fabricated «*dokkha*» flowers made from individual petals or leaves are held together by long thin strands of cotton tied around a red cassava stem.

Far Left: The *dokkha* in the top picture is made from small white gardenias; the one below from the pink flowers of a Rangoon creeper.

Main Image: Varieties of *dokkha* made from plant materials like rose and orchid petals, jasmine flowers, *ixora* flowers, Rangoon creeper flowers, and crown flower sepals.

This Page

«*Thad hu*» – petals sewn on layers of patterned banana leaves (square, circular or pentagonal) – are placed at the points where strings of garlands are tied together, hiding the untidy spots. Plant materials used to create *thad hu* include, *from left to right*: globe amaranth, crown flowers and petals; globe amaranth, crown flower petals and small gardenias; and globe amaranth with orchid and crown flower petals.

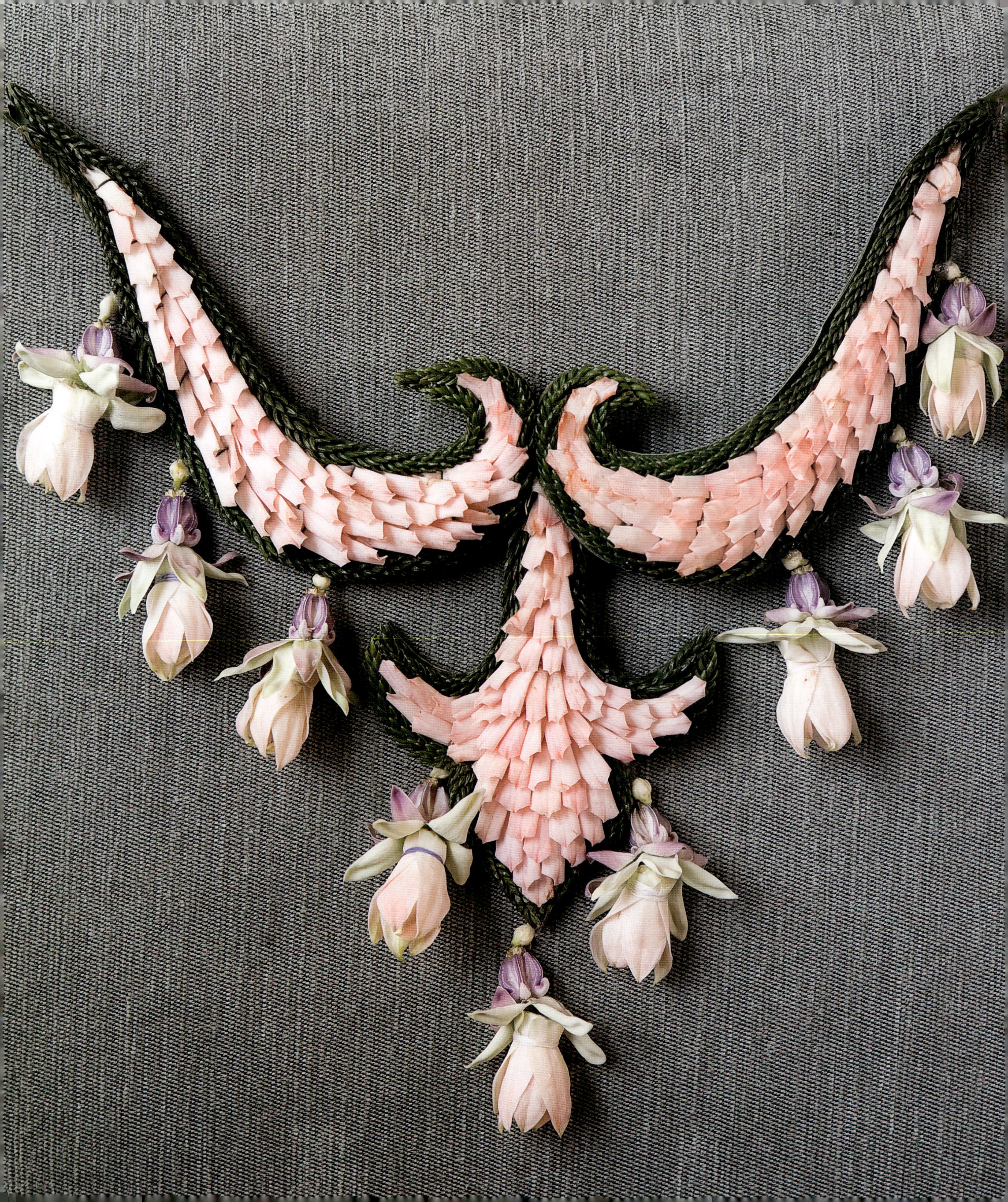

This Spread

The «*bab fuang*» – petals sewn on layers of patterned banana leaves – pictured here are of an extraordinary form and colour combination. The plant materials used to fabricate them are Norfolk Island pine leaves, orchid petals, white crown flower sepals, purple crown flowers and small gardenias. Unseen are layers of patterned banana leaves that form the outline of the design.

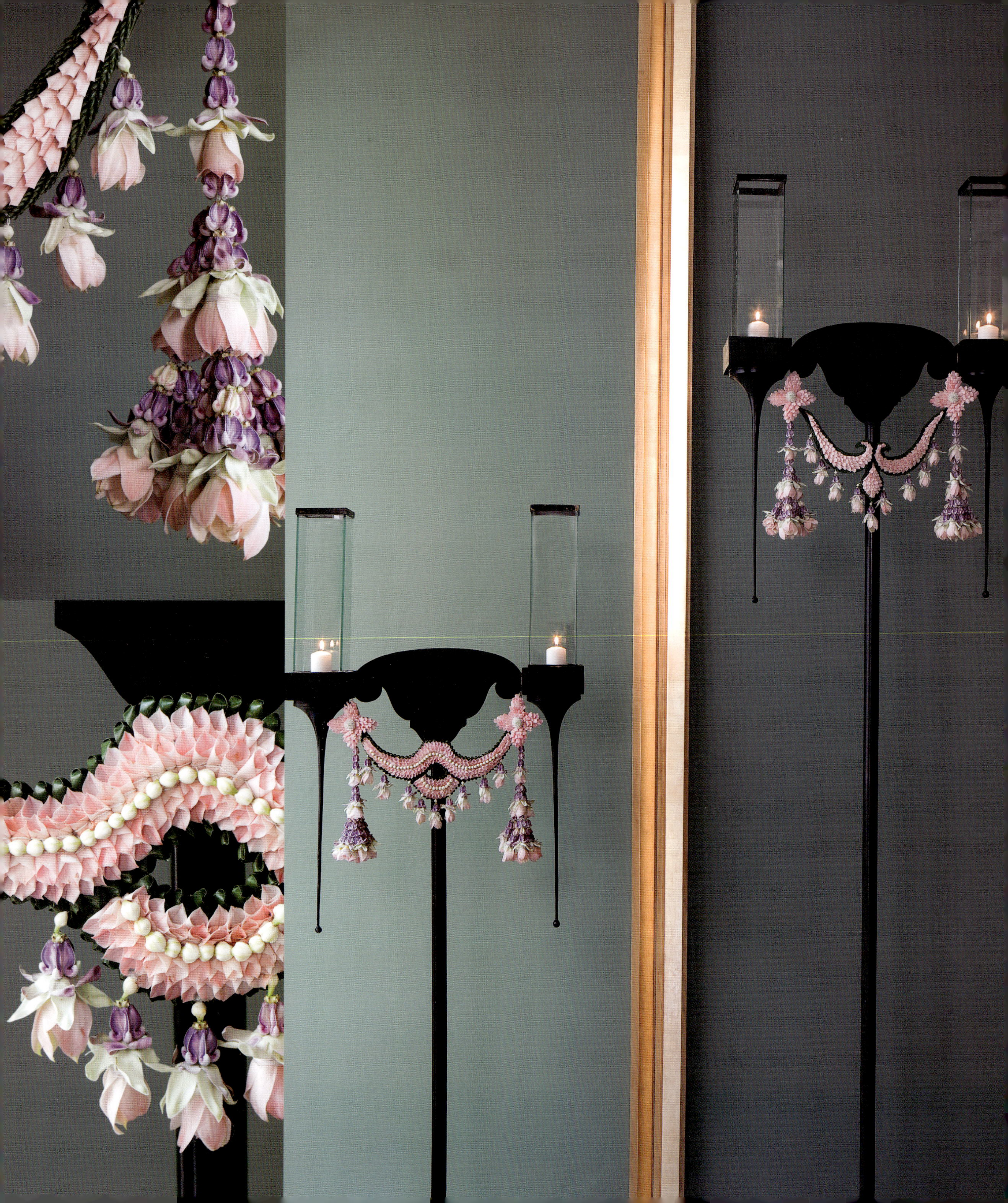

By nine o'clock in the evening on the eve of the banquet, when most of the classical flower arrangement work is completed, intricately made floral accessories arrive in Boromrajasathitmaholan Hall. Here, another team of florists is on hand to incorporate them into the final design. As dawn breaks, the work is done. The flower ladies, who have devoted their lives to this exquisite form of Thai art and contributed much to its existence, stand back and admire their work.

This Spread

«Bab fuang» use the same technique as «thad hu», but in a floral festoon. Thad hu and «uba song-khruang» decorate both ends of bab fuang on these candle stands designed by Sakul Intakul for The Sukhothai, Bangkok.

134 Khruang Tangtua

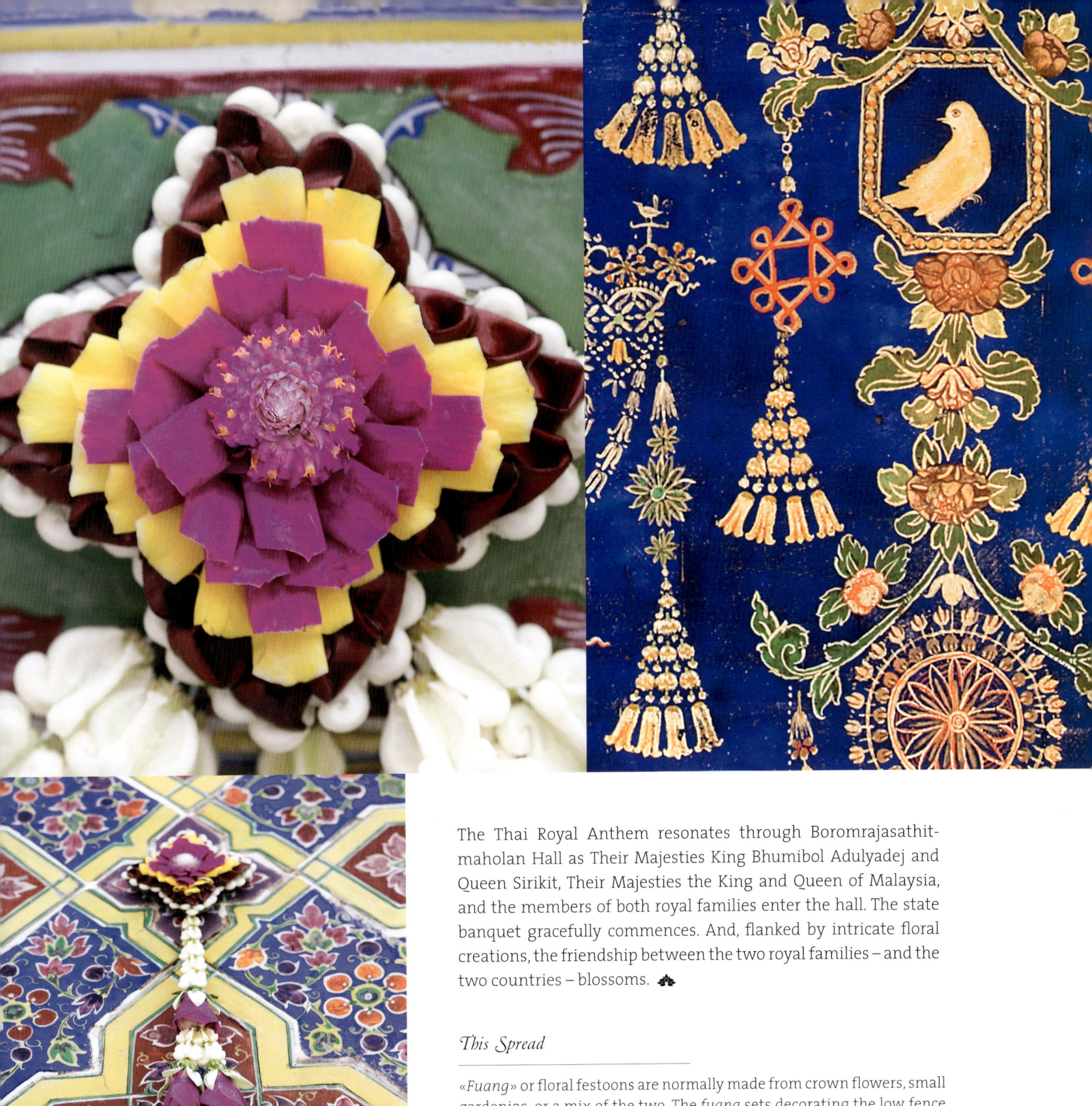

The Thai Royal Anthem resonates through Boromrajasathitmaholan Hall as Their Majesties King Bhumibol Adulyadej and Queen Sirikit, Their Majesties the King and Queen of Malaysia, and the members of both royal families enter the hall. The state banquet gracefully commences. And, flanked by intricate floral creations, the friendship between the two royal families – and the two countries – blossoms. ❦

This Spread

«*Fuang*» or floral festoons are normally made from crown flowers, small gardenias, or a mix of the two. The *fuang* sets decorating the low fence of Wat Ratchabophit Sathitmahasimaram in Bangkok are made from crown flowers and cassava stems. Punctuating these are sets of «*thad hu*» and «*uba song-khruang*».

Top Right: A mural painting from the chapel of Bangkok's Wat Somanasviharn features *fuang* and *uba*.

136   Lanna and Isaan

ล้านนา
และอีสาน

❖ *Lanna and Isaan* ❖
In the Regional Realm

"This country of Lanna makes the stranger feel,

if he must be exiled from his native shores,

he could not find a land of greater charm

and sympathy to spend his days."

So remarked Reginald Le May, an Englishman who worked in the early 20th century as an adviser to the Siamese Government in the northern region. He called this Land of a Million Rice Fields ‹An Asian Arcady›.

Located in a rich plain surrounded by mountainous rainforests that cloak an area which is now northern Thailand and parts of Burma and Laos, Le May's rustic utopia was once a secluded highland region of Southeast Asia, famed for its natural beauty, gentle inhabitants and cultural wealth.

Blessed by a nurturing natural environment and the socio-economic stability of a new kingdom (founded by King Mangrai in 1287), the «*Lanna*» people had, over time, developed a distinctive art and culture, creating the beautiful *Lanna* way of life. Their idiosyncratic customs were such that they could assume a separate identity from the surrounding kingdom's peoples. By the mid 15th century, *Lanna* civilisation reached its golden age under the reign of King Tilokaraja, the most memorable period in *Lanna* culture.

Opening Spread (clockwise from left)

White gardenias decorate a gilded «*sumdok*» – floral offering from the north; «*Tung sod*» – a hanging banner offering – is made from fresh leaves and flowers; a bird made out of dry palm leaves adorns the top of a «*juam*» (where, according to the people of Thailand's northeast, a person's soul resides); pink globe amaranths pierce the tips of «*somdok*» – floral fork offerings made with woven bamboo; and loose local flowers sewn into simple garlands decorate a «*ton dokmai*» (flowering tree offering) in northeastern Thailand.

Despite falling to Burma in 1558, and later fragmenting into small city-states before being officially integrated into the central Thai Kingdom in the late 18th century, *Lanna* was, astonishingly, able to keep its cultural heritage alive. After the Chakri dynasty was founded, Chiang Mai – the capital of the *Lanna* Kingdom – lay in a state of ruin for many decades. Throughout it all, *Lanna* has managed to maintain its own distinct identity.

This Spread

In «Isaan tai», to the south of Thailand's northeastern region, a *juam* is constructed to house a person's soul, as soon as they come of age. It will then be placed on the family altar, at which each family member will make offerings of flowers, incense sticks and candles to their personal *juam*, for their wellbeing.

This Page (top left)

A set of permanent carved-wood offerings in the shape of a gun, a sword, a boat, an elephant and a horse – each made for a personal *juam*. Temporary offerings of flowers, incense sticks and candles are placed within banana-leaf cones.

This Page (bottom left)

Acting like spiritual messengers, birds made from dry palm leaves adorn the tops of these *juam*.

140 Lanna and Isaan

Today's visitors to the mountainous northern region of Thailand are delighted by the beauty of Chiang Mai's numerous temples, the exquisite mural paintings in Nan, the graceful, intricate detail of the stucco and woodcarving in Lampang's Buddhist monastery, and the serenity of Chiang Rai's fertile countryside. But *Lanna's* true charm and beauty emanates from the way of life of its people. The preservation of such delicate cultural heritage is dependent on a continued appreciation by its inhabitants. It is undoubtedly the spirit of the people and the soul of the community which turns the hidden revolving wheel that keeps *Lanna* tradition, with its art and crafts, and religious and domestic rituals, alive through time.

This Spread

Each of these contemporary-style, gilded wooden «*sumdok*» – floral offerings from the northern region – is decorated with one type of flower; traditional *sumdok* are typically decorated with croton or *Polyscias* sp. leaves, together with other flowers. All *sumdok* featured here hail from the private collection of Wiluck and Anchalee Sripasang.

This Spread

«*Khruang sakkara*» – a set of offerings in the *Lanna* tradition – incorporate various accoutrements, including flowers, fresh and dry betel nuts, beeswax and candles. Aside from «*khan dok*» (floral offerings on pedestal trays), *Lanna* offerings normally come in two forms: tree-shaped «*ton*» and pointed-oval «*sum*».

Top Left

A procession of *khruang sakkara* led by a pair of dancers arrives temple-side on a ceremonial day.

Second From Right

A set of *khruang sakkara* placed in front of the Buddha image at Mandarin Oriental Dhara Dhevi Chiang Mai's Prayer Hall.

Lanna and Isaan

This Spread

In the northern dialect, «*khan dok*» is the equivalent to «*phan dokmai*» (floral arrangements on pedestal trays). Flowers, incense sticks and candles are placed in «*suay dok*» – small cones made from banana leaf – then placed on *khan dok* as offerings.

Top Left

Khan dok, made from lacquered bamboo, are usually used as containers on which to bring offerings from home to temple on ceremonial days.

Centre

A bigger and more elaborate kind of *khan dok*, «*khan kaeo tang sam*» is a *Lanna* flower stand traditionally placed in temples on which devotees place incense sticks, candles and floral offerings.

All *khan dok* featured here hail from the private collection of Wiluck and Anchalee Sripasang.

Lanna and Isaan 145

It is a privilege to observe the local religious ceremonies that are performed in village temples on special days of the Buddhist calendar. Such ceremonies are truly a sight to behold and provide a glimpse into *Lanna's* glorious past. Men and women (particularly women) proudly wear their best traditional attire. Offerings of foods and sweets are planned days ahead, while «*khruang sakkara*» – crafts for offerings made from plant materials such as fresh flowers, coconut leaves and betel nuts – can only be prepared one day before. That these traditional crafts differ in design and detail from one community to another adds to the richness of *Lanna* culture.

This Spread

In *Lanna*, «*san kan pao*» are coconut fronds woven into the shape of animals such as fish, crocodiles, snakes and water buffalo. *San kan pao* are prepared prior to religious ceremonies and traditional festivities. The interlaced coconut-leaves' design symbolises fertility.

Top Left

The «*pratu pa*» (forest gate) traditionally marks the boundary between village and forest. In modern times, *pratu pa* are erected at gates or at the beginning of pathways for decorative purposes, especially during festivities.

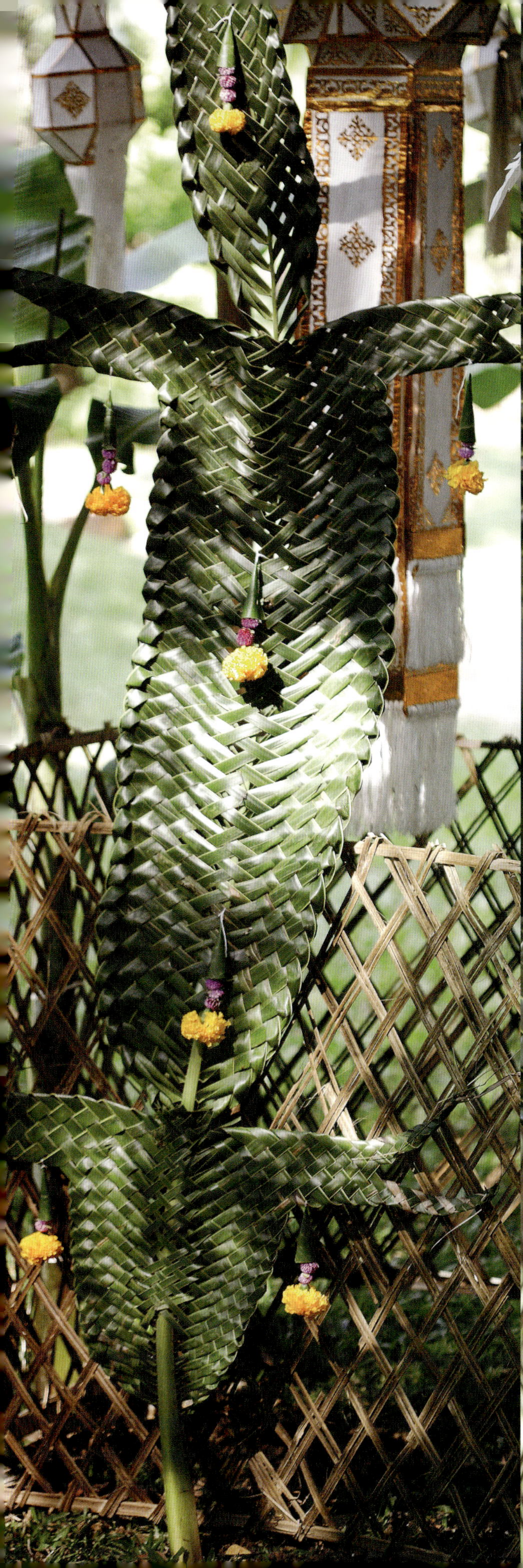
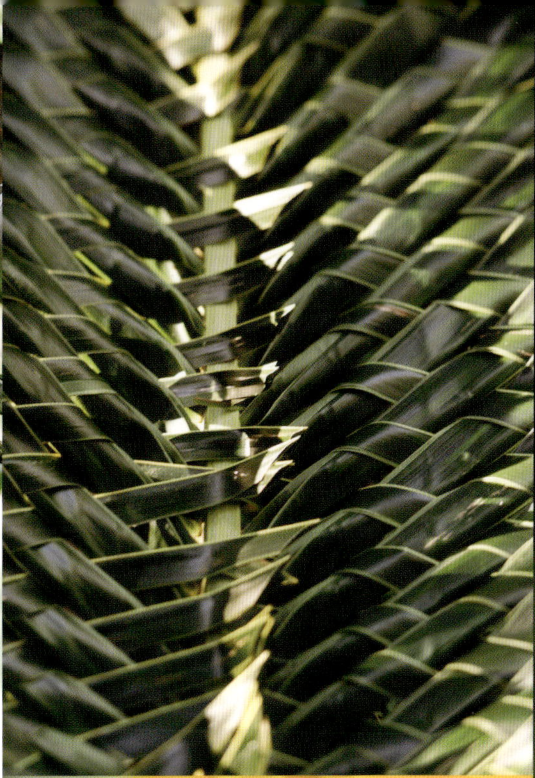
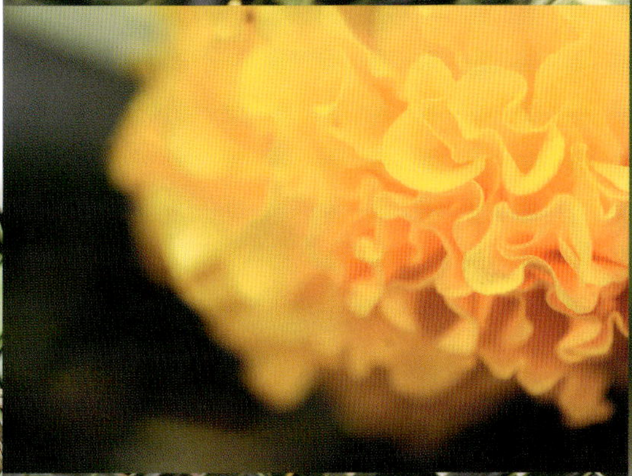
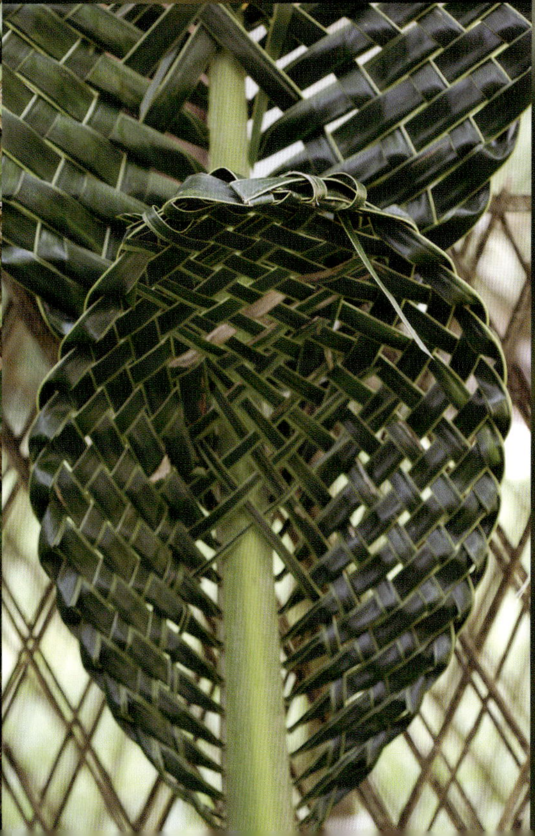
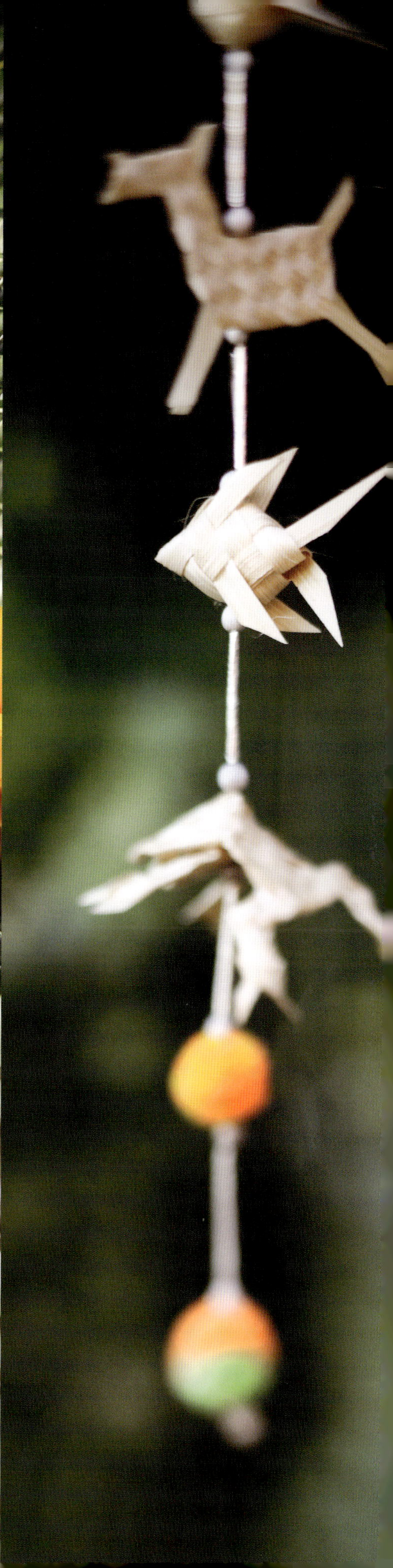

This chapter gives illustrated examples of *khruang sakkara* (including those from «*Isaan*», in Thailand's north east) as they have been passed from generation to generation through *Lanna's* long and colourful history. The diversity of floral art throughout Thailand, as exemplified throughout this book, signifies the wealth of the Kingdom's flower culture.

This Spread

«*Tung*» are banners of different materials varying in size and complexity. As offerings, *tung* are hung in and around temples during ceremonies and festivities in northern Thailand. The *tung* pictured here are made from silver and gold paper, and carved wood.

Opposite Page

«*Tung sod*» is made with fresh leaves and flowers.

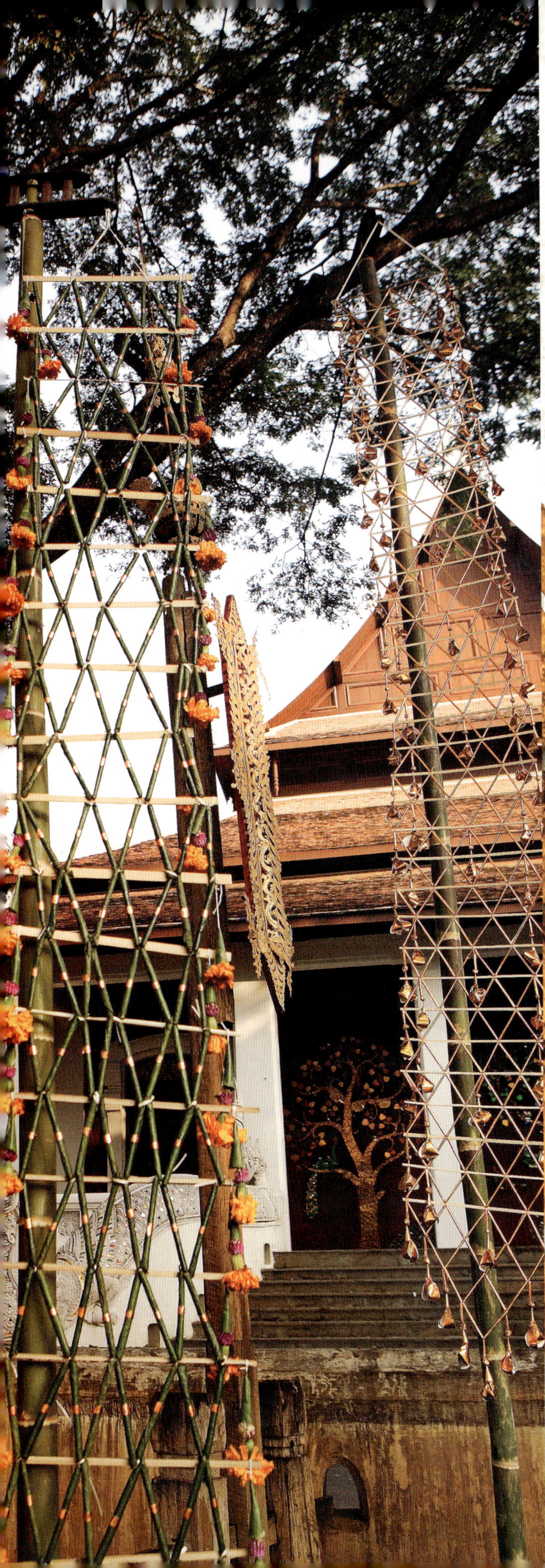
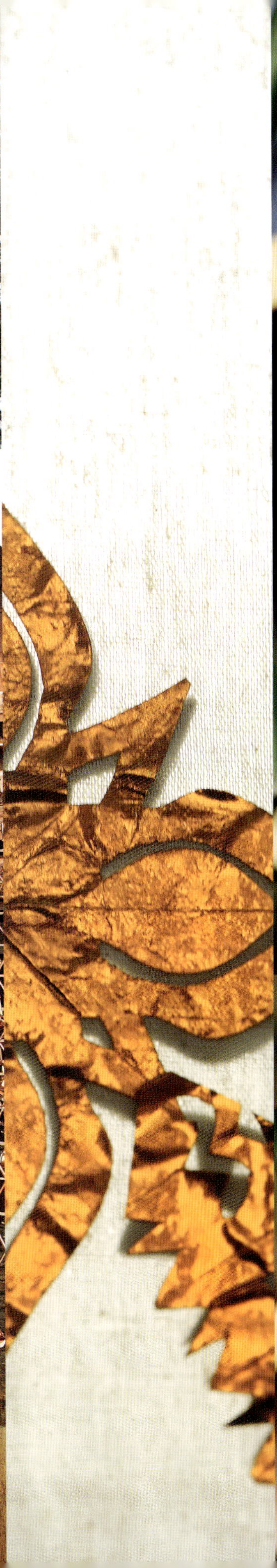
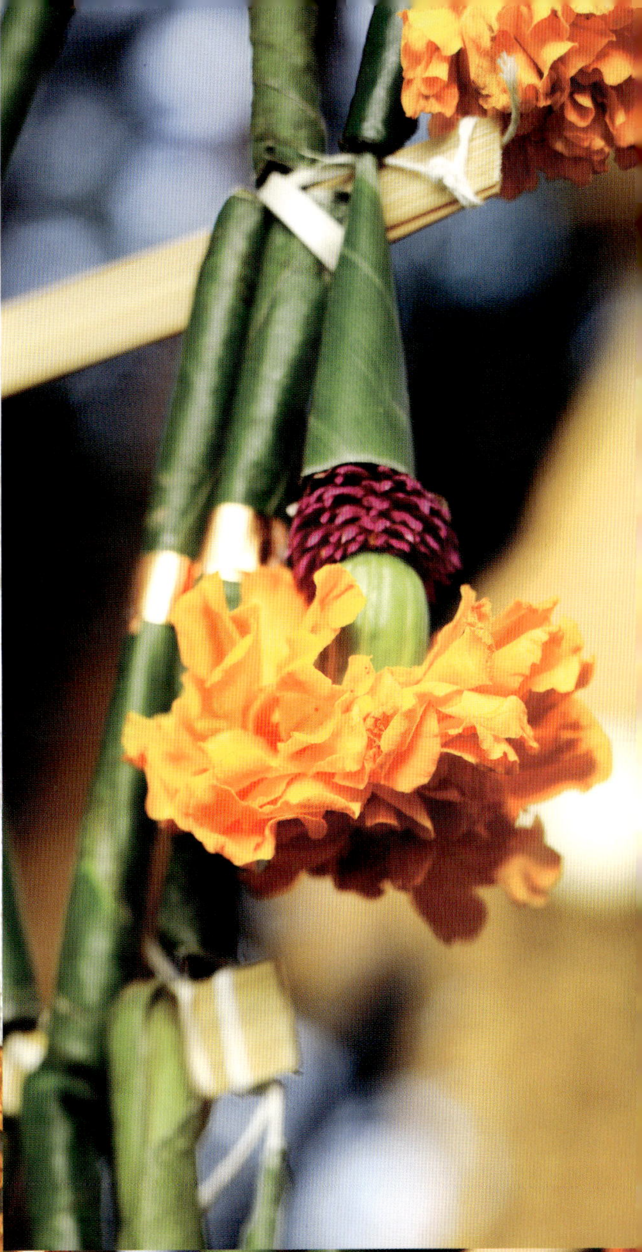
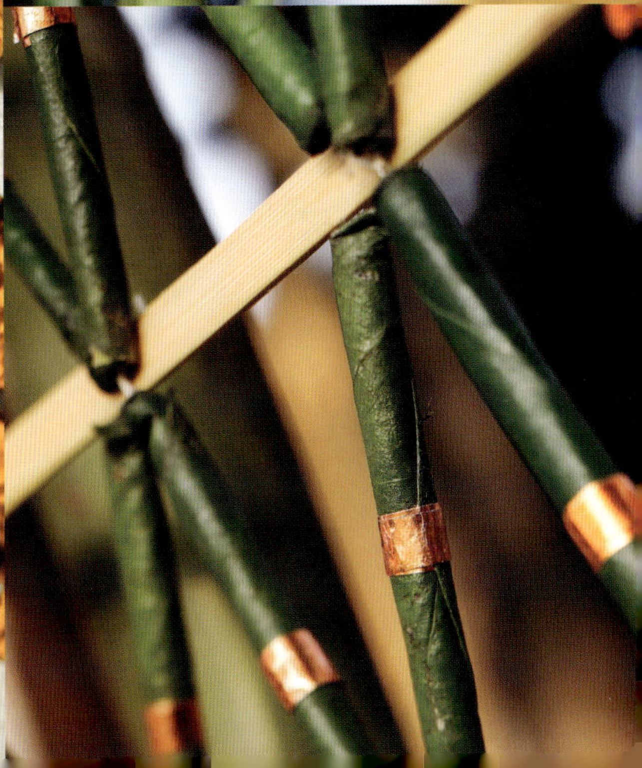

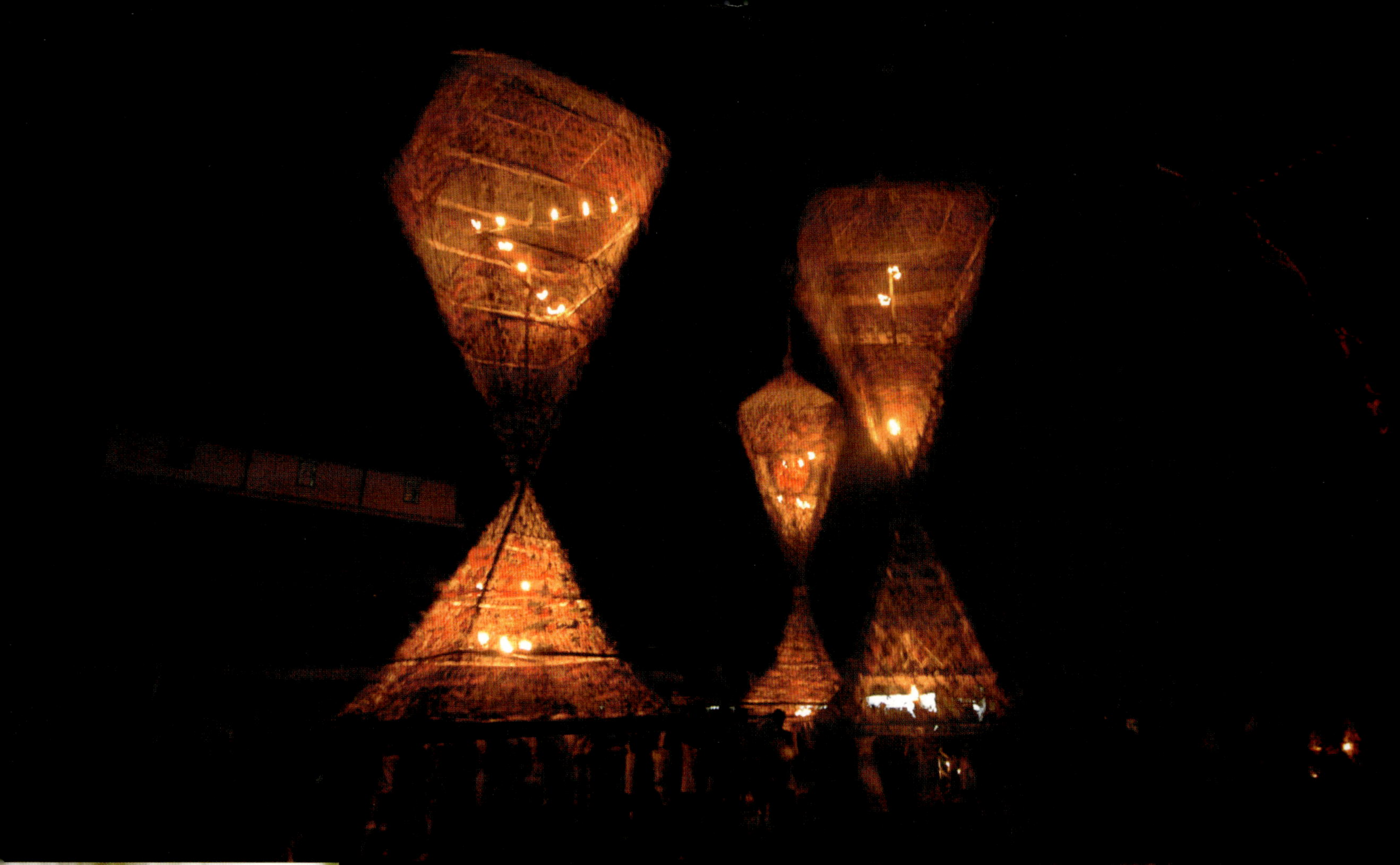

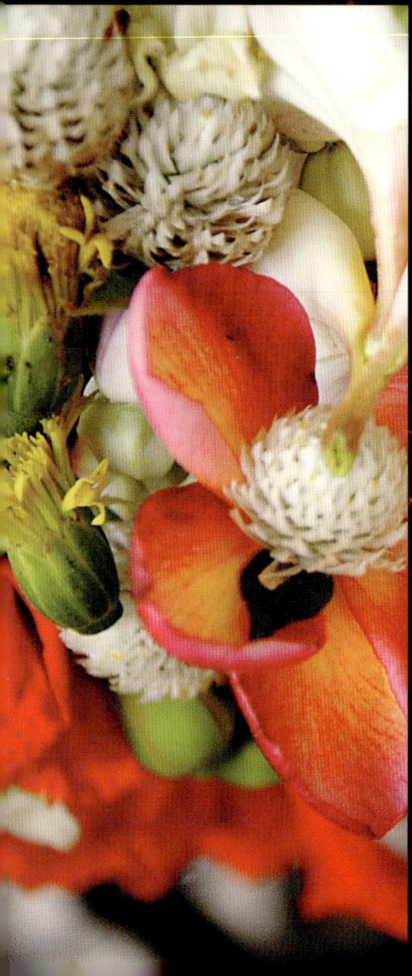

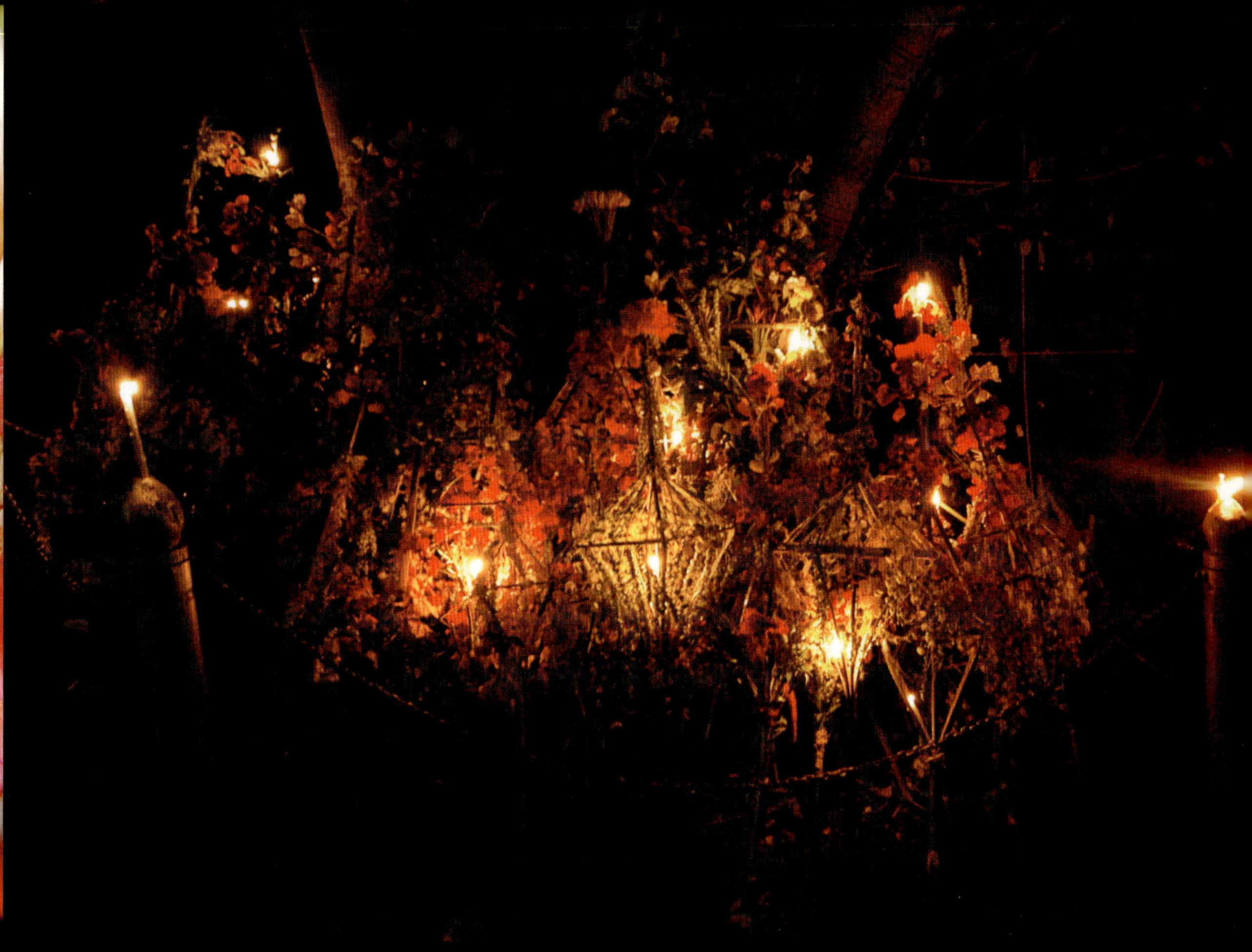

In the year 2000, amidst burgeoning globalisation and the influx of alien cultures, the *Lanna Wisdom School* was founded by a group of local scholars and master-artists to ensure the continuity of *Lanna* knowledge. Taught subjects include *Lanna* language, music, dance, art and crafts. Like many others, Reginald Le May would be thrilled to see that the legacy and charm of *Lanna* – which he fondly described as ‹An Asian Arcady› – lives on to comfort and inspire yet more strangers to the land. ✤

This Spread

Made from bamboo structures, «*ton dokmai*» (flowering tree offerings) are floral offerings unique to Loei Province in «*Isaan nua*» (the northeastern region's north). In the region's Nahaeo District, these *ton dokmai* are prepared annually during the «*Songkran*» Festival (Thai New Year) which falls on April 13. When adorned with fresh flowers, *ton dokmai* are carried at night to Wat Sriphochai for the festivities. Images courtesy of Darin Jungpattanawadee.

Dok Mai Thai Galleries
สมุดภาพดอกไม้ไทย

Malai
มาลัย

Khruang Khwaen
เครื่องแขวน

Dok Mai Thai Galleries 155

Phan Dokmai
พานดอกไม้

Dok Mai Thai Galleries 157

Krathong & Ngan Baitong
กระทงและงานใบตอง

Dok Mai Thai Galleries 159

Baisri
บายศรี

Dok Mai Thai Galleries 161

Ngan Dokmai Lek
งานดอกไม้เล็ก

Dok Mai Thai Galleries 163

Khruang Tangtua
เครื่องแต่งตัว

Dok Mai Thai Galleries 165

Lanna and Isaan
ล้านนาและอีสาน

Dok Mai Thai Galleries 167

Dok Mai Thai
Floral Glossary

- **Bab fuang** แบบเฟื่อง
  Petals sewn on layers of patterned banana leaves using the same technique as *thad hu* but in the form of a festoon

- **Bailan** ใบลาน
  Dry palm leaves

- **Baisri** บายศรี
  An auspicious nutritional offering to the divinities

- **Chaekan dokmai** แจกันดอกไม้
  A vase for flower arrangement

- **Chorakhe** จระเข้
  Two-dimensional floral pendant whose structure resembles the body of a crocodile. Made from three rhomboid shapes fastened to one another, and each nook bedecked with exquisite floral tassels.

- **Dok champa** ดอกจำปา
  Orange champak of the magnolia family

- **Dok khem** ดอกเข็ม
  Flower of the *Ixora* sp.

- **Dok makhuea** ดอกมะเขือ
  Flower of the plate brush eggplant, *Solanum torvum*

- **Dokkha** ดอกข่า
  Fabricated flowers made from petals; each petal is held together by a thin thread, forming a lotus-like bud

- **Fuang** เฟื่อง
  Floral garlands of sewn gardenias or crown flowers

- **Kankluey** ก้านกล้วย
  Banana leaf centre

- **Khruang khwaen** เครื่องแขวน
  Floral pendants

- **Khruang sakkara** เครื่องสักการะ
  Crafts for offerings made from plant materials such as fresh flowers, coconut leaves and betel nuts

- **Khruang tangtua** เครื่องแต่งตัว
  Traditional Thai floral accessories

- **Klin ta-khaeng** กลิ่นตะแคง
  Two-dimensional, six-sided, star-shaped floral pendant, decorated with floral tassels

- **Krabuan khruang phra khwan** กระบวนเครื่องพระขวัญ
  Procession of royal baisri, an auspicious nutritional offering to the divinities

- **Krathong** กระทง
  A container made from leaves

- **Loy krathong** ลอยกระทง
  Ceremony which occurs on the 12th lunar month's full moon night, when offerings are made to the river goddess

- **Malai khor phra korn** มาลัยข้อพระกร
  Hand garlands for royalty

- **Malai mali** มาลัยมะลิ
  Jasmine garlands

- **Malai** มาลัย
  Floral garlands

- **Ngan baitong** งานใบตอง
  Banana leaf works

- **Ngan dokmai lek** งานดอกไม้เล็ก
  Small floral works

- **Pak Khlong Talad** ปากคลองตลาด
  Bangkok's central flower market

- **Phan dokmai** พานดอกไม้
  Intricate floral arrangements set on pedestal trays

- **Phan khan mak** พานขันหมาก
  Wedding dowry tray

- **Phan phum** พานพุ่ม
  Floral arrangements in lotus-bud shape set on pedestal trays

- **Phan thup thian** พานธูปเทียน
  Intricate floral arrangements set on pedestal trays with incense sticks and candles

- **Phithi baisri suu khwan** พิธีบายศรีสู่ขวัญ
  Important ceremony for commoners to call back their wandering souls after a long journey, sickness or frightening episode

- **Phithi baisri thoon phra khwan** พิธีบายศรีทูลพระขวัญ
  Important ceremony for royalty to call back their wandering souls after a long journey, sickness or frightening episode

- **Phithi wai khru** พิธีไหว้ครู
  Traditional ceremony where students pay respects to their teachers

- **Phra kieo** พระเกี้ยว
  Top-knot headdress ornament reserved for royalty

❖ **Phu klin** พู่กลิ่น
Three-dimensional floral pendant/mobile made from small gardenias sewn on five circular pieces of banana leaves; four pieces of banana tree's central core hold it together.

❖ **Phuang kaeo** พวงแก้ว
Three-dimensional floral pendant/mobile made of three hexagonal structures. These large, medium and small structures are linked to one another to create a three-tiered mobile. This is then bedecked with traditional Thai flamboyant design; each nook is fitted with a tassel and a *thad hu*. At its top a string of crown flowers are tied with a floral tassel in the centre.

❖ **Phum dokmai** พุ่มดอกไม้
Floral domes

❖ **Raya noi** ระย้าน้อย
Three-dimensional floral pendant with a six-sided-star structure. The body of the mobile is decorated with floral festoons, tassels and *thad hu*.

❖ **Takhai dokmai** ตาข่ายดอกไม้
Floral nets

❖ **Takraw** ตะกร้อ
Woven balls made from coconut leaves

❖ **Thad hu** ทัดหู
Petals sewn on layers of patterned banana leaves (in different shapes)

❖ **Toh mu bucha** โต๊ะหมู่บูชา
Altar on which Buddha images are placed

❖ **Toom dokmai** ตุ้มดอกไม้
Sewn floral finials

❖ **Uba khaek** อุบะแขก
A kind of intricate floral tassels

❖ **Uba** อุบะ
Floral tassels

❖ **Wai khru** ไหว้ครู
Traditional ceremony in which students pay respect to their teachers

❖ **Wai** ไหว้
Thai gesture; hands are folded together in a lotus-like form as a sign of respect

❖ **Wiman phra-in** วิมานพระอินทร์
Two-dimensional rectangular floral pendant resembling a window frame, inspired by a traditional Thai architectural motif which depicts the celestial residence of the gods. The floral pieces that decorate its top and bottom are triangular floral nets. The pendant's central triangle may be decorated with the flamboyant design, or left plain.

❖ **Wiman thaen** วิมานแท่น
Two-dimensional floral pendant with a double-edged, window-like rectangular frame, topped with a triangular floral net, completed with *thad hu* and floral tassels. The shape was inspired by a traditional Thai architectural motif which depicts the celestial residence of the gods.

❖ **Ya phraek** หญ้าแพรก
Bermuda grass of the *Cynodon* family

The majority of the floral terms in this book follow the spellings used in «Flower Arrangement in Thailand», a book printed in 1954 by the Bureau of Women's Culture, National Culture Institute.

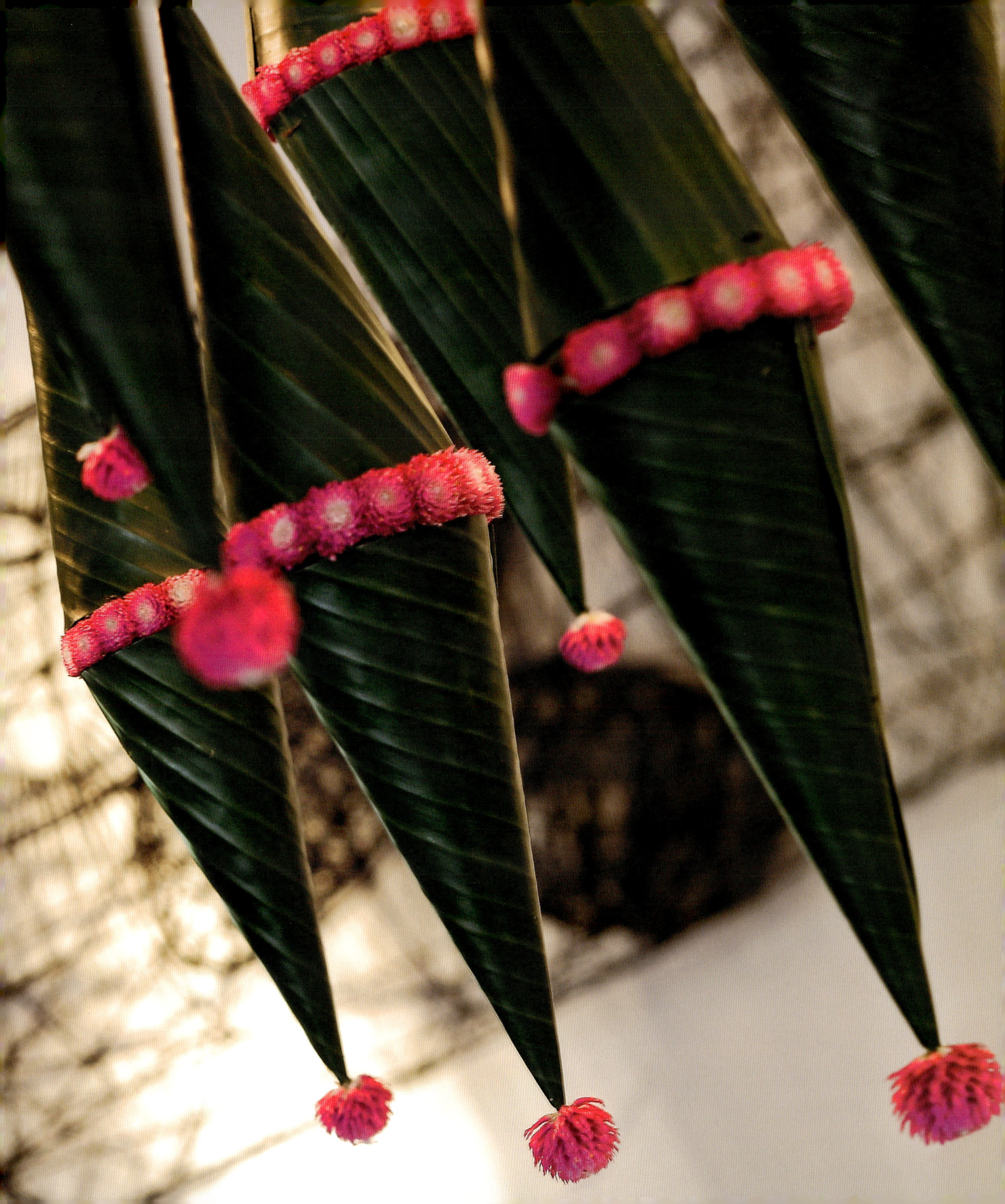

❖ *Dok Mai Thai* ❖
Board of Advisors

Chairperson	**M.R. Yongswasdi Kridakon** Deputy Director-General of The Crown Property Bureau
Vice Chairperson	**Thanpuying Charungjit Teekara** Her Majesty's Deputy Private Secretary
Vice Chairperson	**Thanpuying Supornpen Luangthep** Her Majesty's Deputy Private Secretary
Vice Chairperson	**M.L. Piyapas Bhirombhakdi**
Committee Member	**Mr. Chakrabhand Posayakrit** National Artist, Visual Arts (Painting), 2000
Committee Member	**Mr. Nithi Sthapitanonda** National Artist, Architecture (Contemporary), 2002
Committee Member	**Mr. Chulathat Kitibutr** National Artist, Architecture (Contemporary), 2004
Committee Member	**M.L. Chiratorn Chirapravati** Artist and Illustrator
Committee Member	**Mr. Prathom Lochananond** Thai Floral Master-Artist
Committee Member	**Assistant Professor Wiluck Sripasang** Lanna Culture Specialist
Committee Member	**Ms. Payom Valaiphatchra** Executive Vice President of Expertise Group of Companies
Committee Member	**Ms. Siri Udomritthiruj** Managing Director of Post International Media Company Limited

Platinum Sponsor

Raimon Land is Thailand's premier luxury condominium developer. Listed on the stock exchange of Thailand since 1994, the company has developed renowned projects in Bangkok, Pattaya and Phuket, and won four awards at the Thailand Property Awards 2008: Best Developer, Best Condo Development (Phuket) for The Heights Phuket, Best Condo Development (Eastern Seaboard) for Northpoint and Best Development Website for the second consecutive year for www.theriverbangkok.com. The company strives to provide its customers with innovative products that exceed expectations, to improve the quality of property development in the country through utilisation of best practices in all construction disciplines, as well as through the establishment of new standards in environmental controls and property management. Raimon Land Plc is also a very conscientious member of the corporate community and participates in many socially responsible and charitable causes and events.

Silver Sponsors

Established by Royal Charter in 1907 as the first Thai Bank, SCB is today the leading universal banking group in Thailand, with the highest market capitalization and the largest branch and ATM network. As the country's Premier Universal Bank, SCB provides a full range of financial services, including corporate and personal lending, retail and wholesale banking, foreign currency operations, international trade financing, cash management, custodian services, credit and charge card services, and investment banking services, through its head office and its extensive branch networks. As one of the core elements of its vision, the Bank actively engages in Corporate Social Responsibility (CSR) activities with the aim of promoting charitable projects and activities beneficial to society. The Corporate Social Responsibility (CSR) Committee was established in 2006 as a Board Committee, thus providing a governance mechanism at the highest level as well as the flexibility to develop, optimize, and implement programs for the benefit of the community.

Thai Airways International Public Company Limited (THAI) is the national carrier of the Kingdom of Thailand and one of the world leading airlines. It operates domestic, regional and intercontinental flights radiating from its home base in Bangkok to key destinations around the world and within Thailand. Thai Airways was founded in 1960. At present, THAI flies to 73 destinations including domestic destinations in 35 countries around the world. THAI aims to provide full service to premium passengers, while maintaining its standard of service for leisure travelers. The success of THAI is apparent in numerous customer surveys conducted by well-known institutes both within and outside Thailand. The vision of THAI is to be "The First Choice Carrier with Touches of Thai".

Jim Thompson and a group of his Thai friends founded The Thai Silk Company in 1951 primarily to give Thai people employment, and in doing so, revived the dying craft of hand-woven Thai silk. What was initially a small Bangkok retailer of Thai silk fabrics now has a brand name and reputation that is known and respected worldwide. The Thai Silk Company Limited (Jim Thompson) today employs over 3,000 people in Thailand and has wholly owned subsidiaries in Singapore, Malaysia, Dubai and Brunei Darussalam. It has distributors and showrooms in over 30 countries worldwide for it's home furnishing fabric collections.

Gold Partners

Syllable was officially opened in 1986 as a sister company within the Expertise Group. Firmly committed to the provision of professional services, Syllable takes pride in the fact that it is one of Thailand's leading public relations agencies. The past two decades have seen Syllable play vital roles for its local and international clients, who have clearly enjoyed much success. Their clients represent a wide range of businesses and industries, covering among others the petroleum, entertainment, fashion, sports, education, airline, real estate, hotel and hospitality and retail marketing sectors. Syllable also specializes in the implementation of nationally-run campaigns of various ilk.

The Post Publishing Public Company Limited is the publisher and distributor of the Bangkok Post – an English- language newspaper, Post Today – a Thai-language business daily, and Student Weekly – an English-language magazine. The Company's news and information businesses in the last few years have been expanded to include electronic and digital media. Both bangkokpost.com and posttoday.com aim to be the world's window to Thailand. The Post Publishing is also steadily expanding its multimedia presence through Thai-language TV and radio programme.

The Company's subsidiary companies – Post International Media Company Limited, Post-ACP Company Limited and Post-IM Plus Company Limited – all publish and distribute Thai-language editions of well-known international magazines, namely ELLE, ELLE DECORATION, CLEO, and Marie Claire.

Silver Partners

An Inspirational Resort, in the cultural heart of Northern Thailand, Mandarin Oriental Dhara Dhevi, Chiang Mai offers discerning travelers some of the world's most spacious and luxurious accommodations. Showcasing the beauty of Lanna art and architecture, the resort features spectacular examples of local craftsmanship, design and an extensive collection of museum-quality antiques at every turn. Dheva Spa and Wellness Centre, modeled on the ancient palaces of Mandalay. Its treatment menu draws on the healing traditions of northern Thailand's Lanna culture as well as on those of Myanmar, India and China. Wining and dining options are no less exciting with superb Thai, Chinese and Mediterranean dining venues on offer. Health & Fitness and Cultural Activities are available each day to guests as well as the Lanna Kids Club and the Oriental Culinary Academy. A stay at Mandarin Oriental Dhara Dhevi promises to rejuvenate mind, body and soul in surroundings of unparalleled luxury and beauty.

ELLE Thailand launched in November 1994, is part of a family of 45 editions worldwide. Today, ELLE is published under license by Post International Media Co., Ltd. ELLE is currently number 2 in newsstand sales of international magazines in Thailand.

Launched in Thailand in June 1996, ELLE DECORATION is part of an international network of 28 editions. Currently, ELLE DECORATION is number 2 title on the newsstand among the favourite interior and home decoration magazines. ELLE DECORATION is also published under license by Post International Media.

Marie Claire was launched in Thailand in May 2004 as the 25th Marie Claire worldwide. Marie Claire is well-known for being the fashion and beauty magazine with a plus, the 'plus' being its unrivalled hard-hitting features. Marie Claire is currently published under Post-IM Plus Co., Ltd.

Surivipa, a popular Thai television variety talk show, hosted by Surivipa Kultangwattana. The program aims to inspire the audience with inspirational stories through the interviews with successful personalities. Produced by JSL Global Media, Surivipa is on air every Friday at 10pm, on Modernine TV.

Founded in 1980, JSL Global Media Co., Ltd. currently employs over 400 employees with works spanning from TV drama, special event, rental of studio and equipment to copywriting of foreign animation.

Acknowledgements

In addition to our solicitous advisors, dedicated pre- and post-production team, and ever-supportive sponsors and partners; the publisher, the author and the team behind *Dok Mai Thai: The Flower Culture of Thailand*, would like to extend our gratitude to the many companies, institutes, and individuals for their valuable contributions to the project. We do apologize if anyone has been accidentally excluded from this list.

Key Florists

Bangkok

Anoma Pungpai, Bathaleeya Boonmee, Boonsita Buabran, Kosin Prasarnklieo, Kritsadavan Sangvorasin, Marisa Chuchuai, Niwat Dechkul, Vongsuparp Vorarut, Somsud Suansiri, Wanna Maneenut

Chiang Mai

Boonyuang Manopian, Buasri Somtiang, Jaikham Tapanyo, Jamnean Jinachit, Jaykeaw Khamsean, Krittaphong Chaemchan, Pee Suvan, Phan Jeepota, Phann Chansam, Ta Kajai

Buriram

Cham Kusiram, Saman Nurakram, Saman Usairak, Sattaya Narinram, Yan Nuresram, Yearm Nikulram, Yearn Nukitram, Yen Deelorm, Yord Kusiram

Other Assistance

The Intakul family, who have always given their complete support.

Bangkok

Apaporn Kosolkul, Apichart Intravisit, Arunee Chuboonraj, Benjawan Sudhikam, Chanachai Varamali, Chanasak Niyathirakul, Chatchawan Pisitpaisankun, Chattayom Pengsut, Chavanant Senivongse, Chutima Dumsuwan, Chulita Areepipatkul, Eric Booth, Gregory Meadows, Henri Young, Hubert Viriot, Jittapa Archathawan, Juraruk Cholharn, Julnaj Vongsayan, Kamon Angkavichai, Kanjana Keeratiworanan, Kanjarat Patcharawattanakul, Kantaphon Phanitrat, Kanoklada Rerkasem, Kanokwan Roonbunjob, Korrakoch Charoenplung, Kwanrudee Maneewongwatthana, Phramaha Nabhajala Ghositamedhi, Natteera Yoomongkol, Nontawat Lupautai, Nopamat Veohong, Noppamas Ruayruen, Nopporn and Pornpatr Witoonchart, Nuttha Prathuangsuksri, Ongorn Abhakorn Na Ayuthaya, Orapin Limsakul, M.L. Pattaratorn Chirapravati, Khun Pensri Khiawmeesuan, Philip Cornwel-Smith, Pirakit Valaiphatchra, Prathumthip Saengchan, Puthirak Pensuk, Rangsun Wiboonuppatum, Ratanawalee Loharjun, Salinda Wisutkanchanachai, Sasipen Chansri, Sithidej Mayalarp, Soithong Cholumjeak, Soodrak Chanyavongs, Sorut Sukthaworn, Somnuek Klangnok, Sudarat Pechpan, Sukanya Thummakun, Sumalee Tangjitsin, Supakorn Vejjajiva, Supannee Panichwarong, Supornthip Choungrangsee, Surapat Chaiyongyos, Surivipa Kultangwattana, Thanjija Varamali, Theeranuj Karnasuta Wongwaisayawan, Thirabhand Chandracharoen, Thongchai Truengchitvilart, Thweep Rittinaphakorn, M.L. Varatorn and Padcha Chirapravati, Vichai Boo, Vin Osathananda, Phrakru Vinaithorn Apinya, M.L. Vittratorn Chirapravati, Wachirasiri Thawedeth, Watcharaporn Arjharn, Wipawadee Sirimongkolkasem, Yothin Thamchamrus

Chiang Mai

Anchalee Sripasang, Ampha Chaisawas, Arnut Intrachai, Bhudit Bhiankusola, Chanchayy Manee, Chatchawan Pewwan, Jetsada Chaiwong, Khampan Kantasos, Khannikar Duangjaisak, Laddawan Thamjong, Mayuree Suwawan, Narissa Thaitawat, Nattawut Chantachote, Noi Inchai, Nuchanath Suyata, Pa Boonchai, Piyaphat Srimun, Pornthep Somsri, Ratchaneewan Chantra, Sarayut Boonpan, Savas Rattakunjara, Sommai Lumdual, Sorat Apibal, Thitichai Akarasilapin

Buriram

Adisak Artharn, Boonchuay Subsombut, Chalerm Jarodram, Eien Siwprakhon, Jatupon Narinram, Jintapanee Churnprakon, Khampong Laoaka, Khorb Horaram, Kuan Narinram, Naak Kasemsuk, Niyom Singharn, Pattana Pasorn, Prajim Narinram, Prajuab Narinram, Prakit Deelorm, Rojanachai Sattawaha, Rungthiwa Khantichotiboriboon, Sai Parongram, Samlee Nararam, Samun Parongram, Savong Chaichana, Searn Chumponwong, Sombat Upamaraka, Sonnurk Jamordee, Subin Panthong, Sudjai Nopparam, Suwanna Deejai, Thap Boonkhrong, Thawin Chanaboon, Wannaporn Narinram, Waravithi Poosampao, Wilai Nuresram, Wirojana Tearngtham, Yin Cheonram

Loei

Darin Jungpattanawadee, Neeracha Wongmasa

Tokyo

Daisuke Kamo, Junya Kitagawara, Madoka Oishi

Photographs

The Chakrabhand Posayakrit Foundation, Darin Jungpattanawadee, Jirasak Thongyuak, Kanit Naruponjirakul, Nat Prakobsantisuk (Sakul Intakul's portrait), National Archives of Thailand, M.L. Prangtip Prompoj of Double D Company Limited

Locations

- Ban Moh Palace, Bangkok
- Devarana Spa, The Dusit Thani Hotel, Bangkok
- Jim Thompson House and Museum, Bangkok
- Lanna Wisdom School, Chiang Mai
- Mandarin Oriental Dhara Dhevi, Chiang Mai
- Residence of Chulathat Kitibutr, Chiang Mai
- Residence of Satit Kalawantavanich, Bangkok
- TENFACE Serviced Residence, Bangkok
- The River by Raimon Land, Bangkok
- The Sukhothai Bangkok
- The Sukhothai Residences, Bangkok
- Walai Rukhavej Botanical Research Institute, Mahasarakham University, Mahasarakham
- Wat Benchamabophit Dusitwanaram, Bangkok
- Wat Rakhang Khositaram, Bangkok
- Wat Ratchabophit Sathitmahasimaram, Bangkok
- Wat Ratchaorasaram, Bangkok
- Wat Somanasviharn, Bangkok
- Wat Thepthidaram, Bangkok

Props

- *Khanittha Niyomtham*
  Bailarnpradit
  8/1 Moo 3, Thawasukee, Ayutthaya, Ayutthaya 13000
  Tel: +66 86 407 5563

- *Central Chidlom*
  1027 Ploenchit Road, Lumpini, Pathumwan, Bangkok 10330
  Tel: +66 2793 7777 Fax: +66 2793 7799

- *The Jim Thompson House and Museum*
  The James H. W. Thompson Foundation
  6 Soi Kasemsan 2, Rama I Road, Wangmai, Pathumwan, Bangkok 10330
  Tel: +66 2216 7368 Fax: +66 2612 3744

- *Julnaj Vongsayan*
  Lotus Crystal International Company Limited
  28/6 Soi Ruam Ruedi, Witthayu Road, Lumphini, Pathumwan, Bangkok 10330
  Tel: +66 2255 1930-3 Fax: +66 2253 8434

- *M.L. Varatorn and Padcha Chirapravati*
  Mahanak Palace, Bangkok
  1092 Dumrongrak Road, Mahanak, Pomprab, Bangkok 10100

- *RUEN BOOSSABA The Flowers House*
  21/1 Soi Saladaeng 1, Rama IV Road, Silom, Bangrak, Bangkok 10500
  Tel: +66 2636 3883 Fax: +66 2636 3882

- *Sakul Intakul*
  Pawo Company Limited
  52/1 Rajavithee Road Soi 2, Samsennai, Phayathai, Bangkok 10400
  Tel: +66 2644 9640-1 Fax: +66 2644 9437

- *Anchalee Sripasang*
  Srisanpanmai
  6 Nimmanhemin Road Soi 1, Suthep, Muang, Chiang Mai 50200
  Tel: +66 5389 4717

Team Acknowledgements

Production

Sakul Intakul	Project Director / Creative Director
Jirasak Thongyuak	Photographer
Kanit Naruponjirakul	Assistant Photographer
Santhad Puangpitak	Project Coordinator / Florist
Randorn Saejiw	Senior Florist
Winai Sattarujawongse	Videographer / Documentary Director
Pohnnapa Anahunlipaiboon	Documentary Producer
Tanee Nateepitak	Videographer
Thanest Charnraor	Assistant Videographer
Suchal Chaweewan	Assistant Videographer
Prisana Narinram	Researcher
Kitti Wongsuttipakorn	Financial Controller
Thanakorn Ninprakan	Accountant
Somkid Honganurak	Coordinator
Khaen Krasaetho	Installer
Tee Phokhi	Installer

Editorial Production

Rungsima Kasikranund	Editor
Peter Myers	English Editor
Norranit Suvanich	Assistant to Editor
Carina Chotirawe, Ph. D.	Editorial Advisor
Mali Chaturachinda, Pongpat Klibchan at Be‹our›friend Studio	Graphic Design

Colour separation by
71 Interscan Company Limited
200/15-21 Nares Road, Sipraya, Bangrak, Bangkok 10500 Thailand

Printed and bound by
Sirivatana Interprint Public Company Limited
125 Soi Chan 32, Chan Road, Thungwatdon, Sathorn, Bangkok 10120 Thailand

This edition published in Thailand in November 2009 by
Flower Culture Press
Flower Culture Company Limited
52 Rajavithee Road Soi 2, Samsennai, Phayathai, Bangkok 10400 Thailand

In collaboration with
Sakul Intakul, Pawo Company Limited
52/1 Rajavithee Road Soi 2, Samsennai, Phayathai, Bangkok 10400 Thailand
Tel: +66 2644 9640-1 Fax: +66 2644 9437
E-mail: *sakulintakul@yahoo.com*
www.sakulintakul.com
www.flowerculturepress.com